Growing Up In Pensacola
Personal Essays

by Charlie Davis

East Bay Publishers
2009

Cover photo:
Jack and Tom Davis at Black's Wharf, 1940s.

Illustrations by:
Steve Blair, Crescent Studio Gulf Breeze, Florida.

EAST BAY PUBLISHERS
3650 Ebb Tide Lane
Gulf Breeze, Florida 32563

Printed by
Trent's Prints & Publishing
Pace, Florida

LIBRARY OF CONGRESS CATALOG CARD NUMBER: pending
ISBN 978-1-4392-8889-4
First printing: 2009
PRINTED IN THE UNITED STATES OF AMERICA

PREFACE

Much has been written about the history of Pensacola and Northwest Florida, but I will leave the writing of history to the Historians. It is my wish to share some of the experiences I had while growing up in a Pensacola that was so different and wonderful, beginning with the years prior to World War II, up to the time of the War on Terrorism. I am not a professional writer, but if I were, I would attempt to convey to the readers the indomitable spirit of the community during a time of crisis, especially during the time of World War II. Pensacola was not a sleepy little town, but there were communities within the area that did fit that description, and East Pensacola Heights was just one of them.

I chose the personal essay form for these short stories about my personal experiences while growing up in Pensacola because of its simplicity. As mentioned above I am not a professional writer, so I ask you to overlook the obvious errors, and I hope you will enjoy reading the stories as much as I have enjoyed writing them.

I am deeply grateful to Lyn Zittel, Publisher and Editor of Dockside Magazine, for giving me an opportunity to write for her publication and encouraging me along the way. When I first met Lyn in 2001, I had a strong desire to write, but had doubts about my ability to do so well enough to be published in her magazine. She squashed all my doubts and eventually assigned me a monthly column to write under the byline "Growing up in Pensacola," the source of the title for this book. Thank you, Lyn.

I also want to thank Nancy Newland, Chief of Police at Pensacola Junior College, a great story teller herself, for encouraging me to put into writing some of the stories I shared with her and others on trips and social gatherings over the past ten years. and for a friendship Sandra and I value very much We have been cheerleaders for each other, and I'm looking forward to the day she publishes some of those unbelievable stories she shared with us about her years in law enforcement.

I want to thank Steve Blair, artist and owner of Crescent Studio of Gulf Breeze for creating the illustrations for essays 16, 20, 41, 49, 50, and 51.

My talented grandson, Hayden Davis, a student at Gulf Breeze High School created the illustration for essay #30. Thank you, Hayden.

Of course, I owe more than a thank you to my wife, Sandra, for her years of unyielding confidence and encouragement in my ability to write, and then agreeing to spend the time necessary to prepare the stories and pictures in the proper form for the printer. Without her enthusiasm expertise, and threats of bodily harm, this book would probably still be in the planning stage.

Charlie Davis
Gulf Breeze, Florida
October, 2009

Table of Contents

Chapter Page

1

Pensacola, My Hometown

Webster's Ninth New Collegiate Dictionary defines "home-town" as, "the city or town where one was born or grew up." Well, that's good enough for me, since Pensacola, Florida is my home-town, and it's where I was born and grew up. It's possible, or perhaps very likely that some who know me, will take issue with the term "grew up." For those skeptics, all I can say is, at age seventy-seven I'm still working on it. I consider myself fortunate that God, with help from my parents, decided on Pensacola for my hometown. It's been a great place to live, and I have been able to experience the good times, and the not so good times, with many wonderful people. Over the years, many of my friends and acquaintances were determined to leave Pensacola for a more exciting place to live, and they did. Others left for job opportunities, military service, parents being transferred, and many other reasons. It's impressive how many of those people eventually returned to Pensacola. I did the same thing. I was away for eleven years, living and working in several other states. The longer I was away, the more I realized that my hometown of Pensacola was the ideal place to live. I returned for good thirty-two years ago in 1977.

Pensacola is referred to in many ways. Our former Governor, Reubin Askew, called it "The western gate to the sunshine state," and former mayor, Vince Whibb's description was, "The city where thousands live and play, and millions wished they did." Pensacola has a long, rich history of naval aviation, and is known around the world as "The Cradle of Naval Aviation," and "The Annapolis of the Air." Because of the beautiful white beaches and the clean blue and green waters of the Gulf of Mexico, which extends from Pensacola to Panama City, we are part of what has been called the "Miracle Strip." In more recent years, the area has become known commercially as the "Emerald Coast," and not so commercially as "The Redneck Riviera."

I like Pensacola as it is today, but I loved the Pensacola I grew up in back in the thirties while in grammar school, and the forties and early fifties while in junior high and high school. The fifties are equally nostalgic times for me although I spent much time away in the Navy and in college. It was during my youth that the center of commerce, government and most everything else of importance was in downtown Pensacola. When we walked up or down Palafox Street, in downtown Pensacola, we knew just about every person we met, if not personally, we at least knew who they were. Today, it is possible for me to walk all over downtown and not meet a single person I know. While in junior high and high school, I had a paper route in East Pensacola Heights, the community in which I lived with my parents and five brothers and one sister. I knew every person who lived in the "Heights" and most of the people in East Hill. It was an era when we got to know all of our neighbors well, and established lifelong friendships. During the eleven years I lived away from Pensacola, I lived in neighborhoods in Florida, Georgia and North Carolina where we got to know only those neighbors in the same block. I know that there are neighborhoods in Pensacola where the same conditions would exist today, and it makes me appreciate how fortunate we were to have grown up in Pensacola at a time when life was at a slower pace, and families made a special effort to know everyone in their community.

Polio was the big scare when I was a kid. The kids in East Pensacola Heights practically lived in Bayou Texar. Polio wasn't just a threat from the Health Department, because people were really developing the disease. It was one of the dread diseases my siblings and friends and I grew up fearing. In the summer months, when the temperature reached a certain high level, we were discouraged from swimming in the bayou. On several occasions the various health agencies would visit the schools and demonstrate how the "Iron Lung" worked, and at some of those visits, they would actually bring an Iron Lung with a Polio patient inside. As small kids, we were allowed to talk with the patient, which really got our attention. Thank God for Dr. Salk and his vaccine. It seems that the health care organizations did a good job of prevention, keeping the number of Polio cases at a minimum.

Pensacola probably had no more hobos, tramps and homeless people than any other part of the South during the Depression years on into the World War II period, but many of those that did show up in Pensacola, seemed to know that my dad was a soft touch. It was not unusual for him to come home with a hungry hobo or two for my mother to feed. I remember coming home late from throwing my evening paper route, and finding a whole family sitting in our living room, with the couches and pillows made into beds for an overnight stay. My dad picked up the hitchhiking family at the end of the Bayou Bridge, and brought them home with him. The next morning, on his way to the courthouse, he dropped them off on Scenic Highway, and they continued their hitch-hiking journey. My mom was just as bad as dad about helping desperate people. I came home from school one day, and there was this huge, older man who looked like Santa Claus, or somebody out of *The Grapes of Wrath* movie, sitting at the breakfast table, enjoying a fine meal my mother had placed on the table. I don't believe my parents were exceptions. Many families that experienced the Great Depression reacted the same way as my parents did, when confronted with those less fortunate. We were a kinder and gentler nation back in those days.

Pensacola was no exception back in the late thirties and throughout the forties, when it came to "squatters." I recall the squatters living along the shores of Bayou Texar as well as on the shores of Pensacola Bay, on the south side of East Pensacola Heights. Many families had no choice but to live in the so called, "Hooverville" shanty towns. I recall going to school at Annie K. Suter School with some of the kids that lived in the shanties along the bay and the bayou in the late thirties and early forties. They were good kids, who were victims of their parent's misfortunes. One of those kids, who was a little older than me, is a personal friend whom I admire and respect very much. He served his country in wartime and is retired from a long career in the military. He has a wonderful family and I'm honored to have him for a friend.

There is so much about Pensacola to be proud of, and I hope I've shown some of that pride in some of the essays in this publication. I lived away from Pensacola for eleven years, and most of those years, I traveled throughout the Southeastern states. When someone would ask me where I was from, I automatically said, "Pensacola, Florida," although I might have been living in Georgia, Florida or North Carolina. I always explained where I actually lived at the time, but I was proud of Pensacola, and wanted them to know where I was really from. I now live in Gulf Breeze, Florida on East Bay, where I can walk out on my dock, catch our supper if I want to, and see Pensacola across the Bay. It doesn't get much better than that.

2

East Pensacola Heights

"Blessings On Thee, Little Man,
Barefoot Boy, with Cheek of Tan!"

John Greenleaf Whittier

There could not have been a better community to grow up in than East Pensacola Heights, and I thank God for giving my parents, in 1937, the wisdom to move to the "Heights." It was a decision they never regretted, and one that my five brothers and one sister and I are grateful for. We lived just a block from Walker's Boat House on Bayou Boulevard, and enjoyed a wide view of the bayou through the many beautiful live oaks and magnolia trees. We kept our boats on the beach at the end of Seventh Street.

East Pensacola Heights is a peninsula, surrounded by Pensacola Bay to the south, Escambia Bay to the east and Bayou Texar to the west. "Heights," as defined in Webster's dictionary, is "an extent of land rising a considerable degree above the surrounding country," which is an

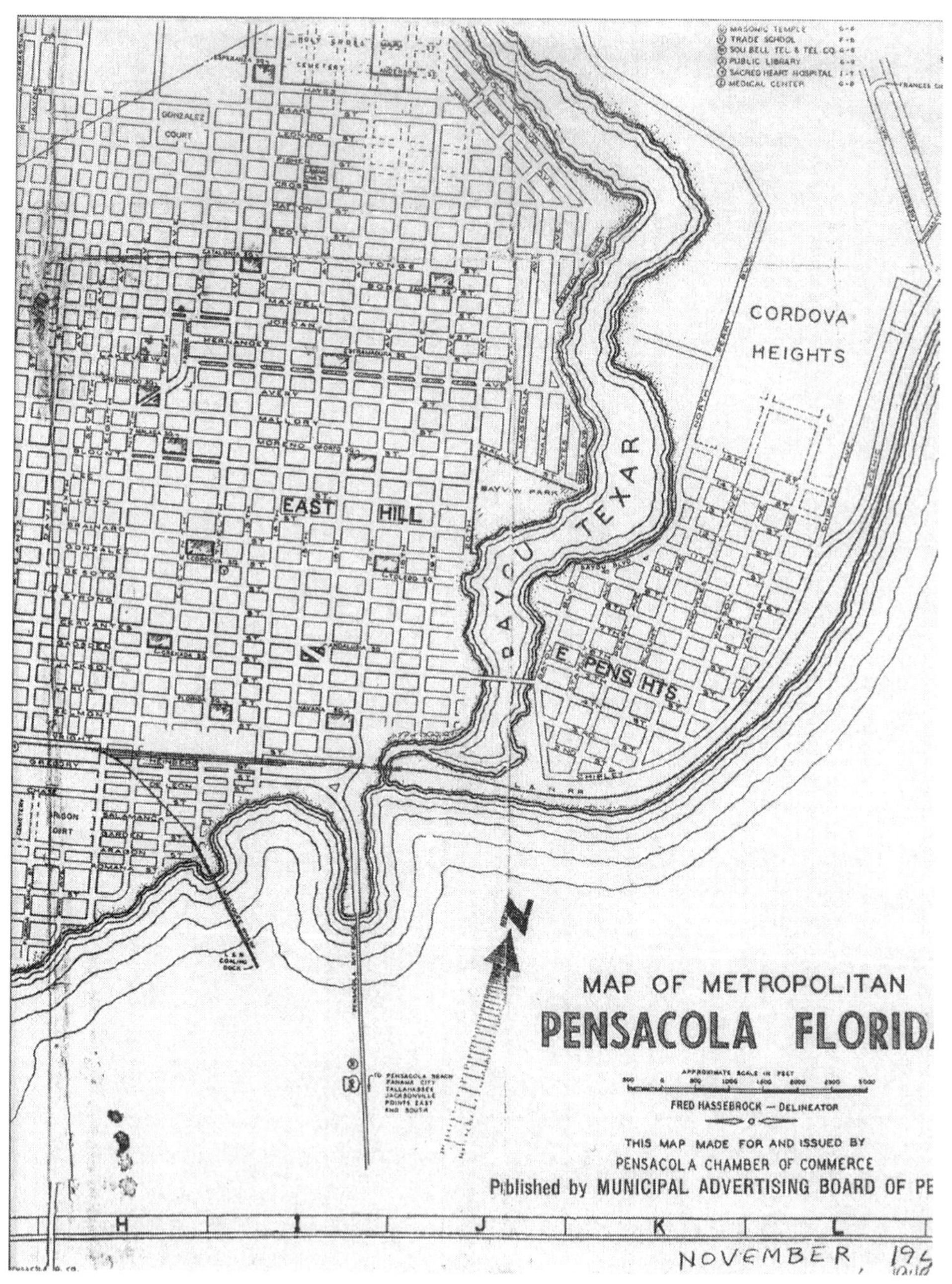

Map of Pensacola including East Pensacola Heights dated November, 1948.
Note: the bridge to East Pensacola Heights is the old Gadsden Street Bridge
Courtesy of West Florida Regional Library

Gadsden Street bridge to East Pensacola Heights. Courtesy of Ed and Jean Wallace

The Mariner Oyster Barn

appropriate description of the area, referred to affectionately by the inhabitants as the "Heights." You have but to visit the "bluffs" along Scenic Highway to realize just how elevated the land is, which provides a spectacular view of Escambia Bay and portions of Santa Rosa County.

It's not clear who the first settlers to East Pensacola Heights were, but the family names that most agree on are, Brosnaham, Hyer, Joseph, Merritt, Sheppard, Nickinson, McCaskill, Thompson, Briggs and Walker. I could get into trouble with that statement, but the facts are, there have been many, wonderful families who were among the early residents of the Heights, and many of their descendents are still residing there. Bob Joseph informed me that his grandfather, Mark Joseph, crossed over Bayou Texar by barge from the Pensacola side. The first wooden bridge was built in 1911. Like other parts of the Gulf Coast, East Pensacola Heights has really grown, and the newer residents are just as proud of the Heights as are the older residents.

The "Heights" is a fisherman's paradise, and a popular location for the fishermen was Walker's Boat House, now the site of the Marina Oyster Barn Restaurant. It was owned by Mr. Willie Walker, patriarch of a pioneering commercial fishing family. Many of us kids worked for him, at different times, doing everything from renting and "bailing" boats, selling shrimp and mullet to customers and selling fish bait to the "city slickers." Most of us knew how to throw a castnet by the time we were teenagers, and could scoop crabs and gig flounders by the time we reached puberty. Throwing a castnet was an art, acquired only after weeks, and sometimes years, of practice. We were judged by our peers on how well we could "spread" our nets when fishing for mullet. Real men won't admit it, but some women could also throw the net well. "Sis" Oliver Beal, whose father,

Evelyn Ann Lee posing with the day's catch of speckled trout from Bayou Texar in 1952. Courtesy of Lavern Goodrich

Inside Thompson's Grocery Store, L to R: Roy, Roy, Sr., Clarence Jetton, and Mary Thompson. Inset: Mr. and Mrs. Thompson
Courtesy of Jackie Thompson

"Sis" Oliver Beal
Courtesy of Chris and Pandora Beal

John Oliver, owned "Nob Hill," could throw a castnet as well as any man her size.

The center of daily activity was around Pfeiffer's, Thompson's and Fullerton's grocery stores and Russell's drugstore. By the time Bob Joseph opened Joseph's IGA on Scenic Highway, all these smaller stores had disappeared. One central gathering spot was the Community House, which was built by the local residents. All types of meetings were conducted there; from Boy Scout Troop meetings to Political Rallies. It's still in use today, under the auspices of the City Recreation Department. To assure success at the fund raisers, such as the school plays and political rallies, many ladies, like Ms. Lena Bradley, Ms. Julia Delahenty and Ms. Jenny Cardenas, cooked their favorite seafood recipes of gumbo or fish chowder, which drew a profitable crowd every time.

Living in the "Heights" meant spending the summers either in or on the bayou. The "ole swimming hole" for most of us was Black's Wharf, but we often swam across the bayou to Bayview Park where we would try to kill each other by "cannon-balling" from the

Joseph's IGA. Courtesy of Bob and Nettie Joseph

Norman Redding riding his bicycle in front of Russell's Drugstore
Courtesy of Emma Jean Redding

three story tower. On Saturday nights, large groups of us walked across the bridge and along the shore of the bayou to Bayview Park for free movies. It's hard to believe that so many of us walked from the Heights to Bayview Park to see the free movies put on by the City. We were a mob of kids of all ages, and the mob sometimes included adults, and we were noisy. The residents along the bayou between the old Gadsden Street Bridge and Bayview Park must have feared for their lives as we walked the bayou beach to the concrete bleachers overlooking the bayou. There was no path, and there was no real beach. It was only reeds, rushes and bushes, but before the night was over we had made a path, because we walked back the same way we came in, usually barefooted and noisy. It won't happen, but if the city decided to resume free movies at Bayview Park, I would bet money that not one kid would walk all the way to Bayview Park from East Pensacola Heights. As I've written elsewhere, most of us wouldn't hesitate to swim across the bayou from the Heights to Bayview Park, but I don't remember any of us swimming the bayou at night. As we got a little older, we had access to skiffs and kayaks, and we thought nothing of rowing or paddling out the mouth of the bayou to the Muscogee Wharf and "Hawkshaw" areas, or up the bayou, beyond the Twelfth Avenue Bridge. I wonder if today's kids would attempt that same journey without benefit of at least a forty horsepower motor on a seventeen foot boat.

Alan Sheppard
Courtesy of Alan Sheppard

During World War II, (1941 -1945) East Pensacola Heights was part of the County, so it had not yet been annexed into the City. Almost all the streets were clay roads, except the Scenic Highway, Bayou Boulevard north to 10th Street and south to Chipley Avenue, all of Chipley Avenue and Stanley Avenue from Scenic Highway to 10th Street. The other streets were red clay roads. The County road graders and dump trucks were constantly busy moving and smoothing the red clay. Red clay was part of our lives, and we kids didn't seem to mind, but our moms did. When it rained, the red clay would wash into Bayou Texar and the whole bayou would turn red. Bayou Boulevard from the Heights to Twelfth Avenue was a red clay road, and there were no houses on that stretch past "Monkeys Camp." When the red clay washed down into the bayou, it stayed red for weeks.

During the war years, everyone had to paint the top half of the automobile headlights black, and Air Raid Wardens were appointed for each block. My dad and a young Alan Sheppard, who today is a retired prominent Pensacola attorney, were the Wardens for our block, and I remember them, standing on the corner during Air Raid Drills, when all the lights were out, and the whole world was dark. At first, all I could see was Dad's cigarette burning, but then I noticed all the fireflies, or as we called them, "lightning bugs." From our house on Bayou Boulevard, all the way down to the bayou through Hyer's Point seemed to light up with "lighting bugs." It seemed the little flying creatures were trying to make up for all the lights being turned off. On such nights, we kids were equipped with fruit jars to put them in. These were the days before DDT and other insecticides.

Johnny Browder with Cobia
Courtesy of Loretta Browder

I mentioned "Monkey's Camp" above, which was a large unimproved track of land situated between Bayou Boulevard and Bayou Texar and north of Hyde Park Road (Ski Jump Road). Monkey's Camp and adjoining property just to the north was the only property between East Pensacola Heights and the airport area that had not been clear cut years before during the timber boom. Most of the property in the area was consistently overgrown with what we called "blackjacks," a specie of oak. It was in Monkey's Camp where my family and others went to find a Christmas tree each

Johnny, Jerry and June Browder
Courtesy of June Browder Merritt and Jerry Browder

holiday season, and it was in Monkey's Camp where many of us went rabbit and squirrel hunting. It was also in Monkey's Camp where Johnny Browder and I went to cook a Sawbill Duck one of us shot while we were duck hunting on Bayou Texar. What I know today and what we didn't know then is that the beautiful specimen we locals call a "Sawbill" is correctly known as a "Redheaded Merganser." The Mergansers are fish eaters, and are not fit to eat. Well, we cooked him over an open fire, using all the culinary skills that two thirteen year old great white hunters possessed. We apparently assumed that if it turned black it was done. Well, it was well done. It was like trying to eat a bag of charcoal. The property we knew as Monkey's Camp is known today as Birnam Woods, an upscale development.

The Bayside Tourist Court, owned by Mr. Earl Browder, was situated in the sharp curve on Scenic Highway, overlooking Escambia and Pensacola Bays. Mr. Browder was an interesting man. Years before, he had made a fortune by inventing a clothes rack, the ones seen in most

Bayside Cottages. Mr. and Mrs. Earl Browder, Owners
Courtesy of June Browder Merritt and Jerry Browder

clothing stores around the country today. The property also included a trailer park, which was crowded with trailers of all different sizes during the war years. Occupants of the trailers seemed to be a mixture of military and civilian, and many of the children residing in the trailer park attended A.K. Suter School. I remember one pretty redheaded girl, who lived with her parents in what seemed to be an extra long silver trailer. I don't believe they were called Travel Trailers in those days. I would find all kinds of reasons why I should ride my bicycle up to the Bayside Tourist Court, but she wouldn't give me the time of day. I don't remember her name now, and I doubt she ever really knew mine. Her family, like thousands of other families, stayed together during the war years by owning trailers that could be moved from town to town, as military personnel and civilian workers alike were transferred time and time again throughout the country. During the same period, Mr. Browder also owned a trailer park several hundred feet north on Scenic Highway, which was also crowded with trailers. I have written elsewhere in this book about the farm Mr. Browder owned in Baldwin County, Alabama.

My sister and brother-in-law, Emma Jean and Norman Redding, lived in East Pensacola Heights soon after they were married in 1945. Norman worked at the Naval Air Station and decided to start a business for extra income. He purchased a lot across from Russell's Drug Store and Thompson Grocery Store on Scenic Highway next to Fullerton's Grocery Store. I was twelve or thirteen at the time, and helped Norman and his dad build a building, and when completed, he opened Redding's Curb Market. It was a great looking little store, but not a successful business venture. Norman thought he was interested in feeding man's

Norman and Emma Jean Redding's Curb Market next to Fullerton's Grocery Store
Courtesy of Emma Jean Redding

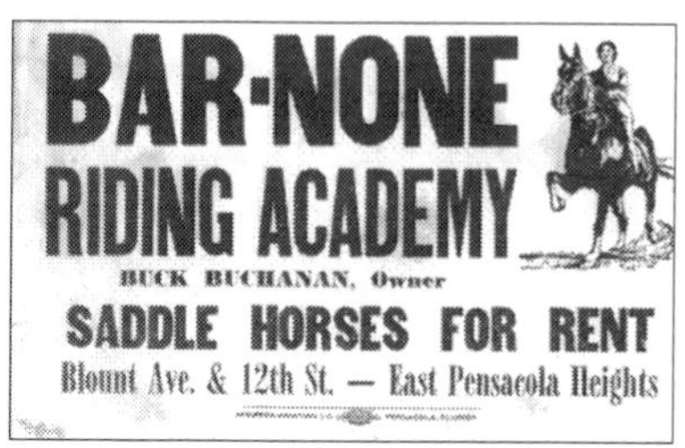

Courtesy of Earline Buchanan Woods Family

stomachs but realized he was more interested in feeding man's soul. Shortly afterwards, he dedicated his life to Christ. He went back to college and obtained a Bachelor's Degree, and, sponsored by the Heights Baptist Church, he attended the Baptist Seminary in New Orleans and received a Masters degree in Divinity. It was quite a jump from peaches to preaching, but he was the right man for the job. After leading several churches, he became a Chaplain at Raiford Prison in Stark, Florida, and retired after twenty-five years, ten of which he was the Death Row Chaplain. The little curb market became the site of Big Lee's Grocery. Several years later, while in Big Lee's store, Mr. Lee, said to me, "Come over here, I want to show you something." I followed him to where his walk-in freezer was located, and he pointed to the floor, where etched in the concrete were the words, "Charlie Davis—1946." Mr. Redding, Norman's dad, had scrawled my name and date the day we poured the concrete floor for the curb market.

Courtesy of Mary Ann Miller

In the days of unpaved streets, many families owned horses, cows and chickens. It was like living in the country, not far from town. In the 40's, the Buchanan and Bonifay families each had stables and folks came from all over to rent their horses. There were many popular businesses in the Heights, such as Philpots Cottages, Chicken in the Rough, Jerry's

Drive-In, the Scenic Terrace, Nob Hill, Simmons Place, LaBounty's and many others. They have all disappeared, except Jerry's Drive-In, and it's still a favorite place for folks from miles around.

The Scenic Terrace was probably one of the most popular nightclubs in Pensacola from the 1940's into the 1960's. Located on the same site where Skopelos on the Bay Restaurant is today, the "Terrace" was the place to go for older teens, college students, young adults and military personnel. The Scenic Terrace was owned and operated by Mr. George Jordan, who was affectionately referred to as "Spade" by his regular customers. The drinking age restrictions were somewhat lax in the 40's and 50's, not only at The Terrace but at most bars and clubs around Pensacola. In other words, teenagers were served adult beverages if they wished. As I recall, the Terrace was raided on several occasions by the local authorities, but before long things would be back to "normal." On the nights that a band was present, there would be a cover charge. Otherwise, the music was provided by the jukebox, and customers came and went as they pleased. There were several waiters, but the one that seemed to be everybody's favorite was known only as "Snapper."

Jerry's Drive-In

Today, East Pensacola Heights is an extension of the City of Pensacola, and all the streets were paved years ago. Annie K. Suter School is still the center of

Hood's Cottoages and Café. Courtesy of Fanny Davis

education, and all the woods, such as Monkey's Camp and the "Gulley's" are now solid subdivisions. It's where the best restaurants are located, real estate values have soared, and most former residents wished they still lived there.

It was exciting growing up in a large family and it just couldn't have been as good anywhere else as it was in the "Heights." We have so many wonderful experiences to remember, and the greatest of these are the lifelong friendships we developed during those years. We didn't realize just how fortunate we were.

Bonifay's Service Station.

Right:
Bonifay Oil Company.
Courtesy of the Clinton Bonifay Family

Left: A model of Brooks Taylor's Ssrvice Station.
Courtesy of Ray Donnelly

3

Annie K. Suter School

In 1938, I entered the first grade at Annie K. Suter School. Over the next six years, my mind was molded to some degree, my fanny was warmed to several degrees, and I fell in love no less than six times, beginning with Miss Johnson, my first grade teacher.

Annie K. Suter School was a one story, brick building, situated on a one block square, fenced yard. There were only three doors, one at each end and the entrance on the south side. It was really a shotgun building. There were six classrooms, one for each grade; two bathrooms, a small lunch room, a small library and the principal's office. Each classroom had a pot-belly stove and a "cloak room." If the cloak rooms could talk, some of us would have been shipped off to the State Reform School in Marianna.

Although there was no central heating and cooling system, the old building was comfortable as well as practical. On cold, winter days, Mr Villenuve, the janitor and Jack of all trades, stoked the fires in each classroom, keeping the whole building warm. In the warm months the windows were opened, so an occasional bird or butterfly flying throughout the building was not unusual. A sliding partition separated the second and fourth grade classrooms, which when opened, served as an assembly hall. We enjoyed school plays, music recitals and a variety of programs conjured up by the school board for our entertainment and edification. Occasionally, a local church, or some other religious group would present Bible lessons, in an attempt to save our souls, which some of us needed more than others. It isn't clear, even today, if the School Board did that for all the schools, or if they figured the kids in East Pensacola Heights needed the spiritual nourishment more than others.

The school ground area was mostly sand with an abundance of oak leaves and pine straw. There were no paved areas, such as a basketball court, nor were there any covered areas. However, there were many shade trees, such as blackjacks, live oaks, and pine trees. The northeast corner of the yard was designated for softball, kickball, and touch football. The southwest corner contained a swing set, two sea-saws and one of those merry-go-rounds that we pushed and then jumped onto. At recess, we just milled around in groups, reminiscent of a prison yard at the "big house," as seen in old movies.

The lunchroom was unbelievably small. We didn't eat in the lunchroom like kids do today. We went through the line to obtain our lunch, and then returned to our class room to eat. Mrs. Roach was the lunchroom lady, and she and one helper did everything. They cooked and served, and I suppose they had Mr. Villenuve to help with the clean up.

The Teachers at Suter School

There were six grades and six teachers. Miss Sadie Coley, the Principal, also taught the second grade. My first grade teacher, Miss Cameron Johnson, was young and pretty, and very likeable. However, I don't recall her being there very long, but seventy-one years later, there are a lot of things I don't recall. She was replaced by Miss Kate Coley, the sister of Miss Sadie

Miss Cameron Johnson Will Be Bride of Frederick H. Babcock

[illegible] interest in the announcement [illegible] today by Mr. and Mrs. Arthur Cameron Johnson of the engagement of their daughter, Miss Cameron Johnson, to Frederick Howard Babcock, Jr., of Santa Barbara, Calif., son of Mrs. Frederick Howard Babcock of New York City and the late Mr. Babcock. The wedding will take place early in November.

Miss Johnson received her education at Florida State College for Women. She is a member of the Delta Delta Delta social sorority and also holds membership in The Spinsters. Mr. Babcock prepared at the Taft school and is an alumnus of Yale university. He served as a lieutenant commander in the naval reserve during the war and was [illegible] for some time at the Pensacola Naval Air station. He is now associated in business in Santa Barbara.

CAMERON JOHNSON

Miss Cameron Johnson's engagement announcement
Courtesy of Ms. Virginia Gomez Newsom

One of Miss Kate Coley 's first grade classes
Courtesy of John "Sonny" Ware

Coley. The other teachers were "institutions" in their own right. Miss Ruth Weller taught third grade. I don't know what all I learned in Miss Weller's class, but it was fun being in her class. I do recall that we read a story about "Ivan the Russian," and it seems like everyone that was in her class remembers reading about "Billy Goat Gruff." I used to think of Miss Weller every time I went under the Bayou Texar Bridge, which is not too often these days.

The fourth grade was owned by Miss Giddens. She was there long before I started at Suter, and she was there long after I left. She had difficulty walking as she wore braces on both her legs, but that didn't seem to slow her down one bit. Miss Giddens was away the year I was in the fourth grade, and Miss Bradley was the substitute teacher. She was older, and very nice, but had no control whatever over us students. The classroom contained a piano and a portable stage, because it was the other half of the "assembly hall," which was created by the sliding partition that separated the fourth grade and second grade classrooms. My most vivid memory of Miss Bradley was her form of punishment,

One of Miss Gidden's fourth grade classes
Courtesy of Jerry Browder

which was to have you extend your hands, palms up, which she would strike with a ruler. On one occasion, as she was about to administer her justice to one of the guys, she deviated from her usual form, and decided to strike his hands with her hands instead of using the ruler. At the last instant he retracted his hands, and she struck the piano, causing the class to laugh. I know for sure I heard her say, "damn!"

Miss Hendricks was the fifth grade teacher for many years, but by the time I got there, Miss Lewis was teaching the fifth grade. We kids really liked her, and I have some fond memories of her class, but I don't remember much about what she taught. Being in Miss Lewis' classroom was like having a Little Theatre Director as a teacher, because she was always recruiting students for some school play or activity.

Over the years, when reminiscing with other former students, even if they had attended years before or years after I did, we always got around to talking about Miss Carrie Williams, the sixth grade teacher. She, like Miss Giddens, was there long before I started, and long after I left. Miss Williams didn't smile too often, and there was no question about just who was in charge of the classroom. She would tear your behind up in a heartbeat if you misbehaved. She perfected corporal punishment, and I was convinced on a couple occasions that when it came to me, she would have preferred capital punishment. On one particular occasion, one of my classmates decided to challenge her authority. It took her about ten minutes to set him straight, but afterwards, it took Mr. Villenuve, the Janitor, at least an hour to clean up the mess and put the pot bellied stove back in the middle of the room where it belonged. She was the warden and we were the inmates, and if we didn't follow the rules, we got the big stick. She had one unusual form of punishment, which she used quite often, which was placing an unruly student under her desk, while she sat at the desk to prevent an "escape." This was early introduction to solitary confinement. One student's mother was really upset over this method of disciplining her son, and one day she stormed into the classroom, ready to do battle with Miss Williams. It was bad timing for everybody concerned, because her son was under the desk at that time, which caused his mom to explode. There was a lot of shouting and finger pointing as she jerked her son out from under the desk. I suspect he would have preferred to stay right where he was. She was irate, and appeared ready to fight. Frankly, my money would have been on Miss Williams. I don't remember if she continued that "under the desk," method of punishment, but I suspect she did.

The Lord gave us The Ten Commandments some time before Miss Williams started teaching at Suter School, but she increased the numbers considerably. She was unquestionably a good person, an outstanding teacher, and even better than that, she was a good Christian lady. She lived somewhere over in the East Hill area, and walked to and from school every day, which helped to keep her in good fighting shape.

My exposure to Miss William's discipline was not only a very traumatic experience, and very humiliating, but had a negative effect on my early romantic life. I was "in love" with a certain blonde in the fifth grade, and her class let out for lunch five minutes before our class did. So, each day, I would strut up to the pencil sharpener about one minute before the bell rang for our class to dismiss for recess, and then I would go thru the motions of sharpening my pencil. The pencil sharpener was next to an open window, and as the bell rang, the class would all jump up and head out the door, and among all the noise and chatter, I would bail out the window, and hit the ground just as my "true love" rounded the corner of the building. This worked great for about a week until one day as I followed my normal procedure, my true love wasn't there, but Miss. Williams was. She caught me in mid-air, and by the time by feet hit the ground she had already gotten in several good licks. Flight would have been in order, but fright, or just plain scared, was in control; besides she had such a death grip on me I couldn't get away. Suddenly, I was no longer interested in romance, because I knew that when I got home, my dad would probably take up where Miss Williams left off, and I was right. Being in love was just too dangerous.

Fighting

Grammar school at that time, or at least grammar school at Suter, was not only an institution of primary learning that developed our minds and bodies; it was also a war college that developed and expounded on the theory of "fight or flight." Fighting was a way of life if you wanted to live to be twelve or thirteen, or if you needed to impress your new girl friend. Otherwise, flight was the preferred choice. Early on, I learned a very helpful rule, the same rule they later taught us in high school, which was: "the shortest distance between two points is a straight line." Our house was three blocks from the school, and I had two choices, and neither was a straight line. I could go north one block to Frank and M. J. Menge's house, turn left and go two blocks to my house; or I could go west two blocks to Walker's Boat House, turn right, go one block and be home. At the time it simply made good sense to me to know my escape routes well in advance.

M. J. Menge
Courtesy of Earle Bowden

What didn't make good sense to me was for a kid to pick a fight with someone that he knew he probably couldn't whip. The only thing dumber than that was to pick a fight with two guys. What really helped a kid grow in stature in the eyes of his classmates was to pick a fight with someone he knew he could whip. The advantages were many. For example, he would announce at recess who he planned to beat up, and the time and place, and by the time school was out, half the kids and most of their dogs would be there waiting for the big event. I employed this strategy when I was in about the fourth or fifth grade, and my intentions were announced well in advance, so naturally by the time school let out a large crowd had gathered. My designated target lived in that straight line between the Menge house and my house, I needed to catch him in that straight line between the school and their house. Now, let me tell you about the guy I had vowed to beat up that day. He was considered a sissy. Why else would I want to fight him? He always carried his books in a satchel. In those days, any guy who carried a book satchel was definitely considered a sissy. Well, the chase began! He knew what was in store for him, so he chose "flight." What surprised me was that he didn't go in a straight line. He went in circles, plus he cut across an open lot that was full of prickly-pears and briars. He made one big sweep around a big clump of blackberry bushes, and I seized the opportunity and circled in the opposite direction, and then I caught him. Well, to tell you the truth, he caught me, up beside my head with that book satchel. I well remember lying there in a bed of prickly pears, and assuming he had escaped. I was wrong, as he came back, charging like he was a bull and I was a red bandana, and then he connected with that book satchel again. I decided to let him go after that. Humility is a wonderful thing, and it will certainly change one's attitude. We became good friends.

The War Years

Our country entered World War II while I was in the fourth grade, and shortly thereafter my two oldest brothers volunteered for military service. Eventually, just about every student and every teacher had family members or relatives who were either in the military, or actively involved in the war effort. There are many things to recall about being a student at Suter during the war years, but most prominent in my memory was the huge pile of scrap metal, collected for the war effort, situated in the southeast corner of the school yard. That scrap pile was ongoing, and everybody contributed. We kids would bring pieces of metal of all kinds to school with us, as well as cans of old cooking grease. During the day and weekends, adults would add to the pile. Periodically, that gigantic pile of scrap metal would disappear, and we would start all over again. We were proud to know that the pieces of metal we would heave onto the

Rita Hayworth poster promoting scrap metal drives during World War II. Courtesy of the National Archives and Records

pile might become ammunition or a part of an airplane or melted down to become part of a ship or tank. We were not aware that this same scenario was going on in every schoolyard throughout the entire country. Those were tough times for our parents, but they, like the rest of the country, showed the resolve that America is known for during tough times. People were proud to be Americans, and they didn't complain about the government. The country was unified against Japan, Germany and Italy.

The Armistice Day School Parade

Annie K. Suter School was always involved in the Armistice Day parade in downtown Pensacola. This was a big event for the students, teachers and parents. Each student was issued a gold and blue cape and hat, and as a group, we looked sharp and colorful. The parade began on South Palafox Street, below Ferdinand Plaza, along about where all the bars, snapper boats, and the old Desoto Hotel were located. The route of the parade was up Palafox Street to Wright Street, back down Palafox Street to Garden Street, and out Garden to about where the old L & N Railroad Engine is situated today. This must have been a pet project for Miss Coley, because she was serious about that parade each year, making sure all six grades were there, not misbehaving and marching with pride. She and the teachers marched right along with us. She taught us to be proud of our school, and we were. Those were the days when we started our school day with a prayer; we stood with our hands over our heart and recited the "Pledge of Allegiance," and sang "God Bless America."

The logistics of getting the kids from all six class rooms to town, in position and lined up in proper order; and then doing all this in reverse, was a monumental task for Miss Coley and the teachers. I don't recall the use of school buses, and I know there were no "portable toilets" in those days. Obviously, there must have been a convoy of private cars, in spite of gas rationing. The "tinkle" factor alone just blows my mind. Perhaps we knew not to wet our pants, or she might "sic" Miss Williams on us.

Eightieth Anniversary and My Day of Infamy

On April 20, 2001, sixty-two years after I first entered Suter School, I returned for the celebration of the school's eightieth anniversary. The reunion proved that true friendships last forever. It proved also that criminals always return to the scene of the crime. It was exciting to be back in that old building, but, like all of my surviving classmates, it had changed considerably. That old vintage structure had been transformed from a wonderful, but old schoolhouse with six classrooms and six pot-bellied stoves into a lively, modern institution with all the latest amenities. Several of us returning dinosaurs decided to take a walking tour of the old building. Each of us had special stories to tell, and memories we cherished about each classroom we visited and the specific teacher we had. The principal's office had not changed in all these years. It was unbelievably small. I stood in the doorway, and suddenly I experienced that same fear I felt the day Miss Coley was pressuring me for a confession. It was not a good day.

My "day of infamy" was when I was in the third grade. After school, I was playing with matches as I walked past the schoolyard on my way to Russell's drugstore. "Doc" Russell didn't exactly give us kid's permission to read without buying, but we managed to keep up with "Captain Marvel," and other comic book heroes while "sneaking a look" at the pages as we devoured our ice cream, drank our cokes or sucked our "Black Cow" candy on a stick. With my dime spent and my mission accomplished, I started home, walking in the direction of the school. As I approached the school, I couldn't believe what I was seeing. The whole schoolyard was on fire, including the fence posts, and smoke was billowing high into the air. The entire neighborhood was filled with smoke, and I could hardly see the flashing lights from the fire trucks and deputy sheriffs' cars. Many people had stopped to fight the fire. I didn't break my stride as I continued through the smoke toward home. I had a lot on my mind. The next day, Miss Coley interrogated me all day. Someone reported seeing "That little Davis boy playing with matches." I denied everything. Now, sixty-eight years later, I want to confess. "I did it, I set the darn schoolyard on fire, but I didn't mean to." Confession must be good for the soul, because I feel better already. Plus, I checked, and the Statute of Limitations has expired.

Group photos of each day of the 80th Reunion, April, 2001
(More photos at the end of this essay)

P.T.A. Meetings, Dogs and School Projects

Suter School apparently had an active P. T. A. group, because it seemed like the moms' were always involved in some project at the school, such as the Easter Egg Hunt, the Armistice Day parade, programs and plays put on at the Community House such as the "Womanless Wedding," and numerous other projects that have faded from memory. When the P.T.A. met back then, it was usually during daylight hours, as I recall, so they must have met sometime after school was out for the day. Otherwise, there wouldn't have been any place for them to meet. The participation must have been very high, because it was always a large number of mothers invading the school on P. T. A. day.

Mr. and Mrs. Tom Brown, Sr.

As explained earlier, half of my time at Suter School was during the war years, and during the early 1940's gas, along with most everything else, was rationed. People had learned to think twice before jumping into the family car to go someplace unless it was absolutely necessary. Unfortunately, most families had only one car, unlike today when everybody in the family over sixteen has their own vehicle. It was rare for each parent to have their own car. So, it was obvious to everyone that the P. T. A. was having their meeting, when all the mothers were observed walking, from all directions in East Pensacola Heights, toward the school. On one occasion, my mother and my aunt, Marie Brown, were standing in front of the school with a group of other P. T. A. members, conversing about who knows what, when the unexpected happened. It was not uncommon for someone's dog to be mixing with the crowd, and unnoticed, a big dog lifted his leg in true canine fashion and tinkled up and down Aunt Marie's leg. If that pooch couldn't tell a post from a leg, he sure as heck couldn't care that there was a war going on, and stockings were hard to get. He would have cared if he had known that my aunt owned a pit bull named "Arco."

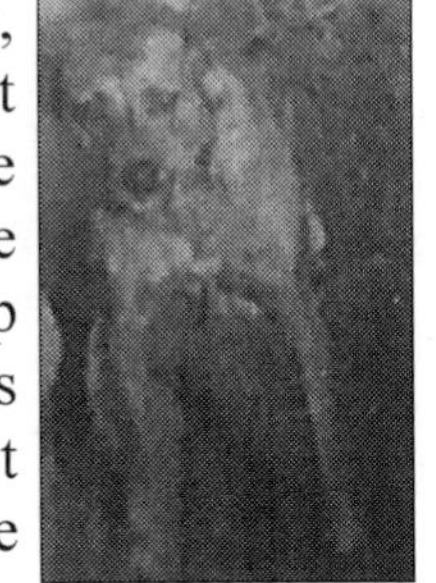
Our Rosie

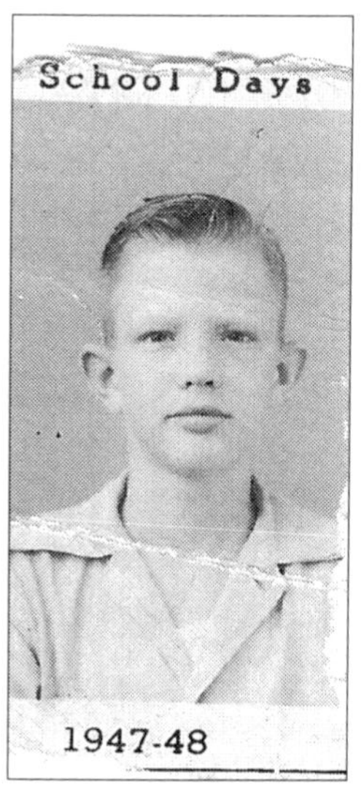

Charlie, Jack, and Tom Davis

Bob Davis

Dogs were part of the scene. We not only knew everybody in East Pensacola Heights personally, but we also knew their dogs. Every family had at least one, and if the kids were not fighting with each other, their dogs probably were. Our dog "Rosie" was a Heinz Fifty Seven breed. Her un-official title was "Rosie, out of Arco." At first, we gave her the uncommon name of "Rover," but had to change it for obvious reasons. We considered her to be the most beautiful dog in the world, but years later, revisiting some old pictures, we realized she was one ugly dog. She loved to fight, and her record of wins was much better than mine. Dogs seemed to know when school was about to let out. Rosie would walk the three blocks to the school yard, and wait for me and my brothers, Jack and Tom. My brother, Bob, had already graduated, and was attending A. V. Clubbs Junior High School. We didn't really need the bell or the clock to tell us school was about to let out; we could tell by the number of dog fights going on in the school yard.

Some of us at Suter were addressed by our nicknames rather than our given first name, and in several cases, we never knew the other guy's Christian name. There were nicknames, such as, "Peter Rabbit" Lee, "Baldy" or "Sonny" Stowe, "Jimbo" Bradley, "Nappy" Goodrich, "Squirrel" Browder, "Bubba" Brown, "Popsey" Schiller "BoBo" Wyse, "Donkey" Williams, "Hoss" Davis, "Snowbird" Early, "Goat" Bonifay, "Beaver" Barber, "Dago" Rhodes and too many more to mention, and several I wouldn't want to put in print.

Easter Egg Hunt

Like other grammar schools in the county, Suter had an annual Easter egg hunt for all the students. Mrs. Stowe, Sonny's mother, who was also the mother of my sister-in-law, was always in charge of the egg hunt and when I say that she was in charge, I mean she was in charge. She was a fairly small lady, born in Scotland, and married to a retired Master Sergeant in the U. S. Marine Corps, which is probably where she got her "Drill Sergeant" attitude. She made the rules, which the students, the other P. T. A. members, and the teachers followed. She was a wonderful lady, very community minded, and talented. Mr. Stowe owned a nursery, so she had access to all kinds of pretty flowers. As we kids grew older and started going to dances, Mrs. Stowe would make our boutonnieres and corsages for our dates, and they were always special, prettier than the ones we would have otherwise bought in town. The best part was that she would never let me pay for the boutonnieres or corsages.

Ms. Agnes McMurray Stowe
Courtesy of Fanny Davis

Sonny Stowe
at 14
Courtesy of Fanny Davis

On the day of the Easter Egg Hunt, she and other well instructed P. T. A. ladies would hide the eggs. She always hid the golden egg. The student who found it won a special prize. One memorable year, Sonny found it, and claimed the prize, which was good for a lot of good natured accusations, and some not so good natured. After the hunt, most of us would "knock eggs," which amounted to gently striking eggs together until one of them cracked, which the owner would forfeit. One year, "Peter Rabbit" Lee and Ray Goodrich ended up with a couple pillow cases full of Easter eggs, because their eggs never cracked. The reason they never cracked was that several days before they had skillfully carved two wooden eggs, which they painted to look like Easter Eggs.

The Womanless Wedding

Several years after I graduated from high school, the P. T. A. decided to produce a play, to be put on at the "Community House," as a fund raising project for the school. The Community House was the meeting hall for residents of East Pensacola Heights, and accommodated all types of functions, ranging from political rallies to Boy Scout meetings. The play they selected was a "Womanless Wedding," which was a tremendous success. Frank Menge portrayed the Preacher, and the groom was played by Barne Morain, Sr. The mother of the bride was played by John Trice. Those two, Barne Morain and John Trice, stole the show. I was a flower girl, and a gorgeous one at that. My aunt, Vera Davis, was the piano player. There were too many in the cast to mention, but the production was a tremendous success, and an example of how well the community and the parents joined together to support Suter School. There were many other projects, before and after our production, to show support for the school. Perhaps it's true, that the community of East Pensacola Heights, as a village did its part to help raise and support the children at Suter School.

I'm pretty sure that the professionals in education, or a least the schools of education at our universities, have some tool for measuring the long term success of education in our grammar schools. Since I'm not in the field of education, I have no clue as to how that could be determined. I believe professional educators would have been impressed with the positive comments made by those former students that returned to Suter School for the eightieth anniversary celebration. It was evident that everyone had a deep respect and love for their former teachers. This was a real laboratory for those interested in long term effects on students. Several former students that attended the open house were there when Suter School opened its doors eighty years ago. One of those was my uncle, Shirley Brown. I attended both open house sessions, and not once did I hear a negative comment about the school or any of the former teachers. East Pensacola Heights was a true microcosm of society, and the makeup of the returning former students was no different, although a large majority had retired from their chosen fields. All of our former teachers at Suter would have been proud of the overall general and specific comments by their former students. The words of Saint Paul are appropriate: "Well done you good and faithful servants" So, if you can measure the success of a program by the gratitude of its recipients, then Annie K. Suter School has been an outstanding success, and will continue to be in the future.

Most Influential Teacher

Most former students could look back at their days at Suter and pick a teacher that was their favorite, or the one that had the most influence on their lives after grammar school. Personally, I liked all of my teachers, but the two who influenced my life the most, and for different reasons, were Miss Carrie Williams and Miss Sadie Coley. Miss Williams was a disciplinarian. Jackie Thompson expressed the feelings of most other former students, when he described her as, "a darn good teacher, but she would put that stick on you." Even though I thought she was going to knock my head off, when she caught me jumping out the window, I know now that what she did was "for my own good." However, I know it didn't hurt her as much as it hurt me, but she usually let the punishment fit the crime. I knew then, she wasn't really mad with me, she was simply disappointed that I would do such a stupid thing, and she had that rare ability to convey that to us. I don't believe any student ever disliked Miss Williams. I believe every student respected her. Her objective was to teach us, and she did. For some of us, she had to teach a little harder. She believed that reading, writing, math and discipline was helped along with a good hickory stick.

Miss Coley was more subtle with her discipline, but she was tough. She had the dual responsibility of teaching the second grade and being the principal, a task which would appall today's modern teachers. I doubt that she had all the paperwork and other responsibilities that are thrust upon teachers and the principal at the current Suter School. She didn't have the benefit of all the testing techniques, the specialists, counselors and agencies; nor did she have all the restrictions placed on the teaching professionals that exist today. She and the teachers made decisions "in the field," and most of those decisions were final. If we had a discipline problem, she handled it, and if we still had a problem, she handled it again. We had to "get over it." Most of our parents backed the teachers when it came to discipline, with the exception of Miss Williams' "under the desk" episode. Frankly, I would have preferred the spankings at school than the one's I got at home. Unfortunately, if my brothers and I got a spanking at school, then we got a spanking at home for getting the spanking at school. Double jeopardy was not a defense in the Davis house.

Occasionally we will come across a quote that we like, and we will lock it away in our memory bank, and we will remember it every now and then for old times sake. Every kid that went to Suter School, while Miss Coley was there, was exposed to what must have been her most effective quote, which was, "Water dripping day by day, will wear the hardest rock away." I remember her uttering that quotation to me numerous times. Obviously, I was not the best student in grammar school, because she seemed to have shared that quote with me an inordinate number of times. In the military, and all thru college, I would recall that quotation, and I would appreciate her a little more each time. After college, and in the business world, that quote would surface when I needed a healthy dose of patience and perseverance. With my family, my four children, my spiritual concerns and with life in general, patience and determination are called upon time and time again, and I would think of Miss Coley and her quotation. That little quote of hers didn't help me excel in any area, but it gave me solace at a time when it was needed, and helped me find a proper prospective on the problems and concerns at the time. All teachers would probably be shocked if they really knew just how much they have influenced their former students through the use of one simple statement, a small encouragement or through the use of a simple quotation.

I suspect that sixty-eight years ago, Miss Coley was ninety-nine percent certain that I set that school yard on fire that day. If she could have gotten a confession from me, I'm not sure what punishment she would have had in mind, but it would have been minor compared to what my dad would have inflicted. Every time I pass by Annie K. Suter School, I think of all those wonderful teachers and school mates I had so many years ago, and whenever I see a Smokey The Bear commercial, I think of that school yard on fire. When I get too impatient with a project I'm working on, or with one of life's little problems, I think of Miss Coley and "Water dripping day by day will wear the hardest rock away."

HAPPY 80th BIRTHDA
HAPPY 80
HAPPY 80

HAPPY 80th

HAPPY 80th BIRTHDAY SUTER

4

Arthur W. Davis

Arthur W. Davis

My grandfather, Arthur William Davis, was an interesting and fascinating man. He became a Pensacola lawyer in 1913, and later served as the U.S. Commissioner for the Northern District of Florida. He was born on August 16, 1857 in Ruthin, Wales. His father, Benjamin Davis, was born at Bolton, Lancastershire, England in 1810, and practiced law for sixty years in Chester, England, near the Welch border. His mother, Susanna Williams Davis, was born in 1820, at Ruthin, Denbighshire, Wales. He had seven siblings, and all but two

Benjamin Davis

remained in England and Wales. His brother Thomas F. Davis, settled in Galveston, Texas, and his sister, Susanna (Griffith Jones), also settled in Pensacola, Florida. I never knew my grandfather, since he died nine years before I was born, but the more I learned about him, the more I wanted to know. When my siblings and I were young, we didn't know much about him, but as we matured we began to acquire bits and pieces about his life as a young man traveling the world over in a seafaring career, being involved for years in hotel businesses in South America and the United States, and as a soldier of fortune in a South American war. Much of what we learned about him was published in the History of Florida, Past and Present, Historical and Biographical, Volume III, The Lewis Publishing Company, Chicago and New York, pg. 34-36, 1923

My grandfather attended schools in Ruthin, Wales and Chester, England, and it was his father's wish that he should become a lawyer. He was disciplined in the reading of the law at too young an age, and at

Arthur W. Davis and his wife, Sarah Emma Foulkes

Arthur and Sarah's home in Ferry Pass

age thirteen, he ran away from home and pursued a seafaring career. He had an adventurous career, visiting many ports throughout the world, including those of South America, ending up in the hotel business in Valparaiso, Chile. His inclination for adventure included his becoming a soldier in the Chilean army from 1879 to 1881, in the "War of the Pacific," which lasted from 1879 to 1884, and involved Chile, Peru and Bolivia. He left Valparaiso, Chile in 1881, and returned to New York, City, where he had previously been in navigation service out from the ports of New York and Boston, on passenger and mail steamers. His connection with the hotel business, as manager, steward or proprietor, continued in several cities along the eastern seaboard.

Arthur W. Davis fishing

On June 26, 1884, at Liverpool, England, my grandfather married Sarah Emma Foulkes, daughter of Robert and Margaret

(Roberts) Foulkes, of Wales. They had six children: Susie (Jim Adams), Elizabeth (Scott Harter), Robert A. (Delphia Ellis), John H. (Vera Creighton), Ben L. (Flossie Johnson), my parents, and William, who died in early childhood. All of the above aunts and uncles, and my parents, are deceased as of this writing.

In 1896, my grandfather accepted employment with Armour & Co. and after assignments in Birmingham, Mobile and Bessimer, Alabama, he was promoted to Branch Manager in Pensacola in 1900, a position he held until 1912. In order to fulfill a promise he made to his father, he resumed his study of the law, and in 1913 he was admitted to the Florida bar. That same year he was appointed Special Agent for the Department of Justice in Pensacola, an office he maintained, in addition to his private practice, until 1920. When the United States entered the conflict in World War I, he found it necessary to devote full time to the official duties of the Department of Justice, in which he had supervision of the territory between Pensacola and Tallahassee. In April, 1920, when the Government wanted to transfer him, he resigned his position, and returned to private practice. In January, 1921, he was appointed United States Commissioner for the Northern District of Florida. The following information was written about my grandfather:

> In January, 1920, the Government sent him to Philadelphia on special service for the Department of Justice, and while in that city he assisted in the capture of Grover Cleveland Bergdoll, the draft evader whose case has been a matter of international prominence.
>
> Mr. Davis is aligned staunchly in the ranks of the Democratic Party, and he served two years as a member of the Board of County Commissioners of Escambia County. He is a member of the Florida State Bar Association and the Pensacola Chamber of Commerce, and is affiliated with the Masonic fraternity, the Woodmen of the World, the Benevolent and Protective Order of Elks, the Knights of Pythias and the United Commercial Travelers. He owns and occupies the fine old colonial mansion erected by the late Judge A.E. Maxwell at Oakfield, five miles north of Pensacola.

> Mr. Davis has written a number of short stories which have appeared in different magazines, and won the first prize for short stories offered by the State Fair, and 'Uncle Jeff's Cabin,' which has appeared in serial form.
>
> *History of Florida, Past and Present, Vol.*III,
> The Lewis Publishing Company, N.Y., 1923, pp 35

My grandfather resigned his position as U. S. Commissioner due to ill health prior to his death on August 17, 1923, at age sixty-six. My grandmother, Sarah Emma Davis, died in 1943, at age eighty-three. They are both buried at Clopton's Cemetery in Pensacola, Florida.

Arthur W. Davis,
Charcoal portrait by G. Fred Brown

DAVIS IS APPOINTED FEDERAL COMMISSIONER

Arthur W. Davis was yesterday appointed by Judge William B. Shepard as United States commissioner of the northern district of Florida, filling the vacancy caused by the death of Judge John C. Avery. Mr. Davis has been a member of the Pensacola bar for several years and during the war was with the department of justice as special agent of the bureau of investigation.

Pensacola News Journal article dated
January 19, 1921
Courtesy of Pensacola News Journal

ARTHUR W. DAVIS IS DEAD; FUNERAL THIS AFTERNOON

U. S. Commissioner Passes Away After Illness Of Several Months

After a lingering illness of several months, Arthur W. Davis, U. S. commissioner and well known in Pensacola business and legal circles, died yesterday morning at his home, Oakfield. He had reached his 66th birthday Thursday.

Funeral services will be held this afternoon at 3:30 o'clock from the home. Rev. J. C. Skottowe of St. Katharine's church will officiate. Burial will be in the Clopton cemetery at Brent.

Honorary pallbearers will be G. Earl Hoffman, assistant district attorney; Fred Cubberly, district attorney; U. S. Marshal Peter Miller, R. P. Reese, T. J. Sullivan and Dr. T. H. Stokes. Deputy marshals and prohibition agents will be active pallbearers. They are R. F. Stearns, Arthur Butterfield, J. D. Knepper, Cuyler McMillan, S. A. Johnson and Archie Odom.

The deceased was forced to give up his position as U. S. commissioner several months ago because of ill health and had been confined to his home since. He was born in Wales in 1857 but came to America when a boy. He had been a resident of Pensacola for 30 years, coming here from Bessemer, Ala. He was admitted to the bar in 1912 and became U. S. commissioner in January, 1921.

Survivors are a widow, three sons, R. A., J. H. and B. L. Davis of this city, two daughters, Mrs. J. M. Adams of Cottondale and Mrs. Scott Harter of this city, two brothers, Thomas Davis of Houston, Tex., and John Davis of England, and two sisters, Mrs. G. Jones of this city and Miss Lizzie Davis of England.

Members of local camps of Woodmen of the World, of which the deceased was a member, will attend the funeral in a body.

CROWDS ATTEND DAVIS FUNERAL

Many Floral Designs At Funeral of U. S. Commissioner Arthur W. Davis.

Funeral services for Arhtur W. Davis, who died Friday morning at his home, Oakfield, were held yesterday afternoon from the family home. Burial was in the Clopton cemetery at Brent with Rev. J. C. Skottowe performing the ceremony.

Large number of the deceased's hosts of friends and relatives attended the funeral and many beautiful floral designs were placed on the bier. Six deputy marshals and prohibition agents were active pallbearers while men prominent in the business and legal world acted as honorary pallbearers.

The deceased was 66 years of age and was U. S. commissioner at the time of his death, though he had been confined to his home for several months through illness. He was born in Wales but had lived here 20 years. Survivors are a widow, three sons, two daughters, two brothers and two sisters.

Above :
Pensacola News Journal article dated
August 19, 1923

Left:
Pensacola News Journal article dated
August 18, 1923

Courtesy of The Pensacola News
Journal

5

Ben L. Davis, Sr.

Ben L. Davis, Sr.
Charcoal portrait by G. Fred Brown

My dad, Ben L. Davis, was born on February 27, 1899 in Mobile, Alabama to Arthur W. and Sarah Emma Davis. Siblings were, Robert, John, Susie, and Elizabeth. His father was associated with Armour & Company, and after a short residency in Bessemer, Alabama, he moved the family to Pensacola in 1900, where he served as branch manager until 1912. In 1913, his father was admitted to the bar, and began the practice of law in Pensacola. The family lived in a large home in the area known as Oakfield, which is situated in the north Brent area. Dad attended Pensacola High School and

Ben L. Davis in his World War I U. S. Army uniform

Pensacola Business College when the normal mode of transportation was by horse and buggy.

During World War I, Dad served in the American Expeditionary Forces in France and Germany, and upon his return to the states, he married my mother, Flossie Aline Johnson, on July 17, 1920. She was the daughter of David Ernest Johnson and Emma Creighton Johnson. Mom's father died when she was very young, and her mother later married Capt. William Ed Brown, who served several terms as Pensacola's Harbor Master. Both my maternal and paternal grandfathers died before I was born, so William Ed Brown, whom we grandkids called "Papa Brown," was the only grandfather my siblings and I ever knew. My parents had eight children: Ben L. Davis, Jr., William A. Davis, Emma Jean Davis (Redding), Robert E. Davis, Charles E. Davis, Fay Aline Davis (my twin sister), John E. "Jack" Davis and Thomas H. Davis. Over the years the family lived in various parts of the county, but for over thirty years the family home was on Bayou Boulevard in East Pensacola Heights.

Dad first went to work as a yard clerk at the old L & N Depot at Wright and Tarragona streets before World War I. After discharge from the army, he returned to his job with the L & N Railroad at the new depot between Wright and Gregory streets. He loved the Railroad, but unfortunately in 1926 he suffered permanent injury to his foot while on the job, and upon his return to work he was relegated to lower paying jobs. During the Depression years, job security was a real concern, as many railroad workers were being laid off. So, in 1932, encouraged by

Ben L Davis and his wife Ms. Flossie Aline Johnson

Dad and his brother, Bob, enjoying one of their favorite pastimes
Note my dad "sculling" his boat

his friends, he decided to try local politics. With the support of his fellow railroad employees, his many relatives and friends, he defeated the incumbent, winning the race for the office of Supervisor of Elections for Escambia County. He remained in that office for sixteen years, although he had strong opposition each term.

In 1948, Dad ran for the office of Tax Collector and won. He was the Tax Collector for Escambia County for the next sixteen years, and ran unopposed the last twelve of those years. He retired in 1965, after

Ben L. Davis' family. Standing L to R: Tom, Jack, Charlie, Bob, Bill, and Ben, Jr.
Sitting L to R: Emma Jean and Flossie Davis

thirty-two years in public office, totally amazed and appreciative of the confidence shown by the citizens of Escambia County.

My father died on April 14, 1969 at age seventy. My mother died on May 8, 1994, at age ninety-three. They are both buried at Bayview Memorial Cemetery, beside my brother, Jack, who died on March 22, 1984, and my sister, Fay, who died January 16, 1935.

Backed Into Office

Ben L. Davis Recalls Railroading and Politics

Ben L. Davis wasn't too perky but the words bounced from him like kids on a trampoline.

Davis, retired Escambia tax collector (as of 1965), and a former railroader and county voter registrar, lay a little squirmy on his hospital bed.

Davis, whose son, William A., banged head first into politics and is chairman of the present County Commission, kind of backed into political office.

"Politics were the farthest thing from my mind as a young man," Davis declared. "I was content then to be a railroader.

By IRA BROCK News Staff Writer

"I was a yard clerk when the old L&N depot was at Wright and Tarragona before World War I. I worked in the yards at Goulding.

"I went into the war and it must have been about that time they were building the present L&N passenger station.

"After the war I came back to the railroad as a clerk and enjoyed every minute of my

Ben L. Davis Recalls Railroading and Politics

FROM PAGE ONE

job until Dec. 18, 1926.

"Before I left the house that day, Flossie (Mrs. Davis) told me to hurry home after work because she wanted to do some Christmas shopping.

"I was riding between two freight cars in the yards and I kicked loose a hitch claw (a coupling) and the car ahead rolled away.

"The jaw of the coupling of car I was on stuck and I kicked it again, just when the car ahead rolled back down the grade and caught my left foot.

"It cut off about two thirds of my foot and Flossie didn't get in any Christmas shopping that day.

"Those railroaders were a great gang but they didn't always accept a man right off the bat, and sometimes a fellow didn't know where he stood with them.

"I found out they had accepted me after I lost my left foot and they passed the hat and gave me $2,700.

"The railroad only came through with $1,500.

"I stayed on with the railroad as a clerk, ticket puncher and down the scale to a watchman as the depression deepened and men were bumped from their jobs.

"I had a lot of laughs with the railroad. One day two sailors watched a cabbage head engine in the Goulding yards.

"One of them said it burned wood and his buddy said it burned coal. The first one said, "I don't care what it burns, it sure make a lot of noise."

"At one time I worked in Nashville. While there I went to Bell College, a girls' school. I got in because I had a ladder.

"Things didn't look too good with the railroad in 1932 and some of the fellows talked to me about running for election as the voting supervisor.

"I didn't know a thing about politics, but my railroad buddies went to work, and they had enough persuasion with their friends to get me elected.

"I don't suppose there were more than 5,000 registered voters that year. If there had been as many as today I might not have been elected in 1932."

Closing of the quotation doesn't mean that Davis had run down. Tumbling of his words like acrobatics going on stage was halted of necessity.

A nurse stuck a thermometer in his mouth to take his temperature.

Interview with Ben L. Davis, Sr. dated March 28, 1969
Courtesy of The Pensacola News Journal.

Ex-Tax Collector Succumbs at 70

Ben L. Davis, 70, retired Escambia County tax collector and a former railroader and county voter registrar, died Monday morning in a local hospital.

Mr. Davis, of 6233 Vicksburg Dr., was a native of Mobile County, Ala. He was educated at Pensacola High School and Pensacola Business College. He came to Escambia County in 1904.

He was an employe in the L&N Railroad clerical and transportation departments for 12 years before becoming county voter registrar.

Mr. Davis was a member of the Masonic Lodge, the Lions Club, Veterans of Foreign Wars and Heights Baptist Church. He was in the Army in World War I.

He was elected tax collector in 1948 and retired in 1965.

Funeral services will be at 3 p.m. Wednesday in Fisher-Pou Chapel with the Rev. Fred J. Martin Jr. and Chaplain Norman L. Redding officiating.

Burial will be in Bayview Memorial Park Cemetery with Fisher-Pou Funeral Service directing.

Surviving are his wife, Mrs. Flossie Johnson Davis of Pensacola; a daughter, Mrs. Emma Jean Redding of Starke, Fla.; six sons, Ben L. Jr., W. A., Robert E. and Tom H. Davis, all of Pensacola; Charles E. Davis of Tampa and Jack E. Davis of Stuart, Fla.; two sisters, Mrs. Susie Adams and Mrs. Elizabeth Harter, both of Pensacola; a brother Robert A. Davis of Pensacola; 23 grandchildren and 11 great-grandchildren.

BEN L. DAVIS

Article dated April 15, 1969
Courtesy of The Pensacola News Journal

6

Big Bird

In 1998, my wife, Sandra, and I completed the construction of our dream home on East Bay in the Redfish Point area. I had always dreamed about having a home on the water, with a dock, so I could simply walk outside and go mullet fishing, crabbing, floundering, swimming, or anything else that has to do with water sports and fishing. We are still in a state of disbelief and euphoria. We had an artist make a wall plaque for us, which contains our names, and the words, "Here We Are Where We Ought To Be." It hangs over the double-doors leading to the deck and the water. Although the property is in Santa Rosa County, the area is a lot like East Pensacola Heights was when I was a kid, with lots of oaks, palmettos, pines, prickly pears, mosquitoes and every kind of indigenous wild animal, fish, fowl and plant imaginable. We enjoy watching all the wildlife, and observing how some animals have adjusted to our encroachment on their habitat. We are especially amused by one street-smart, beautiful, Great Blue Heron, who is closely attached to a neighbor a couple docks from us.

Our neighbor, Lonnie Murphy, retired years ago, and several times each day he walks out on his dock to check his crab traps, and to "see" if the mullet are running. Right behind him, like a shadow, is this

Lonnie and Bobbie Murphy
Courtesy of Mr. & Mrs. Lonnie Murphy

big Blue Heron. It's like they're joined at the hip. We refer to the heron, as "Big Bird." Wherever you see Lonnie, there's "Big Bird." If that faithful bird isn't perched atop the Martin house at the end of Murphy's dock, he's probably under their covered picnic area. A couple years ago, Lonnie built a small covered shelter at the end of his dock, which I assume was just for Big Bird. It's really something to watch during a storm, or on a hot sweltering day, to see that bird hunkered down in the shade, out of the weather. I suppose there's nothing unusual about a buddy looking out for a buddy.

There's one thing for sure. That bird has one heck of an appetite. He'll eat just about any kind of fish or small crab you give him. When Lonnie's not around, he will panhandle all the other fishermen. All I have to do is appear on my dock with a castnet, and Big Bird is immediately on the scene. He won't come as close to me as he does to Lonnie, but he will follow behind me from dock to dock as I try to catch him a meal. Fortunately, he's not too choosy, because I once fed him an old ugly toad fish as well as a small sting ray. I have no idea how much he can eat, but one day I fed him five regular size mullet, one after the other, and he gulped each one down, head first, and then flew back to his perch, and harassed the Martins. It's an interesting sight to watch him duck as the little Martins dive at him. It's obvious when he's irritated, because he lets out a shriek that can be heard up and down the bay.

Charlie and Big Bird

Lonnie once told me how persistent that ole Blue Heron can be when he's hungry. As I recall the story, Lonnie was working on something in his garage, and Big Bird came into the garage and kept glaring at him and talking to him. He actually has a kind of growl when he's trying to get your attention. Lonnie said he chased him out of the garage, and later while on the other side of the house working on his truck, his winged friend lit on top of the truck and wouldn't leave him alone. "So," Lonnie said, "I got my castnet and we went out on the dock. I wanted to catch him something to eat, so he would leave me alone. I threw and threw that darn castnet, but I couldn't even catch a choaper."

"Charlie" swallowing his fish

We both laughed, and I asked him, "What did you do then?"

"The only thing I could do," he answered. "I went up to Winn Dixie and bought him some mullet."

Now that's not just true friendship, that's true love.

When I shared the first draft of this article with Lonnie and his wife, Bobbie, I learned some interesting facts about that Great Blue Heron. I was quickly informed that the big bird's name was "Charlie." named after the late Charlie Kinsley, who was an avid mullet fisherman and a resident of East Pensacola Heights for many years. When ole "Charlie" showed up at the Murphy dock 26 years ago, he was just a small, immature bird that was being abused by an older Blue Heron, who was protecting his territory. Lonnie felt sorry for him, and made sure the youngster got his share of the fish. That's all it took, it was love at first fish, and he's still around after all these years. Now, he protects his territory, with an attitude. He hangs out with the Murphy family, like all their other pets, on the dock, on the patio, and he would probably walk into the house if they would let him.

Charlie Kinsley
Courtesy of Lonnie & Bobbie Murphy

"So, Bobbie, why did ya'll name him after Charlie Kinsley," I asked? I'm glad I asked her and not Lonnie, because he might be reluctant to explain the real reason.

"Well", she said, "Charlie Kinsley taught Lonnie how to throw a castnet years ago, and they used to fish together all the time. One day, years after Charlie died, Lonnie was cleaning fish, and that bird was right there with him, as usual. Later, Lonnie came into the house and told me a strange story."

"What kind of story?" I asked.

"He said, 'Now, I don't think I'm crazy, and I know that birds can't talk, and I don't believe in reincarnation, but, either I'm crazy, or that bird just spoke to me.'"

"Really," I asked? "What exactly did he say to him?" I laughed, but realizing she was being serious, I silently waited for her answer.

Her response was that Lonnie told her, "I heard that bird say just as plain as day in Charlie Kinsley's voice, 'you (Bleep), I fed you mullet for years, now, it's your turn to feed me!"

"Was he serious?" I asked, then quickly added, "I mean, was Lonnie Serious?"

"Just as serious as he could be, and he really believes that bird is the reincarnation of Charlie Kinsley," she answered.

Who are we to say it didn't happen? Why couldn't it have happened just like Lonnie said? Big Bird, I mean, "Charlie", is really Charlie Kinsley! I can't help but recall that about twenty-five or thirty years ago, Charlie Kinsley was a frequent writer of letters to the Editor of the Pensacola News-Journal. His letters were well written and very poignant. I suspect that those who bore the brunt of his letters were relieved when he died and the letters stopped. If they only knew.... he's back! If the Pensacola News-Journal ever changes its policy regarding anonymous letters, maybe he'll peck out a few more.

Even though, ole' "Charlie" continues to eat the goldfish from our neighbors, Harry and Becci Kaeser's, little lily pond, I will treat him with more respect in the future. I just wish he would talk to me! I have lots of questions.

In 2001, a revision of the above article was published in Dockside Magazine. In 2003 hurricane Ivan destroyed the Murphy's home and dock. They built a new home on pilings, but at the time of this publication (2009), they had not replaced the dock; but I'm happy to report that our friend "Charlie" is still around. Wouldn't it be nice if he could tell us, in Charlie Kinsley's voice, of course, how he survived the ravages of hurricane Ivan when all the houses in the neighborhood were either destroyed or heavily damaged?

Today, as we drive past the Murphy's house, it's a common sight to see that beautiful Blue Heron patiently waiting at the front door for his daily ration of chicken legs. He still patrols the neighborhood for a handout. One of his favorite perches is in a pine tree in our yard, which positions him just above our front deck. Occasionally, about daybreak, he will let out one of his blood-curdling screeches, which we are used to now, but it does drive our neurotic cat bonkers each time.

Sadly, Harry and Becci Kaeser died a couple years ago, not too long after they rebuilt their home. We miss them very much. The new owners, Pete and Melanie Whitehouse have rebuilt the little fish pond, and recently, Melanie was showing off the new stock of goldfish. I didn't have the heart to tell her that ole "Charlie" would be mighty pleased also.

Pete and Melanie Whitehouse (inset) and their goldfish pond
Courtesy of Pete and Melanie Whitehouse

Paintings of Big Bird "Charlie" by
Gloria Nobrega
Courtesy of Len and Gloria Nobrega,
New Wave Engraving & Painting
Gulf Breeze, Florida

7

The Big Little Book

I'm surprised how many people in my age group don't remember the "Big Little Books" that were so popular when we were kids around the time World War II came and went. Just about everybody remembers the comic books which are still going strong today, but for many, the cute little Big Little Book has faded from memory. I remember that the movie, *The Biscuit Eater* was playing at the Florida Theatre one Saturday morning back in the early forties, and the admission price to see it was one Big Little Book. The books were sent to the guys and gals in the military. A gigantic cardboard box was positioned near the door, and as we

From the Duane H. Siers Family Collection, Bienes Center for the Literary Arts
Courtesy of the Broward Library, Ft. Lauderdale, Florida

entered, we tossed our coveted Big Little Books into the box. When my brother, Bob, and I, and our three cousins, Jack, Bubba and Tom Brown, entered the theatre, the box was overflowing. *The Biscuit Eater* is a story about two kids who adopted a bird dog they named Promise, who refuses to hunt for anything but its own food. All the kids in the theatre fell in love with the dog, and when the dog was accidentally shot and killed, it seemed like every kid in the theatre was bawling. When the lights came on, each of us tried to hide our tears, and not one of us, to this day, would admit to crying.

A kid just wasn't with it back in the thirties and forties if he didn't have a drawer full of Big Little Books. It's interesting that the comic books are still around big time with collectors, but publishing the Big Little Books, a part of the comic book industry, stopped years ago. I often wondered how they got started and why they didn't last. I found the following answer to the first part of the above question on the internet:

> *In 1919, Captain Joseph Patterson of Chicago's Daily News sought to increase readership by creating comics that appealed to the public's morbid fascination with crime. Soon after, "Dick Tracy" was created. Following the success of the "Dick Tracy" strip, its artwork was recycled into a cheap but unique book form in 1932. And Big Little Books were born.*
>
> *Redskins Are Dangerous and Other Lessons,*
> Stephen Ausherman, 1998

The little books were indeed unique. As I recall, most of them were hardbacks, text was on the left page, pictures (a comic strip frame) was on the right page, and some books ran up to as much as 500 pages. They covered everything from Little Lulu to Little Women, and Terry and the Pirates to Flash Gordon. Picture, if you will a 500 page book that measures about four inches square. An added feature were the small, separate drawings or pictures on the upper right hand corner of each page on the right side, which became animated when flipped rapidly with the thumb. These books originally sold for five and ten cents, but through collectors and traders, they now sell from $8.00 to $1,600.00.

The books were a successful, short lived, commercial venture. Kids could read about the exploits of their favorite hero in the Sunday "funny papers," buy a big little book, tune in to the afternoon radio program, and for a dime, they could watch the movie...all about the same hero. That was four media outlets for the same series or character. Multimedia "hype" had arrived. Today, comic characters enjoy three of the above media forms, plus T.V., Internet, CDs, DVDs, live concerts, action figures and video games. The poor little Big Little Book became obsolete, a victim of high tech.

After all these years, the characters are still familiar: Betty Boop, The Phantom, The Green Hornet, The Shadow, Captain Marvel, and the ones that are still going strong, Superman, Batman, Tarzan, and Spiderman. Wouldn't it be nice to visit the old Walgreen's Drug Store, downtown, and just to have something interesting to read while enjoying one of those big milkshakes made with real ice cream and real milk by a real "soda jerk," we could "borrow" from the huge rack of comic books, our favorite Big Little Book?

An Exhibition from the Duane H. Siers Family Collection,
Bienes Center for the Literary Arts.
Courtesy of the Broward Library, Ft. Lauderdale, Florida

8

Black's Wharf, the Old Swimmin' Hole

Oh! The old swimming'-hole! In the long, lazy days
When the humdrum of school made so many run-a-ways
How pleasant was the journey down the old dusty lane,
Whare the tracks of our bare feet was all printed so plane
You could tell by the dent of the heel and the sole
They was lots o' fun on hand at the old swimming'-hole.
But the lost joys is past! Let your tears in sorrow roll
Like the rain that ust to dapple up the old swimming'-hole.

The Old Swimmin'- Hole
James Whitcomb Riley

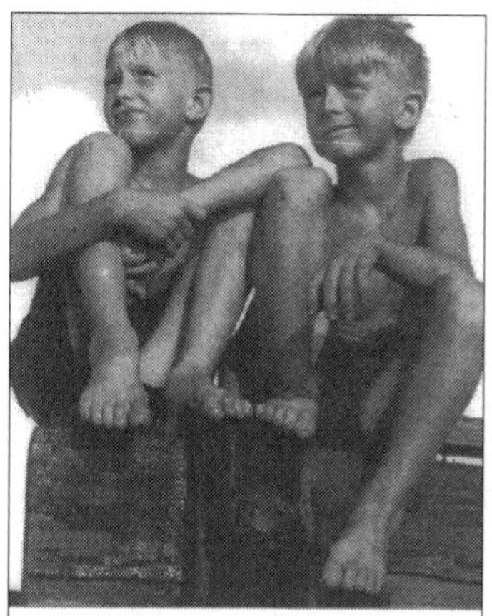
Jack and Tom Davis perched like pelicans on Black's Wharf, circa 1940s.

When James Whitcomb Riley wrote The Old Swimmin'-Hole, he didn't have Black's wharf in mind, but when I remember the great times my siblings and I had at Black's wharf from the late thirties into the sixties, I can't help but think of Riley's poem. Black's wharf was our swimming hole in East Pensacola Heights, situated on Bayou Texar, across from Bayview Park. I don't know for certain who built the wharf originally, but we always assumed it was built by the previous residents of the big house across the street from the old wharf. The family name was Black, and the wharf must have been built prior to the thirties because it was just a skeleton of a dock in 1938 when my family moved into our new home just two blocks away. The Lavender family lived in the house during most of the years that my siblings and I were kids and spending time at Black's wharf.

There were many other places to go swimming, because the Heights is a peninsular, surrounded by two bays and a bayou. Still, most of us preferred to go to Black's wharf, on Bayou Texar. We could look across the bayou and see and hear the people enjoying themselves at Bayview Park, which was always crowded in the summer months. When old friends get together, and talk about the good times we had growing up in East Pensacola Heights, Black's wharf will always be a favorite subject.

L to R: Fred Keller, George Van Metre, Trent Van Matre, Bob Keller, Mary Ann Keller Kickliter. (circa 1940s) Courtesy of Mary Ann Keller Kickliter

It is strange that Black's wharf was such a popular place to swim and gather, because the wharf itself was in terrible shape. The wharf's structure was substantial and was constructed of creosote timbers and posts, but all that remained of what once must have been an attractively built dock or wharf was a skeleton of timbers full of rusty, dangerous nails and spikes. No one, as far as I can remember, ever made an attempt to nail new decking other than a few boards at the end of the dock. But, did that stop us from running back and forth on it like a bunch of monkeys? Heck no!! You can always identify a person who grew up in the Heights by looking at their scarred up feet. Occasionally, when someone did add a board or two out on the end, some of us would take turns showing off our version of the swan, jackknife, cannonball or the belly bust. Anytime we could get our hands on a large plank, it became our diving board, the source of a lot of cuts, bruises, and busted behinds.

It's a wonder that many of the adults didn't get together and repair the old wharf, because many of our friends would come to swim or picnic for hours at a time, and others would come to go crabbing or fishing. The beaches and the clean water were much more attractive to some than the old wharf, but many of us kids loved that old wharf, even though it was indeed dangerous to climb upon.

Black's Wharf, circa 1940s
Courtesy of Mr. & Mrs. Ben Kickliter

We usually couldn't get through the day without somebody getting splattered up beside the head with a combination of mud and seaweed. Once it started, everybody got into the act. Normally, though, it was quiet and peaceful at Black's wharf, and most of us had a healthy respect for each other. It was really an enjoyable place to be on a hot summer day, at a time when hardly any of our homes were air conditioned. Often, especially during the weekends, entire families would come, and cars and bicycles would be parked along the road and in the woods, causing traffic problems along Bayou Boulevard. It was at Black's wharf where many of us learned to swim, and where we taught our younger brothers and sisters and nieces and nephews how to swim. Mary Ann Keller often brought her siblings, Susan and Billy with her to Blacks wharf. Two of my nieces, Marie and Margaret, my brother Ben's oldest daughters, would often accompany me to Black's wharf. It was interesting to watch how my two nieces and Mary Ann's two siblings would risk all when attempting to out do each other. They would attempt any challenge; dives, flips, cannonballs, you name it.

Many of us would often swim across the bayou to Bayview Park, a city maintained recreation park where we could meet up with our city friends on the other side of the bayou. We would enjoy the many amenities such as the three story dive tower, diving boards, swings, the small city zoo, the bathrooms and ice cream, if we had any money. When we were ready to go home we would simply swim back across the bayou. We had the best of both worlds. As we got older some of us would prefer going to Pensacola Beach or Bayview Park, perhaps because of the excitement of the larger crowds. But if we just wanted to be with our friends, in our own neighborhood, then we had Black's wharf to enjoy.

Mary Ann Keller Kickliter and sister , Susan Keller Fillingim
Courtesy of Mr. & Mrs. Ben Kickliter

Margaret and Marie Davis
Courtesy of Margaret Miller

9

Bob Davis the Inventor

When my five brothers and one sister and I were growing up in East Pensacola Heights in the 40's and 50's, we boys always had one or more projects going on at the same time. Our yard looked like a school for industrial arts students. All my brothers were good at building things. For my brother, Bob, there always was more than one way to skin a cat. It didn't mean much to him if somebody said something couldn't be done. If he couldn't do the job himself, he got somebody else to do it. He has always been resourceful, even as a kid. If he wanted something, and

Bob Davis

he couldn't buy it, and he couldn't get somebody to give it to him, or lend it to him, then he would build it. He could build just about anything.

Bob Davis as a teenager

Bob kept us well supplied with kayaks at a time when it seemed like every kid in East Pensacola Heights and East Hill owned a kayak. He made a wood frame, covered it with canvas, and painted the canvas with what we called "dope," a paint that was used on airplane skins. That was the only dope we knew of in those days, except for a few friends. He also made a diving helmet from an old galvanized water tank, by first, cutting it in half and then cutting out on each side for the shoulders, so the tank/helmet rested on both shoulders. Next, he cut out a square in the front and welded on a face mask with a glass front. Finally, he attached one end of a long air hose to the helmet and to the other end he attached a bicycle pump. He, Bob LaBounty and Freddie Cleaveland would each take turns walking all around the bottom of Bayou Texar while the others would stay busy in a boat pumping air into the helmet.

Freddie Cleaveland
Courtesy of Helen Cleaveland Simmons

Bob also built what might have been the world's first "Outboard Motor Bicycle," or, it was the first that any of us had ever heard of, by attaching a twelve horsepower air-cooled "Water Witch" outboard motor to the handlebars of his bicycle. He accomplished this by replacing the propeller with a bicycle

Bobby LaBounty
Courtesy of Gail & Bobby LaBounty

sprocket. He then connected the regular bicycle sprocket and the improvised outboard motor sprocket with what must have been an extended bicycle chain; then he and Fred Cleaveland rode all over East Pensacola Heights until something broke, or they ran out of gas or into something or someone.

On another occasion, he built a "bullet" ride in the side yard of our home, which like the "Bullet" ride at the county fairs, rotated on its axis. He counterbalanced the "ride" by fashioning a huge box on each end for us kids to sit in, and it worked. He charged each kid in the neighborhood a nickel, and did a booming business until Dad made him tear it down, even though we had not yet become a litigious society at that time.

Bob with brother, Ben prior to establishing Bob Davis Realty.
Courtesy of Margaret Miller

Bob is an avid hunter, which may have started with the crossbow he built from an automobile spring's leaf, mounted onto a homemade gunstock. He made arrows from steel rods and the string was a stainless steel cable. It took two guys to cock the thing and once cocked and loaded it was lethal, and once demonstrated to Dad, it was gone. He once built a kite about six or seven feet tall. He borrowed his buddies' belts to use as a tail, which they last saw crashing into Pensacola Bay.

Most of his creations worked to some extent, but not his homemade parachute. Fortunately, he tested it from the top of a large pine tree before giving it the ultimate test. He drew a large crowd that day. His parachute opened....just after he hit the ground, and then everybody was patting him on the back, not to congratulate him, but to help him get his breath. I think he was taller before his jump.

Bob always had money in his pockets. As a small kid he worked at Walker's Boat House selling shrimp and renting boats. He also worked for Captain Maurice Walker on board the charter boat, *Patsy*, cutting bait on trips into the Gulf of Mexico. When he was a lot older, about twelve, he first worked at Pfeiffer's Grocery Store, and then at Philpot's Restaurant and Cottages, doing just about everything. He had his own business at age sixteen. Today, he is a semi-retired Real Estate Broker. Unfortunately, the beautiful waterfront home Bob and his wife, Marilyn, shared near the mouth of Escambia River was destroyed by Hurricane Ivan; putting a crimp in his habit of fishing for mullet almost every day, which he dearly loved to do so he could share his catch with his many friends.

Bob & Marilyn Davis

Bob Davis Family.
L to R Bob, daughters Scotty, and Lynn, her husband, Moe Hayes, grandbaby, Tracy, wife, Marilyn, and oldest daughter, Susan

10

Bob Joseph

Bob Joseph, U. S. Marine
Courtesy of Bob & Nettie Joseph

During the Korean War, I was a U.S. Navy Dental Technician attached to the U. S. Marine Corps at Parris Island, South Carolina. On one of those typically hot days in the summer of 1952, while walking in the direction of the chow hall, I observed a Marine walking in my direction, and thought that there was something familiar looking about the guy. Now, in that time period, on a Marine Recruit Depot that was bursting at the seams with recruits, and a war thousands of miles away going badly, there were many things that I could have been thinking about other than that approaching Marine. Besides, all Marines looked alike to us Navy guys especially when they're fresh out of boot camp. He looked familiar in spite of the "skin-head" haircut and "spit-shined" shoes. We Navy guys took pride in our shoes looking good, but the Marines were not happy unless they could see their reflection in their new, government issued, plain-toed, cordovans. Well, the sun was shinning bright on the guy as he got closer, and his shoes were sparkling. He was looking good like a Marine should. We recognized each other about the same time.

"Bob Joseph," I said, excitedly, as I was glad to see him "What are you doing up here?" I asked. It was a crazy question. I don't remember what his answer was, but it was obvious, because guys our age in 1952 had to be somewhere, like in the Army, Navy, Air Force or Marines. It was great to see another friendly face from home, although I had been seeing a lot of young men my age from Pensacola as they went through boot camp at Parris Island. In the weeks prior to seeing Bob, I ran into John Farebee, Billy Harrison, Billy Tummler and others. Fortunately, all of them survived the war and returned home safely. It was especially good to see Bob Joseph, because he was from the neighborhood, East Pensacola Heights. Bob's family was among the early pioneers of East Pensacola Heights. His grandfather, Mark Joseph, settled in the "Heights' long before the first bridge across Bayou Texar was built. According to Bob, his grandparents crossed the bayou on barges to get home. Bob's father, Millard Joseph, Sr. helped build the Community House, the gathering place for East Pensacola Height's residents for many years. Bob and I grew up

Charlie Davis & Billy Harrison

Charlie Davis, Billy Tummler, and Charlie's 1939 Packard

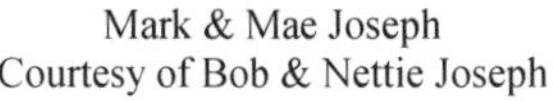

Mark & Mae Joseph
Courtesy of Bob & Nettie Joseph

Marian & Millard Joseph
Courtesy of Bob & Nettie Joseph

together. We were in Boy Scout Troop 101 at the same time, and we had great times at Camp Big Heart. I'll always be indebted to him because on a beautiful moonlit night on the beaches of Pensacola Bay he introduced me to the wonderful game of "Spin the Bottle." It was like reaching a new milestone in life, finding out that you could kiss a girl without making her cry. I don't know what Bob promised the girls, but they all showed up. He was a master of the game, and organized the events with great enthusiasm, just as he organized his life after returning home from the military and began building his successful retail grocery businesses.

His first grocery store was "Heights Grocery" at the corner of Knowles Avenue and Lee Street in East Pensacola Heights, which he opened in 1957 at age 26. Bob told me the story about how a friend, a successful business man, loaned him money to purchase the existing neighborhood grocery store from Mr. and Mrs. T. H. Blackmon, Sr. His many years of working in the grocery business, especially his fourteen years with Delchamps, provided him with the necessary knowledge and

Bob and Nettie Joseph

experience to succeed in his first entrepreneurial venture into a very competitive field. Those who know Bob would not be surprised to learn that he repaid the loan long before it was due. Well, we're all familiar with the old, well worn saying, "Behind every successful man, there stands, a surprised mother-in-law" or a nagging wife," but that wasn't the case with Bob. His secret for success was, in his own words, "The love of my life," who is, of course, his wife and partner, Nettie.

Nettie is a southern belle from Mobile, Alabama, and it was a case of one belle ringing another's bell. Bob said, "It was love at first sight," and he's never been the same since. The truth is, she hasn't either, but that's getting ahead of an interesting story. Bob's pursuit of Nettie is a classic study in the philosophy of "Definiteness of Purpose," which is defined in most first class sales manuals. Bob said to me recently, "I had made up my mind that she was going to be my wife, and on the day she graduated from high school, I gave her an engagement ring." Talk about "robbing the cradle," but that's no problem when you're out of your mind in love. A short time later, sixteen year old, Nettie, returned the ring to Bob, saying she just didn't want to get married. Bob reacted like most broken hearted guys would, he joined the Marine Corps. Did it change his position about "having Nettie as his wife someday? No way! He had already made up his mind; he had "definiteness of purpose" engrained under that Marine Corps helmet. He then did what most successful people do when complications arise; he went to Plan B, which was a letter campaign to Nettie's mom. Did it work? Of course it did, and they were married on April 5, 1954. They have two wonderful children, Melissa and Robert, Jr., plus three grandchildren. Like their family, their business continued to grow.

Robert Jr., Nettie, Bob, and Melissa Joseph

After operating Joseph's Grocery for seven years, Bob and Nettie expanded in a big way. In 1964, they built a new, modern building on Scenic Highway in East Pensacola Heights, and opened Joseph's IGA. For the next thirty-three years their business thrived, meeting the grocery shopping needs of their many friends in East Pensacola Heights and customers from other neighborhoods, throughout Pensacola. In 1997, Bob and Nettie sold Joseph's IGA to David Apple, and the tradition of good service continues

Joseph's IGA

today under the business name, Apple Market. A huge expansion was completed in 2009.

Today, Bob and Nettie are happy retirees, and active in many endeavors. They attend the First United Methodist Church in Pensacola, where Bob is an usher and has been the chef for the Joe Harrell Men's Bible Breakfast for several years. He loves to fish for mullet, and you should know he still keeps his shoes shined, even though his hobby is "Wood Turning." Nettie is active in several areas of the church, including the United Methodist Women, and the church library. Her hobby is obviously gardening, since she is a certified Master Gardener. East Pensacola Heights is part of the city of Pensacola, but if it were a separate city itself, Bob Joseph would have been a likely Mayor. He did a lot for the "Heights."

11

Bodie

Bodie at his typewriter at The Pensacola News Journal
Courtesy of the McCrory Family

It was 1951, a time during the Korean War when most of us in the Naval Reserve unit at Ellison Field were ordered to active duty. Many of us received individual orders to report to Boot Camp, and Vernon "Bodie" McCrory and I traveled on the train together from Pensacola to Harve de Grace, Maryland. The U.S. Navy was kind enough to provide us transportation in one of their old World War II buses to the U. S. Navy Training Center at Bainbridge, Maryland, situated along the beautiful Susquehanna River. It was there, on

October 21, 1951, that we ceased to be civilians and became the property of the United States Navy. We were in boot camp, and our butts belonged to a handful of previously retired Navy chiefs who were quite unhappy about having been called back to active duty.

It was obvious that Bodie wasn't too excited about boot camp, or being away in the Navy. It interfered with his job as a sports writer at The Pensacola News-Journal, and more importantly, it kept him away from his true love and future wife, an attractive nursing student by the name of Helen Holman. About the only thing Bodie had in common with the chief's was that none of them wanted to be there. As for me, I found the whole

Bodie McCrory and Charlie Davis

Back Row L to R: Charlie Davis, Carl Burkhart, Francis Davis, Bodie McCrory.
Front Row: 2 unidentified fellow sailors

experience exciting and interesting.

Bodie was the epitome of a sports fanatic, and on our long trip to Maryland, he was constantly scouring the train and train stations for the sports sections of available newspapers. I heard the life story and stats on just about every sports figure from Ty Cobb to Mickey Mantle and Charlie "Choo Choo" Justice to Eddie Arcaro. I was amazed at just how much sports knowledge and trivia he had stored in that brain of his. It was no surprise to me or anyone else, that he later was considered one of the best in his field of journalism. He would have been much happier as a professional baseball player, his childhood dream, but a bum shoulder put an end to those ambitious thoughts.

If the authorities would have listened to Bodie, the Korean War would have ended quickly, perhaps on a Saturday night at Yankee Stadium, the house that Ruth built. He would have organized one hell of a baseball game between the North Koreans and the U. S and our allies, and the war would have ended in nine innings. Unfortunately he never presented such a proposal, especially since the salty chief's were telling us we would be in "this man's navy" for years to come. One pot-bellied old chief suggested that we write our girlfriends and, "Tell 'em not to wait on youse, 'cause this war's gonna last for years and years." Well, I didn't have a girlfriend at home, but I knew Bodie didn't cotton too well to the chief's suggestion, because he talked about Helen about as much as he talked about sports figures.

Bodie was a teaser, and he would cause some of those guys from the big cities, who were real Dodgers and Yankee fans, to get all excited when he would take a position against, or for one of their teams or players. He could switch his position back and forth, and by the time the shouting was over they would be completely confused. He had that "gotcha" smile along with his loud, infectious laugh. He was in his element when discussing sports, especially baseball, and there was no doubt that he enjoyed what he was doing, and the guys knew that he knew what he was talking about.

We were given a two week leave from boot camp in December, 1951, and Bodie and I boarded a crowded train in Baltimore for a long trip home. We changed trains in Birmingham, and prepared for the usual layover in Flomaton, Alabama, where we would catch another train into Pensacola. We spent more time than we should have in the club car on our way to Flomaton, and had a few more beers than we should have, and

Neither one of us could find our seabags with both hands. With the help.from other G I's, we managed to exit the train, and to our surprise, or shock, both our dads were there to greet us. I don't know how the conversation went in the McCrory car on the way to Pensacola, but it was a bit quiet in our car.

After our return to boot camp, Bodie's bum shoulder was giving him problems. His shoulder would "slip out of joint," and he would be in excruciating pain. This happened several times, and he was later discharged from active duty and sent home. I missed him. He was a lot of fun to have around. He returned to his old job at The Pensacola News-Journal as a sports

Bodie and Helen's Wedding
Courtesy of the McCrory Family

Bodie and son Pat
Courtesy of the McCrory Family

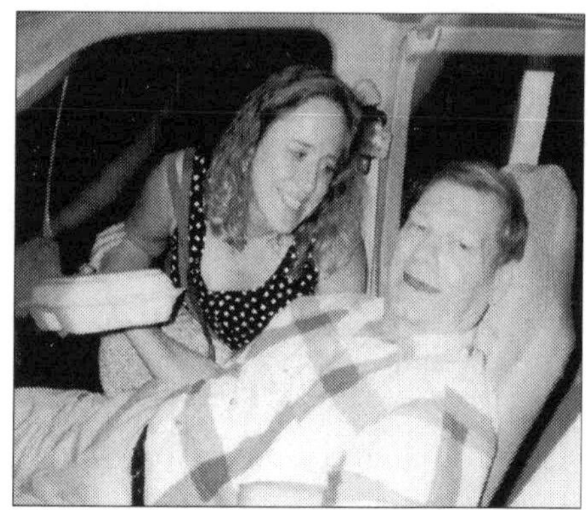

Bodie and daughter, Susie
Courtesy o f the McCrory Family

Bodie and Helen with daughter, Tracy
Courtesy of the McCrory Family

writer, married Helen, and they subsequently became the proud parents of son, Pat, and daughters, Susan and Tracy. Several years later, after I graduated from college, and he was the manager of the sports department, he offered me a job as a sports writer with The Pensacola News-Journal. I thought he was crazy, since I had no experience whatever at writing. He was confident I could do the job, but I turned him down, of course. In retrospect, I wish I had accepted his offer.

Bodie had a distinguished newspaper career, which began as a sports writer for The Pensacola New-Journal in the forties while still in his teens. He was hired by Wesley Chalk, a popular, sports writer, and he began his career by, in his words, “shagging balls for Wesley.” After twenty-eight years with the Pensacola News Journal, he left his position as Sports Editor in 1979 to become the Executive Editor of the Monroe News-Star in Monroe, Louisiana. He retired as Editor and Publisher in 1988, but continued to write a weekly column for the Monroe News-Star. Bodie was active in many civic organizations and community affairs and served as President of the Monroe Chamber of Commerce. He was a member of the Legislative Committee of the Louisiana Press Association, several professional organizations, and served on the Advisory Council of the L.S.U. School of Journalism. His activities and accomplishments placed him in contact with state and national

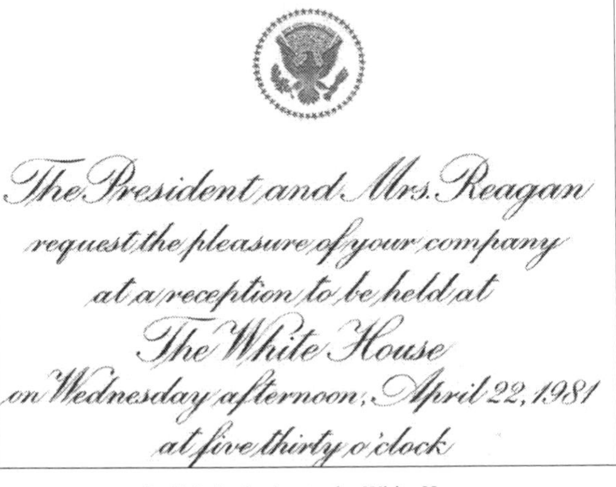

The President and Mrs. Reagan
request the pleasure of your company
at a reception to be held at
The White House
on Wednesday afternoon, April 22, 1981
at five thirty o'clock

Bodie's invitation to the White House
Courtesy of the McCrory Family

leaders, and earned him an invitation to the White House from President Reagan in 1981.

The last time I saw Bodie was June 1, 1991 at the Pensacola Yacht Club at the wedding reception for my son, Frank, and daughter-in-law, Meredith Stanhagan. Bodie's daughter, Tracy, was the maid-of-honor, as she and Meredith were best friends, and still are. I don't know if Bodie ever got that bum shoulder fixed, but a bigger problem was his heart. Doctors couldn't fix it, and it finally gave out at age sixty-three in 1993. Pensacola and the Gulf Coast lost a great citizen, Helen, Tracy, Pat and Susan lost a wonderful husband and father, and I, and many others, lost a good friend.

Meredith Stanhagen and Tracy McCrory, best friends
Courtesy of the McCrory Family

Above: Bodie McCrory, Editor and Publisher of the News-Star World
Courtesy of the McCrory Family

Right: Helen and Bodie McCrory
Courtesy of the McCrory Family

Left: Bodie giving the Commencement Address at Tracy's Graduation from NLU in 1988. Courtesy of the McCrory Family

Right: Bodie and former Governor of Louisiana, Dave Treen
Courtesy of the McCrory Family

Left: Bodie and former Governor of Louisiana, Edwin Edwards
Courtesy of the McCrory Family

12

Brooks Taylor's Service Station

Brooks Taylor at his service station
Courtesy of Joyce Bennink

A few years ago the pop song, *1432 Franklin Pike Circle Hero*, recorded by Roger Miller and others, was about a guy who went out of his way to help all of the kids in his neighborhood. Each time I heard that song, I thought about the late Brooks Taylor, who owned and operated a service station in East Pensacola Heights back in the fifty's and sixties. "Running" a service station is tough, but Brooks managed to provide a good living for his wife and five kids. During those years, he endeared himself to the community, especially the young teenagers with automobiles. He was known to be a soft touch and often gave a "little credit until payday." At times, he also allowed them to use his tools and his facilities to work on their own cars.

To some, he was the "father image" they didn't have at home. Some of the guys that hung around Brook's station back then are now grandfathers, and were eager to share their feelings about Brooks. Wesley "Tal" Chalk, whose father, Wesley Chalk, the well known Sports Writer for The Pensacola News-Journal, died when Tal was only twelve, said "Brooks was the father I didn't have. My love for old cars and the ability to repair them, I owe to Brooks. After I was married, I would often go to Brooks after dinner, not knowing why, I just did. My wife used to say, "Going to kiss Brooks good night?" My daughter, Tina, was born on March 9th, same as Brook's, so each year we always went to his station and shared her cake with him."

Brooks, his wife Helen, children, Nita, Ken & Joyce
May 7, 1943
Courtesy of Joyce Taylor Bennink

John, "Sonny" Ware, wrote, "I remember that Brooks would stay late just to get our cars fixed. He was like a big brother to us. If you had a

Wesley "Tal" Chalk

John Sonny Ware
Courtesy of John Ware

Jerry Browder
Courtesy of June Browder Merritt

Ben Early
Courtesy of Ben Early

problem, ole Brooks would try to resolve it for you. Brooks was a good person and is still missed." Ray Donnelly said, "I had a red, 1940 Chevy with "Big Lee's" air horn on top. Brooks did a good job of painting it red. He trusted me enough to give his two daughters a ride to Pensacola High School every day. At times, a few of us hanging around would decide to drag the main, and bring Brooks back something he wanted from the Famous Drive-In or the Milk Bottle (Pensacola Dairy)." Ray, who has an infectious laugh, added, "I remember one night when a few of us were at Brooks, and Jerry Browder and Bennie Early went to get Dixie Cream Donuts in Brownsville...about six dozen, and

Ray Donnelly, Ronny Pfeiffer, Tom Davis, Bennett Orr, and Charlie McLemore at Ronny Pfeiffer's Wedding
Courtesy of Charlie & Nan McLemore

several of us got milk at Big Lee's and then there was a real eating frenzy."

Tom Davis shared their feelings, and added that, "Brook's wife brought him lunch every day." After his death in 1983, his wife received numerous letters, extolling the positive influence Brooks had on their lives. His daughter, Joyce Bennink, said, "In recent years I've come to realize that my dad had a sense of mission."

Hopefully, he took comfort in knowing he did more than just "stoop" to help young men. Tal Chalk best expressed the thoughts of others, by saying, "My one regret...was not telling Brooks how much he meant to me." Brooks probably knew how each felt, which was his reward for being a good person.

Brooks working at his desk.
Courtesy of Jimmy and Diane Carter

A model of Brooks' service station by Ray Donnelly
Courtesy of Ray Donnelly

13

Brother Bill's Eulogy
William A. Bill Davis
1923 - 2003
Funeral Services
Harper-Morris Memorial Chapel
October 10, 2003
Eulogy

Good Morning, Everybody!

I'm one of Bill's five brothers, and...On behalf of Dickie, Billy, Ken, Barbara, Chris, Fanny and their families, I want to thank you for joining us today to celebrate Bill's life.

Each of us will, of course, mourn Bill's death, but we'll do that in our own way...in our own privacy...but, today, we're here to celebrate his life...his long and active life...and we have many, many reasons to celebrate.

We can celebrate because Bill not only had a long, active and

Bill and Fanny and their sons standing L to R Rusty, Ken, Billy and Dickie
Courtesy of Mrs. Fanny Davis

productive life, but he enjoyed good health almost all of his life. There's an old saying that, "you get out of life what you put into it," and Bill Davis put a lot into life...and he got a lot out of life. He probably got more out of life in his eighty years than most people could get in a hundred and eighty years.

It's quite possible that when the Lord created W. A. Bill Davis that He really did throw away the mold...perhaps the Lord was thinking that one "W. A." every few generations was enough. Whatever the Lord had in mind for Bill, I'm sure he exceeded His expectations, because Bill took life and ran with it.

Bill believed in shortcuts. A good example was when he told me and my cousin, Jack Brown, that he was going to teach us to swim. We were young, and Bill was a young teenager. We all got into a rowboat, and he rowed across the bayou towards Bayview Park, where we thought we were going for swimming lessons. However, he began laughing, and then he threw both of us overboard, out in the middle of Bayou Texar, and said, "Okay, boys, swim or drown." He then rowed back toward

Walker's Boathouse. We learned to swim in one short lesson. That was a perfect example of how Bill Davis "conducted business." He cut through a lot of details, time consuming tasks, and unnecessary paperwork in most activities in his life, and it worked for him.

If Bill had chosen a theme song, it might have been "The Wabash Cannonball," because I remember hearing him sing that song, when I was just a little kid. That's why I requested they play "The Wabash Cannonball" by Boxcar Willie prior to the services. As his little brother, I thought any person that could sing the "Wabash Cannonball," yodel, and blow smoke rings, was some kind of great man. He had his own version of "Dangerous Dan Magrew." but unfortunately, I can't quote him publicly. If title means anything, the proper song for Bill could have been "I Did It My Way."

Bill was an avid sportsman. Fishing was his passion...both fresh and saltwater fishing...and he was darn good at it. He was the catcher on the Catalonia Park team years ago. Two of his former team mates were here at the funeral home last night during visitation, and both said, "He was a darn good catcher." That was a little before my time, but I do remember him as a catcher on several sandlot games in East Pensacola Heights. I thought he was good too, but what the heck, he was my big brother.

I remember when he used to take Dickie, Billy, Ken and Rusty rabbit hunting, when they were small. Back then, the area between East Pensacola Heights, the airport, and Scenic Highway was all woods. He would hunt at night, using the car's headlights...which was not legal, of course. They just about wiped out the rabbit population in East Pensacola Heights. He did the same thing with his grandchildren and nephews & nieces up in Alabama, when he and Carol lived there.

Let me share with you a few things about Bill which most of you already know: Bill was born in 1923...just five years after the end of World War I...just in time to be old enough to go to war in World War II.

A. He enlisted right after Pearl Harbor was attacked...leaving his wife (Fanny) and baby (Dickie) at home. He came home a couple times while going through training, but once he was sent overseas, he remained until the war was almost over.

B. He was in the Army Air Corps...and completed fifty-five missions over Nazi Germany. I'm told that they were all daylight missions.

Bill in uniform
Courtesy of Mrs. Fanny Davis

C. Bill was probably the only American G. I. to take a real live monkey aboard a B-17 Flying Fortress on a bombing mission over Germany.

D. Toward the end of the war, his crew went on a humanitarian mission somewhere in Europe to rescue and repatriate a group of American P.O.W."s. One of those P.O.W."s was Philip Beall, Jr., who later became a State Senator as well as our neighbor in the "Heights."

E. Four years ago, Tom Brokaw wrote a book, entitled. "The Greatest Generation." He shared the feelings of most grateful Americans, when he wrote about the American men and women in uniform during World War II, stating, "I think this is the greatest generation any society has ever produced." He also wrote that, "The sad reality is that they are dying at an ever faster pace...and the Department of Veterans' Affairs estimates that about thirty-two-hundred World War II Vets die every month." Bill is simply part of those statistics.

As for his work ethic, Bill was never afraid of work...

A. Not long after he was discharged he purchased a Service Station in East Pensacola Heights. It was about that time that he and several longtime friends and fellow veterans formed the "Psycho Motorcycle Club." The term "Psycho" was appropriate.

B. He worked at the Naval Air Station for a short period of time.

C. He and his older brother, Ben, owned and operated a Ferry Boat Service in Mobile, until their boat, the *Flossie A*, was damaged by fire.

D. He retired from the Escambia County Health Department, where he held several supervisory positions.

Bill in his office at the Health Department

E. While still working at the Health Department, he founded Pensacola Insecticide Company, and Davis Pawn Shop. He later sold both businesses.

F. Also, while still employed at the Health Department, he threw his hat into the local political ring. He ran for Escambia County Sheriff in 1964, but was unsuccessful. In 1966 he ran for County Commissioner in District four, and defeated the incumbent. He remained on the Board of County Commissioners for one term.

Vote For And Support

W. A. (Bill) DAVIS

FOR

SHERIFF

I Pledge A Business Administration:

The Escambia County Sheriff's Office operates on a budget of more than a half million dollars annually, employing from 75 to 100 people.

If I am elected as your Sheriff, I pledge myself to practice every possible economy that does not impair the quality of the law enforcement and protection you are paying for through the expenditure of this large sum of your money.

To this end I Plan to:

1. Carefully budget the requirements of each department and place upon the department head the responsibility of staying within his budget.
2. Eliminate the controversial car allowance at a saving of thousands of dollars yearly.
3. Put every purchase on a strict bid basis, again effecting a yearly saving of thousands of tax dollars.
4. Seek the co-operation of all other law enforcement agencies — city, state and federal — and avoid any duplication of their efforts. This will save money and will free men and equipment for the performance of the prime duties of the Sheriff's Department.

Sincerely,

W. A. "Bill" Davis

W. A. (Bill) Davis

G. Bill always had a love affair with boats, and I can't remember when he didn't own a boat of some kind. After retirement, he purchased a commercial fishing boat, which he continued to operate, even after he and his second wife, Carol, moved to Alabama.

H. The move to Alabama was a great experience for Bill and Carol. They built a new home on the several acres they acquired, and eventually Bill started two more businesses. First he tried his hand at being a pig farmer, and built a large, modern pig parlor on their land. He didn't particularly like the pig business because of its sensitivity to the market and the economy, so since he couldn't control it, he sold it. Afterwards, he got into the junk car business, and built a large, successful junk yard.

Bill on his boat *The Rampage*
Courtesy of Chris and Sharon Bridges

I. On a fishing trip to

Gautier, Mississippi, he fell in love with the area, eventually bought property on Sioux Bayou, and built a nice waterfront home. He sold his business and property in Alabama, and he and Carol moved to Gautier. He soon purchased another commercial fishing boat, and for the next several years he followed his passion, fishing, which he was darn good at.

Bill and wife, Carol
Courtesy of Chris and Sharon Bridges

J. He had recently sold his farm, but on one of his fishing trips, he almost "bought the farm." He had developed the bad habit of fishing by himself, and on one of those occasions, he was anchored about seventy miles offshore in the Gulf of Mexico, when he was "run down" by a large Gulf shrimper. Bill's boat sank instantly, with him inside. He was able to free himself at a depth of about fifty feet. By the time he popped to the surface, all he could see was the stern of the shrimper, rapidly moving away from him. Fortunately, the captain turned his boat around, and literally jumped overboard to help rescue Bill. It turned out that the captain was a cousin. The company that owned the shrimper was glad to settle with Bill right away, and he soon purchased another boat.

K. Bill loved buying and selling things, from plastic jugs to road graders, and like fishing, he was good at it. He usually gave away about half of everything he bought. You just couldn't visit him without being loaded up with all kinds of things. Sandra and I stopped by to visit, and ended up with a pool table, which we didn't even want.

L. He had a way with kids...he was great with kids. He just had a knack for making kids feel good. He would ask kids a silly question...that demanded a silly answer...that evoked laughter. Kids liked being around him. His grandchildren, as well as his nephews and nieces,...and his little brothers...loved going to his house. His granddaughter, Deneese, probably summed it up for all the grandchildren, when she told her dad, a few days ago, that "some of the best memories of growing up was at her grandpa's house, the farm in Alabama, or out on one of his boats."

M. Bill was always a good host, at home or on his boat. Several years ago, we brothers got together for a fishing trip aboard his boat to the Chandelier Islands. On the way down we got into some pretty large waves, making it difficult to move about on the boat. It was then that Bill, being the perfect host, decided to make some banana pudding. He was able to get most of the ingredients into the bowl, and we did have banana pudding, which was good, since there is no such thing as a bad banana pudding. It was interesting to observe Bill's dress code on that trip. He wore Bermuda shorts, and a pair of high top tennis shoes with no socks or shoe laces, and his underwear hung out about six inches below his shorts.
That was typical brother Bill.

N. He was a practical jokester....with no limits. His friends had to be on guard at all times.

1. On fishing trips with his friends around the Southeast, nobody wanted to stay in the same cabin with him...they were afraid they might go to sleep before he did...and that would have been dangerous.

2. A coworker at the Health Department was bragging about how good the gas mileage was on his new Volkswagen. He swore it didn't burn any gas at all. What he didn't know was that Bill was adding gas to his tank every day. The following week, he siphoned gas from his tank each day.

3. Bill had a houseboat, which he had moored at Conway Creek, near Mobile. His friend, Jim Peaden, had joined him and others for the weekend. Jim was a big eater, and wanted more than just fish, which they planned to catch. He offered to buy steaks if Bill would go to the store and get them, and he gave Bill a blank check...which was a big, big mistake. Bill came back with huge steaks, wine, candy bars, cakes, candles, and a gift for everyone...and the gifts were gift-wrapped, all at Jim's expense.

4. Back when there were no roads on Santa Rosa Island, the Health Department's Mosquito and Rodent Control Department built a cabin several miles east of the Casino. Legend has it that there is a headless woman who walks the beaches at night. I've forgotten the origin of the legend, but Bill intentionally blew it out of proportion, while

explaining the legend to one of the employees he had assigned to spend the night in the cabin. After dark, Bill sneaked back and hid behind a sand dune near the cabin. With a sheet over his head, and disguising his voice as a woman, he called out to the employee several times. The employee, who by that time was scared to death, responded with, "Leave me alone woman, I ain't coming out!" Bill decided not to stretch his luck, because he knew there was a gun in the cabin. These episodes were typical Bill Davis.

Carol & Bill, in his usual dress
Couresy of Chris & Sharon Bridges

O. I talked about Bill's dress code aboard his boat, but it wasn't much better on land. For example, a few years ago, the teller at Bill's bank was hesitant to cash a check he had received on some business transaction, so Bill asked to see the bank's president. Sometime previously Bill had acquired a pair of yellow, high top basketball shoes, which he wore as he strode into the bank, oblivious of onlookers reactions. The bank president, familiar with Bill's good banking history with the bank, said,

"Mr. Davis, we will be more than happy to cash that check, but would you do me one big favor?"

"What's that?" Asked Bill.

"Tell me, please, where in the world did you find those shoes?"

William Arthur, Bill, Davis left a healthy legacy to his children & grandchildren:

A. Five Sons
B. Fourteen Grandchildren
C. Seven Great-Grandchildren......and counting
D. He loved them all....and they loved him!
E. They will always cherish the memories of being at their grandpa's house...his farm...or on his boat.
F. Those wonderful memories will never disappear....for any of us.

Thank You!

Fanny Davis and sons,
L to R Dickie, Ken, and Billy. Inset: Rusty
Courtesy of Bob and Marilyn Davis

Chris, Carol and Bill Davis
Courtesy of Chris & Sharon Bridges

Sharon, Davis, and Chris Bridges
Courtesy of Chris & Sharon Bridges

14

Camp Big Heart

CAMP EMBLEMS

Here's how Camp Big Heart veterans indicate that they have attended the Gulf Coast Council summer Camp.

Attractive red and blue embroidered Camp Emblems are available at the Trading Post to all Scout Campers who have spent one week or more in the Council Camp.

Worn on the right pocket of the Official Uniform Shirt, they proclaim to all the world that you have had this high experience of Scout camping. Each year a Scout spends in Camp is also recognized with an emblem bearing the numerall indicating the number of years experience.

Watch for this sign on the Uniform as the Scouts go by!

Courtesy of The Flori-Bama Scouter

When I was twelve years old, I was a member of Boy Scout Troop No.101, and we had out troop meetings at the Community House in East Pensacola Heights. I believe every boy benefits from being involved in scouting, regardless of how far he advances, or how many merit badges he earns. I didn't advance too far, and I didn't earn too many merit badges, and I'll admit that even though I tried, I haven't always been faithful to the scout motto of "Be Prepared." Like most of my fellow scouts, I can still give the "Scout's Oath" without error, but at age seventy-seven, the part about "keeping myself physically strong and mentally awake" has taken on new meaning for me. Just about everything I remember about scouting was good, with the exception of the "Belt Lines" and the "Snipe Hunts," but what I remember best were the trips to Camp Big Heart, located east of Gulf Breeze on property that is now part of the Gulf Islands National Seashore's Live Oaks Reservation.

Camp Big Heart, the camp ground for the Gulf Coast Council of the Boy Scouts of America, was nestled among the naval live oaks, on the narrow strip of land, south of Highway 98. The center of activity was the large, steep-roofed, unpainted frame building with a wide, covered porch across the south side of the building, and the two massive chimneys' at each end. The rustic structure primarily housed the kitchen and mess hall. No scout could forget the large moose head mounted above the fireplace at one end of the mess hall. The building faced south, overlooking Santa Rosa Sound, and Santa Rosa Island in the distance. Also, visible was the old wooden bridge that crossed over the Sound to Pensacola Beach. Much of the grounds were heavily wooded, mostly with live oaks and magnolia trees, but just under the leaves, weeds and bushes, was pure white sand, just like the beautiful white beach along the entire south boundary of the camp. The camp was situated on high grounds, and to get to the clear, salty water and the long, wide dock,

Bob Joseph, Boy Scout
Courtesy of Bob and Nettie Joseph

Camp Big Heart Is In Santa Rosa State Park

Camp Big Heart is located in Santa Rosa State Park, just seven miles east of Pensacola on Highway 98, which crosses the camp property on the peninsula between Pensacola Bay and Santa Rosa Sound.

The site comprises 300 acres of wooded land and white sandy beaches on two excellent waterfronts. These provide ideal swimming, boating, fishing and other water sport facilities.

Native live oak trees abound in the State Game Preserve maintained by the Florida Park Service. One of the last remaining natural wildlife areas in West Florida, it is truly a haven for Scouts and their camping friends.

Formerly under jurisdiction of the Federal Government for many years, the Navy used the area in World War II as a rest camp, and it is still referred to as the Naval Live Oak Reservation. It was here that choice timbers were marked in the old days for use in building the old wooden Naval vessels, some even being used in "Old Ironsides", the USS CONSTITUTION.

Courtesy of The Flora-Bama Scouter
The Official Bulletin of the Gulf Coast Council-B. S. A.

Above: Main Dining Hall. Courtesy of S. Willard "Vic" Vickery
Below: Cabins in the woods. Courtesy of David P. Ogden, Park Ranger/Historian/Librarian, Gulf Islands National Seashores, Florida District

Above: Inside the Main Dining Hall. Below: Bunks in the Cabins.
Courtesy of David P. Ogden, Park Ranger/Historian/Librarian, Gulf Islands National Seashore, Florida District

Campfire area
Courtesy of David P. Ogden, Park Ranger/Historian/ Librarian, Gulf Islands National Seashore, Florida District

we had to descend a well worn path of white sand to where the dock began. Several small, but well built cabins were situated east and west of the central building.

For many of us, our first visit to Camp Big Heart was our first trip away from home without our parents, and it was exciting. I thought about my first night at Camp Big Heart on my first night in Navy boot camp seven years later. The Scout Officials and the Scout Leaders kept us busy with projects, such as life saving, first aid, knot tying, as well as competitive sports, and time to work on our merit badges. We had lots of free time, so we went swimming and on hikes. We also did things we were not supposed to do.....like, sneaking down the beach to Camp Isabel, the Girls Scout

Activity at the Main Dining Hall
Courtesy of David P. Ogden, Park Ranger/Historian/Librarian, Gulf Islands National Seashore, Florida District

camp also known as Camp Inky, less than a mile east of Camp Big Heart. Of course, we got caught by the adult leaders, who fussed at us and made sure we headed back to our camp. When we got back, the Scout officials, our Scoutmaster and the Scout leaders were waiting for us. It was like being AWOL. On several occasions, we hunted for Indian pottery, or chards, which were bits and pieces of Indian pottery. One fellow scout found a well preserved lid. The handle to the lid was a replica of a bear on all fours. Years later, my wife, Sandra, and I went back to the same area prior to it's becoming a National Park, and found several pieces of pottery and a musket ball.

It was during the time of World War II that I was a scout, and our troop's first Scoutmaster was a Navy pilot, by the name of "Buzz" Sawyer. He was a great guy, very patient and interesting. He must have been transferred, because Mr. "Rags" Diamond, a long time resident of East Pensacola Heights, became our Scoutmaster. They were both very good men, and we liked and respected both of them. Another resident of East Pensacola Heights who was of tremendous help to scouting in general, was Mr. Wallace King. As kids, we didn't fully appreciate all the responsibilities a Scoutmaster has. I learned to appreciate them more after I became a Scoutmaster in 1957 for a troop sponsored by the Downtown Rotary Club. Bobby Kahn and Jack Papador were the advisors from the Rotary Club, and both were generous with their time and help with the troop. It was a great troop, with a great bunch of kids. Years later, while living in North Carolina, my son, Frank, became a scout in the Daniel Boone Council, and I knew exactly how he felt, when his mother and I drove back down the mountain, leaving him on his first night at camp.

On one visit to Camp Big Heart, our troop was involved in a "Camporee," and we were not allowed to stay in the cabins; we had to sleep in our pup-tents in an area away from the main camp. We had to be self-sufficient, doing our own cooking, over an open fire, etc. Bob Joseph, Jack Brown and I, as well as several others, decided to make a bed out of palmetto fronds and Spanish moss, on top of which we laid our sleeping bags. How were we supposed to know that the palmettos and the moss were infested with red bugs? We found out real quick, and we continued to know several days later.

When our troop had a week long stay at Camp Big Heart, our parents were invited to visit on one of the days, which was probably the last day, so they could take us home. I never went to a "Campwoebegone" type camp for kids, so I don't really know how going off to a Boy Scout camp differs, but I wasn't expecting my parents to visit, but they did. I'm glad they came, because I know they enjoyed being there, and they got to witness something that I thought was very, very funny. One kid, who was not in our troop, was, like the rest of us, all squeaky clean, a clean uniform, our teeth brushed, and our hair slicked back. We were ordered by everybody that had any authority, that we were to look good and be sharp, and of course, "Be Prepared." It was like having inspection in the military. It was like the Admiral or the President was coming. Anyhow, this kid looked good. He was clean, and he was fascinated with an eagle that was in a wire pen in front of the central building. My parents and I were looking at the eagle also, but we were observing him from the front of the pen, but the clean, ready to see his parents, kid was behind the bird. I doubt that the eagle planned his next move, and he probably didn't even know that the kid was there, but, if he did, then it was obvious he didn't care. I never was real smart, but even I knew that when a bird, a chicken or a monstrous size eagle lifts it's wing about half way, that it's either going to fly, or let something fly. He did the latter, and he must have been saving up for several days, and my squeaky clean fellow scout wasn't clean anymore, from the top of his head to the top of his shined shoes. I personally would have headed for Santa Rosa Sound, but he hunkered down under a water spigot. The eagle, like all American Bald Eagles, seemed to have a look of pride in himself...perhaps in a job well done.

Today, across the sound from the spot where Camp Big Heart was located, you will see a crowded Santa Rosa Island, replete with many homes, businesses, condos and water towers. At the time I was at Camp Big Heart, the only visible structures on the Island were the Pensacola Beach Casino and the "Fish Hatchery." The old wooden bridge, leading to the Island from Gulf Breeze, was a great place to fish from, and, unlike today with high traffic, a special area was provided for fishing from the bridge. Several scouts slipped away and fished from the bridge, and caught a good mess of croakers, spots and spade fish. They brought them back to the mess hall to be cooked, and those of us who were lucky got a sample to taste. Why is it that normally I would throw those kinds of fish back, as not worth cleaning, but fought all the other kids just for a taste?

I remember the singing at night around a large bonfire and music provided by a scout leader named Alden Langford with his accordion. I don't remember if the singing was good or bad, and frankly I wouldn't have known the difference, but it was such a wonderful experience for me as a twelve year old kid. I have a lot of good memories from my youth, and I never bothered to classify them, but if I did, being in the Boy Scouts and sitting around a big bonfire at Camp Big Heart with dozens of other scouts, would be right up there at the top.

Another thing that stands out in my memory of Camp Big Heart has to do with the guys who were there at the time, who later became leaders in our community and beyond. It's an example of how scouting builds character and leadership in individuals who strive to succeed in scouting, and later exhibit those same qualities of leadership in all that they do. There are many examples, but I can't think of anyone who better demonstrates these attributes than T. A. Shell. He was one of the scout leaders who was on hand the summer I first attended Camp Big Heart. "T. A." was about fifteen or sixteen at the time, and was everywhere and involved in everything regarding Camp Big Heart. He had probably earned all the known merit badges at that time, was an Eagle Scout, and it was either shortly before or afterwards that I read in the Pensacola News-Journal that he attended a World Jamboree of Scouts in one of the European countries. Today, Thurston A. Shell is a senior partner in one of the area's most successful law firms, Shell, Fleming, Davis and Menge, and has unselfishly served his community and his church in countless ways. He is the embodiment of the scout oath, and that torch has been passed on, and on, and on as all three of his sons, Steve, Scott and David are Eagle Scouts. In addition, and no surprise to anyone, his grandson, Jon Shell is also an Eagle Scout. That's five Eagle Scouts in one family, which has to be some kind of record in the annals of scouting since the day Sir Robert Baden-Powell started the movement in 1908.

Camp Big Heart doesn't exist in Gulf Breeze today, but when I visit the former site at the Gulf Island National Seashore's Live Oaks Reservation to fish or go crabbing, I can easily recall the laughter and shouts of the kids swimming in the sound, the jubilant and disappointing yelling of troops in competition, the loud noises in the chow hall and the quietness late at night when exhausted kids are sleeping. But, above all, I can recall the singing of dozens of young voices, and I can almost feel the heat from the gigantic bonfire. What I can't hear, but I know it was there, is the positive developing of young minds and bodies, preparing them to meet the challenges of God and Country.

Courtesy of T. A. Shell

15

Owen T. "Casey" Cason, Capt., F.H.P., "The Best of the Best"

Portrait of Capt Cason which hangs in the Owen T "Casey" Cason building in Pensacola, Florida Courtesy of Florida Highway Patrol

To the average motorist driving along a stretch of Navy Boulevard around the end of the Christmas Holidays in 1959, Sgt. Owen T. "Casey" Cason was just another Florida Highway Patrolman doing his duty. I was helping my friend, and fellow F.S.U. student, Charlie Evans and his new wife, Betty, load an air conditioner into the car for transport back to Tallahassee. My son, Chuck was two years old, and his mother and I neglected to keep an eye on him as we loaded the car. About the same time we both

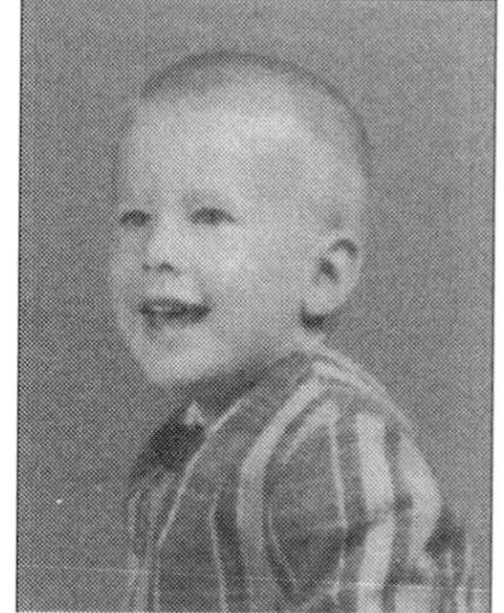

Chuck

Charlie and Chuck and Lolly (behind screen door)

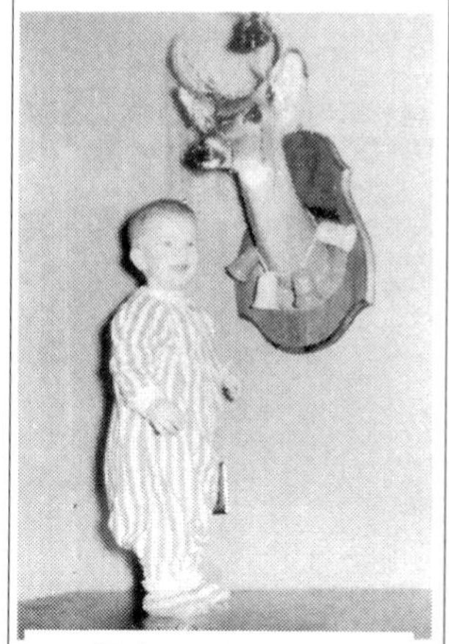

Christmas Card 1959

missed him, we heard the horrible sound of auto tires screeching and horns blowing, which seemed to be coming from all directions. As we looked through the smoke and dust, we saw this big, tall Highway Patrolman standing out in the middle of Navy Boulevard, holding Chuck in his arms, safe and unharmed. The lecture we received from Sgt. Casey Cason was well deserved. I remember him saying to both of us, "If you're not more careful, you're going to lose this child!" We were all in shock, and we

Betty and Charlie Evans, then and now
Courtesy of Mr. & Mrs. Charles Evans

Capt. Casey Cason
Courtesy of the State Archives of Florida

couldn't thank him enough. We were, of course, grateful that he had just saved our son's life. We couldn't know, as we watched him drive off to continue "doing his duty," that he wasn't just another Highway Patrolman, but that he was to become a legend with the Florida Highway Patrol, to be considered "The Best of the Best" by his fellow Highway Patrolmen, and a close personal friend and protector of five future Florida Governors.

In my research to learn as much as I could about this giant of a man who saved my son's life, I talked to many individuals who knew him personally, and some who just happened to be on the receiving end of his style of doing his job as a Florida Highway Patrolman. Everyone I spoke with about Casey said without hesitation, that he was "tough," but always finished the sentence with, "but fair." That was his reputation throughout Northwest Florida. There were many stories about traffic violators attempting to run, on foot, and Casey personally chasing them down. The one story that I thought might just be part of his legend, turned out to be true, and was covered by the news media. It's the story about a truck driver accidentally driving off the Pensacola Bay Bridge, and Casey jumping into the water and rescuing him. So far, I haven't heard of a report of him arresting his own mother, but I was told that he did give a ticket to the brother of a fellow F.H.P. Officer in DeFuniak Springs.

Earle Bowden, Editor Emeritus of The Pensacola News Journal, told me about an incident he had with Casey many years ago. Earle had received a call from his wife, who was visiting her sick mother in Panama City, suggesting he should "come right away." Earle left his office, drove through Gulf Breeze, and continued traveling east on Highway 98 toward Panama City. That area of South Santa Rosa County was sparsely populated back then, and there was very little traffic on the

Earle Bowden
Courtesy of Earle Bowden

highways. He didn't travel very far out of Gulf Breeze before he was pulled over by Casey who, according to Earle, "took a lot of time before he got out of his car." As he approached Earle, he asked, "You're in a big hurry aren't you, son?

"Yes Sir," replied Earle.

"Did you know you were speeding?" asked Casey.

"Yes Sir, I suppose I was," answered Earle.

According to Earle, Casey proceeded to write the ticket while leaning on the hood of Earle's automobile. After he finished writing, he walked over to Earle, who was still sitting in his car, and asked, "Where were you going in such a hurry?"

"Panama City," replied Earle.

"Why are you in such a hurry? He asked.

"I'm going to visit my sick mother-in-law," Earle answered.

"You're what?" He asked, as though he had been given a smart-aleck answer.

"I'm going to visit my sick mother-in-law," Earle repeated.

Casey simply stared at Earle for what seem to be a long time, as if in disbelief. He then did the unexpected; he tore up the ticket, and said as he walked away, "Well, I sure don't want to stand in the way of a man visiting his sick mother-in-law!" He then got into his cruiser and drove away. Surprised, but pleased, Earle continued on to Panama City and visited his sick mother-in-law.

Michael Ferguson, Brigadier General, U.S. Army, Ret., a Civilian Aide to the Secretary of the Army and currently a Pensacola attorney, is the stepson of Capt. Owen T. "Casey" Cason. He spoke respectfully of his stepfather, describing him as being very athletic and having played tackle at the University of Oklahoma. Gen. Ferguson also spoke of Casey as having been "a very dedicated officer," and said, "When the job required eight hours, Casey would spend twelve hours." Such dedication to his job is what made Casey successful in his law enforcement career, but it had an adverse affect on his marriage. He had spent his early adult

Brig. General Michael Ferguson
Courtesy of BG and Mrs. Michael Ferguson

years as a bachelor, and married late in life. The "wear and tear of the job" eventually destroyed the marriage, and Gen. Ferguson's mother and Casey were divorced in 1965. He was later selected by Governor Reuben Askew in 1971 to be his bodyguard and head of security, promoted to Captain, and transferred to Tallahassee. He remained in Tallahassee for the rest of his law enforcement career, and it was there that he earned the respect of his peers and his superiors, and his legend was enhanced.

"Owen T. Cason was a man's man," according to Colonel Joe Henderson, Florida Highway Patrol, Retired. Col. Henderson is the historian for the F.H.P. and was a personal friend of Casey. I talked to Col. Henderson several times by telephone, and it was obvious that he knew Casey well, and held him in high regards. "Owen T. was one hell of a man," he said, adding, "He had a reputation for doing his job" He always referred to Casey as "Owen T," and while discussing his assignment to the DeFuniak Springs area, he said, "Owen T was hardnosed but fair," and "He always did the right thing." Col. Henderson shared a story about a trip to Palm Beach, Florida that he and Casey attended together on Florida Highway Patrol business. The meeting was at the luxurious Colony Hotel, and he said. "Owen T. was awed by the beauty of the place," and "I knew he was a genuinely good person,

Governor Reuben Askew and Capt Cason outside the Capitol after a bomb threat. (circa 1970s)
Courtesy of the State Archives of Florida

Col. Joe Henderson, F.H.P. (Ret.)
Courtesy of Col. Joe Henderson,

and was grateful for what he had." As we ended our telephone conversation, the Colonel said, "He was such a nice person," and paused, and then added, "He was the best of the best."

Both General Ferguson and Colonel Henderson made reference to Casey's athletic ability and his physical attributes. Each talked about how Casey worked out all the time, doing hundreds of sit-ups and push-ups, and how he always kept bar-bells in his patrol car. They also talked about his reputation for running up and down the twenty-two flights of steps, for a total of one thousand steps, every day, in Florida's Capitol Building. It became a tradition of his throughout the time that he personally served the five Governors. "He started his tradition soon after the building was completed in 1977," according to an article about Casey in the St. Petersburg Times, dated February 10, 1999.

Capt. Cason running the stairs in the Capitol in Tallahassee
Courtesy of the State Archives of Florida

Capt. Cason running with Governor Bob Graham
Courtesy of the State Archives of Florida

There is much written about Casey's physical attributes and his dedication to law enforcement, but I soon learned that there was another aspect of leadership:

> One of the contributions Casey was known for was his lifelong work with the American Legion's Boy's State. His presence and energetic entertainment and leadership led many young people in Florida to continue political and other careers after their education. As his stepson, I had the privilege of being at Boy's State with Casey as a high school representative from Pensacola High School, as a Cadet, speaking about my West Point and Boy's State experience, my application of Boy's State leadership principles as a Lieutenant in the Army, and as an Assistant Counselor, once I retired and began my practice of law in Pensacola.
>
> Brig. Gen.. Michael L. Ferguson (Ret)

Owen T. "Casey" Cason served five Florida Governors as their personal bodyguard, including Governor Wayne Mixon, who served as Governor for only three days. Although the mandatory retirement age for Florida Highway Patrol officers was age sixty-two, the State of Florida made Casey an Agent with the Florida Department of Law Enforcement (F.D.L.E.), allowing him to continue his position. The Governors he served and their terms of office were:

1.	Reuben Askew	Jan. 5, 1971	To	Jan. 2, 1979 - 8 years
2.	Bob Graham	Jan 2, 1979	To	Jan 3, 1987 - 7 yrs. 11 mo. 27 days
3.	Wayne Mixon	Jan 3, 1987	To	Jan. 6, 1987 - 3 days
4.	Bob Martinez	Jan. 6, 1987	To	Jan. 8, 1991 - 8 years
5.	Lawton Chiles	Jan. 8, 1991	To	Dec. 12, 1998 -7 years, 11 mo.

On September 3, 1991, on his eightieth birthday, a big birthday party was held for Casey on the 22nd floor of the State Capitol Building. A large crowd attended, and included former Governors, Reubin Askew, U.S. Sen. Bob Graham, Wayne Mixon, Governor Lawton Chiles, Comptroller Gerald Lewis and Secretary of State Jim Smith, and many other friends and state officials. Each of the above officials spoke, honoring Casey for his many years of service to the State of Florida. Casey's grandson by marriage, Michael Ferguson, Jr., gave a talk and presented a plaque, honoring his grandfather.

Capt. Casey Casons's eightieth birthday party at the Capitol Building
Guests: Former Secretary of State Jim Smith, Former Governors Wayne Mixon, Lawton Chiles, Bob Graham, and Reuben Askew
Courtesy of the State Archives of Florida

Casey remarried and lived out his retirement years in Central Florida near Orlando. He died in 1992 at age eighty-one. A memorial service was held in Tallahassee, Florida, and speakers paying tribute to Casey included Gov. Lawton Chiles, former Gov. Wayne Mixon, Secretary of State Jim Smith, and reporters, Dick Kane and Jim Story. Pastor Robert McMillan of First Baptist Church of Tallahassee officiated.

I suppose everyone can think of something important they put off doing until it was too late. In my case, I put off getting in touch with Capt. Owen T. "Casey" Cason to personally thank him for rescuing Chuck almost fifty years ago. I'm not sure I thanked him at the time back in 1957, but I hope I did. We all live with our regrets, and not contacting him over the years is one of mine.

Law enforcement people routinely do things in the course of their responsibility that affects other people's lives in various ways, often jeopardizing their own lives or health. Unfortunately, they don't always get the recognition, praise and show of appreciation they deserve. Obviously, Casey Cason jeopardized his own safety fifty years ago, and our family would like his family and friends to know that we are grateful for his actions. My son, Chuck, and his wife, Laura, have a wonderful, Christian family consisting of two daughters, Julie and Ashley, and a son, David. Chuck earned a Master's Degree in Music Education, is a classical guitarist, and previously taught music at Stetson University. He currently teaches music at Warrington Middle School in Pensacola.

Chuck, wife, Laura and their children David, Ashley and Julie

16

Chicken George

Frank Davis

In the late seventies, my son, Frank, a student at Brentwood Middle School, was into raising quail. For his age, Frank was a good bargainer; however, in one of his swapping sessions with a local hatchery owner, I believe he came out second best, ending up with a chicken. Well, it really wasn't a chicken, it was just a "biddy," a baby chick. The little, fuzzy thing was about three inches high, and looked like a piece of cotton with eyes and a beak. It was exalted as a "Full-Blooded Rhode Island Red Rooster," with such enthusiasm, that Frank was allowed to keep the little ball of downy feathers in his room. He christened him "Chicken George."

Frank and Chicken George
Illustration by Steve Blair,

"Chicken George" wore out his welcome after a few weeks when he began making peculiar sounds, which Frank could imitate quite well. The two of them, talking in young rooster talk, earned "Chicken George" a transfer to the back yard. However, they continued conversing through the bathroom window each morning as Frank was getting dressed for school. He grew into the largest and most beautiful rooster I have ever seen, and became our "junk-yard dog." He loved Frank, and he hated me. Each time I arrived home, I had to devise a new way to enter the house safely, without being attacked by "Chicken George." His usual tactic was to cock his head and freeze as I drove into the driveway, then as I exited the car he would drop one wing and charge toward me with "fire" in his eyes. We would go from tree to tree until somehow I would make it into the house without injury from his three inch spurs.

One day, while I was planting Ivy near the side of the house, I kept "Chicken George" at a distance with a broom. I felt safe as long as I could see him, but he sneaked around the house and attacked me from the other direction. I didn't see him coming, and he was on me like a wild thing, scaring the heck out of me. I instinctively grabbed a fallen limb, and started swinging it, hoping only to scare him away. The limb connected with his neck, and poor ol' "Chicken George" flopped around, and then after laying still, his eyes closed. Shocked, I wondered how the heck I was going to explain to Frank that I had killed "Chicken George." I resumed planting, and minutes later, without warning, that darn rooster attacked again. He wasn't dead, he was mad. It was "deja vu all over again," me and that "dead" rooster, going from tree to tree.

Later, Frank gave "Chicken George" to a friend whose family had chickens, thinking that perhaps a few hens would improve his attitude. During summer vacation, Frank ran into his friend at the mall.

"How's Chicken George doing?" he asked.

"He's dead," his friend replied.

"What happened?" Frank asked, consolingly.

"We ate him," replied his friend, as he continued walking.

Left:
Frank and friend working on his boat, The Native

Left: Frank fishing with me Right: Frank with a redfish.

Frank, Meredith, and sons , Hayden and Hunter
Frank, a graduate of the University of West Florida, is a building contractor and owns Sanddollar Construction Company, Inc. in Gulf Breeze

17

Christmas, Way Back When

I have wonderful memories of Christmas in Pensacola, especially the many Christmas' we seven kids and our parents enjoyed in our home in East Pensacola Heights; singing Christmas Carols and exchanging gifts at A. K. Suter School, and going downtown during the holiday season.

Our family lived in East Pensacola Heights for thirty years, beginning in 1937. That house on Bayou Boulevard is gone now, but the memories, especially the memories of Christmas in that house, will last as long as we last. We never had an artificial Christmas tree, and I doubt

Tom and Mother opening presents Christmas morning

that we ever had a "store bought" tree, because we usually went out into the woods and cut our own tree. Our favorite place to hunt for trees was "Monkey's Camp," which is where "Birnam Woods" subdivision is located today. I can still smell those pine trees when I reminisce about those "good old days."

By the time Christmas Eve arrived, the Christmas presents were stacked almost as high as the tree. My mother believed that everybody in the family, and that included all the aunts, uncles and cousins, and those who were not family, but were like family, should receive a gift. She shopped for bargains on socks, gloves, handkerchiefs and ties, and she wrapped each one with love, in inexpensive paper, as if the contents were expensive keepsakes. All those gifts, which she piled up as she was wrapping them, was as large as the pile of coal delivered in our yard each winter. We always kidded Mother by saying that the cousins probably said, "Well, let's go to Aunt Flossie's and get our socks," because socks were her favorite gift item. Her philosophy was, "Everybody can use a good pair of socks."

People didn't decorate their homes as much back then as they do today, but there were places and areas we always wanted to see. So, Dad and Mother would drive us around to see the decorations. First on the list was always the Coca Cola Company on north Palafox Street, where each year they displayed a large, lighted Santa Claus and his reindeer on top of the building. We would then ride around North Hill and East Hill before going downtown. It was a ritual that was part of our Christmas.

The teachers at Annie K. Suter School primed us with the Christmas spirit each year by deciding who would and who wouldn't sing and participate in the Christmas plays. It didn't take much effort to convince Miss Lewis, our fifth grade teacher, that I couldn't sing or act, and that I was best at just "watching." Each classroom drew names, and we exchanged gifts before going home for the Christmas Holidays. Naturally, some of us grumbled about giving better than we got. We had not yet learned that it was "more blessed to give than to receive."

Christmas dinner at the Davises

When we were young, the typical gifts left by Santa Claus were skates, BB guns, bicycles, tricycles and dolls. Half the kids in Pensacola got skates for Christmas, and the other half got BB guns. A typical scene was dozens of kids on skates, snaking through all downtown areas that had sidewalks, doing the "Hucklebuck" on skates. The "Red Ryder BB Gun" probably did more for the corporate stock of the major glass companies and General Electric's light bulb division than any other economic factor. The albino squirrels at one time existed only in East Hill, but they are now plentiful in East Pensacola Heights. I can think of only one thing that would make a squirrel cross over the Bayou Texar Bridge, and that would be a kid with a BB gun.

As a paperboy I looked forward to Christmas, because some of my customers gave me money and some gave presents. The Pensacola News-Journal helped us by printing Christmas cards that included our individual picture, which we delivered a couple weeks before Christmas. It worked, but those customers, whom I thought were big tippers were not, and vice versa. I still thought, at that time, that "it was more blessed to receive."

If you really wanted to get into the Christmas spirit, downtown Pensacola was the place to be during the holidays. I worked at Douglas-Allen while attending P.J.C. That was 1955, when everything was downtown, including most of the people of Pensacola during the holidays. The sidewalks along both sides of Palafox Street were jammed with shoppers, walking in both directions. People bunched up at the corners, waiting for the traffic light to change. It was the time of year that you saw people you hadn't seen since last Christmas. There was the miracle of Santa Claus being at both Sears and Penney's at the same time, the Salvation Army's music and carols permeating the downtown area, and the ever-present "Gus, the Peanut Man" wearing a Santa Claus hat. For some, the holiday season included joining family and friends at one of the downtown restaurants, such as, the Driftwood, the San Carlos Hotel, Child's, The B & B, the Embassy Cafe and The Dainty Del. For those in a hurry, there was always Bill's Grill and Angel's Chili Bowl.

As I got older, Christmas took on a different meaning, and my friends and I looked forward to attending the parties and dances, including the New Year's Eve festivities. We were, and still are fortunate to have some outstanding bands in the area. A great night was attending a couple parties, and one of the big dances, then having breakfast at Cagles Restaurant... if we could get a table.

Now that I'm old, my good memories are of having watched my own children and grandchildren enjoy the wonderment and joy of Christmas. Along the way I've realized the true meaning of Christmas, and discovered that "it really is much better to give than to receive."

18

Churches

Our family began attending East Hill Baptist Church when we moved to East Pensacola Heights in 1937. Its location on Gadsden Street and 13th Avenue was convenient for those of us in East Pensacola Heights, as there was no church of any faith in the Heights until sometime in the late forties when East Hill Baptist Church sponsored the Heights Baptist Chapel. I was too young to remember, but prior to our moving to the Heights, my family attended Brent Baptist Church, when it was located on the northeast corner of Davis Highway and Kilbee Lane. My mother was a charter member of the Heights Baptist Chapel, so our family began a long time affiliation with the Heights Baptist Church. My mother was a proud Baptist and loved the Baptist Church, but she truly believed it didn't matter what church you attend, just so long as you attend a church. There was no question about her strong feelings for the Baptist Church, and in her faith in the teachings of the church, which she maintained until her death at age ninety-three. She did, however, believe that when Jesus spoke to Simon Peter, saying "Upon this rock I will build

East Hill Baptist Church Sunday School classes, mid 1940s.

my church," that Jesus probably meant the Baptist Church. Although she had her strong feelings about the Baptist Church, she was somewhat ecumenical in her Christianity in many ways. When Pope John Paul II was first chosen by the Catholic Church in 1978, she commented, "I think we've got a good one this time." As usual, she was right.

Rev. W. G. Stracener Of East Hill Baptist Church

My dad's parents migrated from Wales, where they were members of the Church of England, so naturally my grandparents joined the Episcopal Church once in this country. My dad was never an Episcopalian as far as I know, and he was rather slow in becoming a Baptist. He did, early on, attend church and Sunday school with my mom, but an unfortunate incident one Sunday morning caused him to stop attending church. Early in his political career, while attending Sunday school with my mom, a gentleman, upon seeing Dad, said, "Well, hello, Ben, this must be election time!" My dad was embarrassed and didn't attend church for several years afterwards. Fortunately, time takes care of a lot of things, and years later, after he retired from office, he began attending church again. A few hours before he died in 1968, although unaware just how sick he was, he said, "I'm going to heaven." I believe he did. He was a good man, and I take comfort in my belief that he is in heaven right now, with Mom.

I was baptized by Reverend Stracener, whose son, Larry, attended Clubbs Junior High School at the same time I did. I don't really know what prompted me to "come forward" that Sunday morning and agree to join the church and be baptized, but I'm glad I did. I liked East Hill Baptist Church, and I liked Reverend Stracener, and although I don't remember much about his sermons, I do remember most of the girls in attendance. Some of the things I learned won't help me much when I get to the "pearly gates," but there were incidents that I have enjoyed recalling over the years.

As a young teenager, I never felt comfortable when asked to participate in Sunday school. It was a stage in my life when I was shy, and lacked self confidence. I recall an experience one Sunday morning that scared the heck out of me. Our Sunday school teacher had us form a circle, and asked each of us to pray out loud as it became our turn. I didn't know how to pray, and as it got closer to my turn, I was looking for the door. I was terrified. I didn't know what to say or how to say it, so I decided that when my turn came, I would bolt and run. There was no doubt in my mind that that was what I was going to do. I was going through that door…and I was going to run all the way to East Pensacola Heights. The guy next to me must have been as scared as I was, because when it was his turn, he hesitated, and was silent for what seemed a long time, and then said, "Amen." That stopped the praying. I didn't have to run after all. I was so relieved. I could have hugged his neck.

Johnny Browder
Courtesy of Loretta Browder

East Hill Baptist Church

On another Sunday morning, I was sitting with my friend, Johnny Browder, during the services. We didn't come together; we just met at church and decided to sit together. We were sitting toward the rear of the church, and after the services were well underway, he said, in a loud whisper, "I've got something to show you, Hoss."

"What?" I whispered back, placing my fingers to my lips. At the same time the two ladies in front of us turned around and looked directly at Johnny, but didn't say a word. He got the message.

"This," he said, as he extracted a small mayonnaise jar from inside his shirt. He had punched several tiny holes in the lid.

"What is it?" I asked, prompting the two ladies to turn around and give me the *eagle eye*.

"It's a green snake," he replied. "I caught it this morning at home."

What I thought were green leaves was all green snake, and it filled the entire small jar. Green snakes don't get very big, but this one had maxed out.

It was only natural that we both were more interested in the snake than we were in Reverend Stracener's sermon. It didn't take Johnnie long to get bored with the snake being in the jar, so when he unscrewed the lid, the snake began exiting the jar. Johnny held his head in the jar, but he came all the way out, tail first. People on each side of us began to move. The snake didn't want any part with being put back in the jar, which we were both trying to do when the jar slipped out of Johnny's hand, and crashed to the floor. It didn't break; it just rolled, making that strange noise that jars make when they roll on oak floors in quiet churches. We both stopped giggling, and got serious about trying to get the snake to agree to go into Johnny's shirt pocket. It wouldn't, and in the excitement, the snake slipped out of John's hand onto the floor, and slithered toward the front of the church. Several people were already looking under the pews because of the noise made by the jar, and when they spotted the snake as it streaked toward the pianist, a weird thing happened. It was like the wave at a football game, people jumped up as the "serpent" passed under their pews. This was long before the days of Marlin Perkins and the "Crocodile Hunter," but Johnny must have read some of the same books they did. Some people had their feet up in their pew seats and some had rushed out into the aisles, but Johnny got to the snake and scooped it up. He held it about midway, so both ends were flailing, as I followed him up the aisle and out of the church. We walked home to East Pensacola Heights. I don't remember if Johnny was concerned about lightning that morning, but I was.

Another incident happened at a Sunday evening service. A group of young boys were sitting together at the front of the church, and they were getting ready to sing. They were not being very attentive to the lady directing them, and consequently they got off to a bad start, so she stopped them. She quietly whispered something to them and the sanctuary got very quiet. Then, just as they were about to start, one of the kids "stepped on a frog," and all the kids cracked up, laughing and pointing fingers at each other. The adults, at first, acted like they didn't hear a thing, and then bowed their heads or covered their mouths so nobody could see that they were laughing also. The Organist quickly began playing and the kids giggled their way through the entire hymn. I was so busy watching the kids, that I didn't see the preacher's reaction. I wish I had, because I often wonder how preachers handle those kinds of situations that surely must occur occasionally during their careers.

First United Methodist Church in Baghdad, Florida

So, I began my walk with Jesus at East Hill Baptist Church, but while attending college, I became an Episcopalian, the church of my paternal grandparents. I was proud of my membership in the Episcopal Church, but rules forbade me to remarry in the church, so forty-five years ago, I became a Methodist, where I am very comfortable and happy. I've been a member of First United Methodist Church in downtown Pensacola, for over thirty years, and on May 24, 1986 Sandra and I were married in the quaint, historic First United Methodist

St. Christopher's Episcopal Church

Church in Bagdad, Florida. We enjoy our membership, the fellowship and worshipping at our big, one-hundred year old stone church on Wright Street. Pardon the pun, but it's the Wright place for us. We are both active in our church. For the past several years, both of us were Stephen Ministers, a lay program, which is not unique to Methodist, as it was designed by the Lutheran Church, but adopted by most other denominations. Sandra had to become inactive when she became the church's Librarian. I've been involved for over twenty years with the Joe Harrell Men's Bible Breakfast, a non-denominational, weekly Bible study group named for a prominent Pensacola attorney who was a leader in the church. Also, for the past several years, I've been involved with the Methodist Men's Group, well known for a monthly dinner at the church, highlighted with prominent speakers on various subjects.

Rev. Van Davis
Pastor of St. Christopher's Episcopal Church

While on the subject of churches, I would like to share with you some of my experiences with one individual who impressed me a great deal on what it means to be a Christian, and how he handled his responsibility of being a Christian. At the time, I was a Realtor in North Carolina, and became close friends with a man by the name of Ken Harris, who along with his wife lived in Florida half the year and in North Carolina the other half. This was a common arrangement among families who owned

First United Methodist Church and the Wright Place
Courtesy of the First United Methodist Church

Charlie and Sandra in Orlando at the Stephen Ministry Leaders' Training Workshop

property in North Carolina and another state. Ken was a former homebuilder, and owned a lot of property in both states. Thanks to Ken, I was able to sell additional real estate during the mid to late 1970's when the economy was in bad shape, especially in the real estate business. The economy was almost as bad then as it is today (2009). There was no mortgage money available from local lending institutions. Home sales were difficult and at a record low. Many old, established local Real Estate agencies had gone out of business, so I concentrated on land and

Joe Harrell Bible Breakfast Group
Front row L to R: Larry Davison, Bob Joseph , Bob Espersen, Clay Schilling, **Second row** L to R: Chuck Rogers, Dixon Moseley, Joe Herrington, Alex Ferry , **Third row:** L to R : Wendell Lovan, Charlie Davis, Buzz Windham, Tim Price-Williams, Bill Espersen, **Last Row** L to R: Frank Brown, Anthony Wingo, George Ricketson, Jim Murphy, and Gordon Towne

commercial properties where owner financing was possible. This is how I met Ken, who owned a lot of real estate. Owning a lot of real estate is not what made him unique, and is not the reason I've chosen to write about him. What made him unique in my mind was that he was a born again Christian and he didn't mind telling you about it. He didn't just talk the talk, he walked the walk.

Ken was a Presbyterian, but I would have never known it if he hadn't told me, because to my knowledge he never visited a Presbyterian church while he was in North Carolina. He did visit the smaller churches, no matter what the denomination was, especially those in the rural mountains of Western North Carolina. It was not unusual for him to give his truck or car to a church, or purchase a van or a piano, or just whatever he thought the church might need. I never knew what he might be driving, because he was always giving his vehicles away. He was a close personal friend with the owner of a successful auto dealerships in town, who also was a born again Christian. Those two, very successful business men, were always visiting churches and individuals to share their faith with anyone who would listen. I was a member of a local Methodist Church, and Ken was always kidding me about being a Methodist, saying I should join a church that believed in a strict interpretation of the Bible. One day, I challenged him to attend my church with me, and he laughed, and said, "Charlie I don't need to join the Methodist church, I already belong to the Lion's Club." If anyone else had made that statement, I would have been offended, but I knew he didn't mean it in a hurtful way. I knew from the many previous conversations we had, that he thought many churches, including the Methodist church, did not concentrate on, as he said, "The teachings of Jesus," but was more concerned with social issues. I was not as involved as much with my church in North Carolina, as I am with my church in Pensacola, so I didn't know for sure if perhaps there might be some truth to what Ken was saying about the Methodist church in general. I was determined to find out, and I did.

Well, I know now, thirty years later, and I have known for years, that it certainly isn't true insofar as my church here in Pensacola is concerned. The First United Methodist Church of Pensacola is a teaching church, so if a member of our congregation wanted to learn more than what they could learn by attending services each Sunday, the possibilities are unlimited. There are too many volunteer classes to enroll in, programs to participate in, and Sunday school classes to attend, to mention. I know, because Sandra and I have enrolled in most of the classes that are available, have participated in numerous programs within the church, and will continue to do so in the future. We have learned more about the New and Old Testaments and their application to our Christian faith than we ever imagined possible. I wish I had known about all this thirty-three years ago, when Ken was pulling my chain and putting doubts in my mind. I could have set him straight; but I suspect he knew what he was doing. Perhaps he knew I would find out and discover that if I really wanted to learn the bible, that I would find a way.

Joe Harrell
Courtesy of First United Methodist Church

Ken is in heaven now, and reaping the benefits of being a good Christian. I think of him often, how he goaded me on, always with a smile or a hearty laugh, to be serious about my Christian faith. Occasionally he would tell me I needed to rededicate my life to Jesus. I always retorted with, "I've been baptized already, Ken, at East Hill Baptist Church." This went on and on, until one day, he won out. I obviously had weakened. Ken and I had met for breakfast at a new, but large restaurant because I had an appointment with the chef. I had recently sold the chef a house, and needed his signature on some additional paperwork. I don't remember exactly what led up to it, other than a friendly challenge as usual from Ken. What I clearly remember now is that we were standing in the middle of that new, modern kitchen, with the chef, cooks and waitresses running all over the place. I also remember the loud noises of pots and pans, and everyone shouting at each other. It was typical kitchen noise found in any large, busy restaurant, and there I was, standing there with Ken, my head bowed, repeating what must have been a typical "Sinner's Prayer." It's was a very, very short prayer, but about half way through it, the noise almost stopped completely. Everyone in the large kitchen seemed to have stopped what they were doing. The talking ceased. They waited until we were through, and then they all applauded. I thought to myself, "What the heck just happened?" My client, the head chef, came over, shook my hand and congratulated me. All three of us laughed, and the activity and noises resumed. I suppose it's true that the Lord works in mysterious ways, and unusual places.

My Pastors at First Church
Courtesy of Pensacola First United Methodist Church

Rev Dr. J. B. Nichols

Rev. Bob Dickerson

Rev. Dr. Henry Roberts

Rev. Dr. Wesley Wachob

Joe Harrell Men's Bible Breakfast Group

Standing L to R: J. Stringfield, Jim Pace, Lee Mundy, Miles Davis, Maurice Davis, Joe Harrell, George Cowen, John Gavin, Dick Horten Moose Harling, Bert Lane, C. D. Lamar.
Seated: L to R: R. G. White, Clarence Lloyd, Bill Spain, John Hoefflin, and Calvin Todd.
Photo by Frank Horne. Courtesy of the First United Methodist Church, 1981-82

Front Row: Frank Horne, Richard Perry, Jim Brinson, Dudley Jarvis, Homer Cole
Second Row: Carlton Handcock, Dudley Cowley, George Cowlin, George Stringfield, John Griffin, Lee Mundy, Jack Cowley, Dick Hootin, Abe Abrams, Jim Crooke, Bill Conner, Moose Harling, George Olliff,
Third Row: John Susko, Jurgen Multoff, Walt Cline, Calvin Todd, Jim Pace, Walter Perry, John Hoefflin, Bill Griffin, Charlie Davis, Ellis Sellers, Unidentified, Buz Windham, Ralph Merrill, Joe Tarbuck and Bill Spain. Late 1980s

Joe Harrell Men's Bible Breakfast Group

Front Row: Dale Willis, Charlie Davis, Bob Espersen Tim Price-Williams, Jerry Mitrovich, Clay Schilling.
Second Row: Bob Strange, Bob Joseph, Bill Morris, George Ricketson, Dixon Moseley, Charlie Smith, Buz Windham , and Gordon Towne.

L to R: Bob Joseph, Jim Murphy, Dale Willis, and Jerry Mitrovich, and Clay Schilling

Joe Harrell Men's Bible Breakfast Group

Frank Brown and Bob Joseph

Jim Murphy, Dixon Moseley, and Charlie Davis

L to R: Charlie Davis, Wesley Odom, Bob Joseph, Jim Murphy, and George Ricketson

Frank Brown and Buz Windham

Bob **Joseph**

Joe Harrell Men's Bible Breakfast Group

First United Methodist Church Volunteers

Victor Kalfus and "Famous Vic's Cookies", an FUMC tradition

Micki Kuba

L to R: Bob Joseph, Jerry Mitrovich, Jim Murphy and Dixon Moseley

First United Methodist Church Volunteers

Mary Percy, Nettie Joseph and Carla Mitrovich

Dixon Moseley, Jim Murphy, Bob Joseph, Jerry Mitrovich, and David Crow

Methodist Men's Dinner Group

Dr. Clarence Elebash, guest speaker

Charlie Davis introducing the speaker

Pat and Jim Brinson,

Bob Espersen

Joe and Shirley Reed

L to R Sharon Espersen, Libby & Tom Mayhugh, and Les & Sue Butsch

Pat and Jim Brinson with Nettie Joseph

Bob Espersen and Charlie Davis

Dixon and Janie Moseley

Methodist Men's Dinner Group

First United Methodist Church Library

Jeanne and Ron Tew

Quentin Roosevelt, Karen Evans and Betty Roosevelt

Nettie Joseph, Sue Glenn & Bob Joseph

Betty Roosevelt, Barbara Vititow, Mary Wesley, and Nettie Joseph

Anna Spain, Sue Nicholson, Barbara Vititow and Mary Walton

Sarah Frances Mosley, Karen Evans, Rick Potter , and Nettie Joseph,

First United Methodist Church Library

Sue Butsch, Bill Brown, Myra Martin and Debra Tallman

Mary Walton, Quentin Roosevelt, Wesley Wachob, and Betty Roosevelt

Betty Hyatt, Mary Walton, Mary Wesley and her daughter, Irene Christian

19

The Day The War Ended

On August 14, 1945, I was thirteen years old, and I was at Walker's Boat House when we heard the news that Japan had surrendered and the war was over. It was V-J Day as far as most people were concerned, although the official date would come a little later. The war with Germany and the Axis powers had ended less than three months earlier on May 8, 1945, a date to be known forever as V-E Day. The radio in Mr. Wilmer Walker's boat was turned up as loud as it would go. I don't remember who all was there at the time, but I do remember that my brother, Bill, was there along with a lot of our friends. Bill and my brother, Ben, had only recently been discharged from the Army. We sat on the deck of the *Flossie A* our family's boat, which was also tied up at Mr. Walker's dock, undergoing major repairs and being refitted from a pleasure boat to a commercial fishing boat. I don't recall who the newsman was, but I do recall that he was a well known commentator, and he was excited, just like the rest of us were. At that point in my life, World War II had taken place during almost a third of my whole life. It was only a few days earlier that my parents, along with my aunt and uncle, Tom and Marie Brown, were sitting on our screened porch at our home on Bayou Boulevard, just a block away, discussing the recent allied bombing raids on Japan. They were talking about a new type of weapon, called an "atomic bomb." I remember my uncle saying the bomb "was not much bigger than a football."

That night Mother and Dad took me and my two younger siblings' downtown to experience first hand, what was probably the largest crowd that ever assembled in downtown Pensacola. It was a celebration of the triumph of good over evil, and a celebration of a victory by our nation and our allies over unbelievable madness and cruelty. It was the end of a global war that snuffed out the lives of over thirty million men, women and children. It was, the world thought, a war to end all wars, and the local citizens, like the rest of the world, were ready to celebrate.

Dad's office was on the second floor of the court house, and faced Palafox Street, which was full of people and cars. We had a bird's eye view of cars and people going up and down Palafox Street, where there was a constant flow, in both directions, of honking horns, and jubilant shouting voices. Most automobiles were equipped with running boards back then, and just about all running boards were crowded with men and women. Palafox Street was bumper to bumper in both directions, with vehicles of all makes, and the sidewalks on each side were packed with happy, jubilant people. I don't recall when we left for home, but I'm sure the celebrating continued on into the wee hours. I'm also sure that there were a lot of hangovers throughout the world the following morning.

20

A Different Discipline

Ben L. Davis

My dad was a tough disciplinarian. He had to be, with seven kids, and especially so, since six of us were boys. People were always asking us how many kids there were in our family, and we didn't help much with our standard answer of "there are six of us boys, and we each have a sister." We boys were as different from each other as night and day, but we did have one commonality, we looked and acted like brothers. We had a lot of energy, and occasionally that energy got us into trouble, not with the law, but with our dad. Frankly, our dad was the law! No, he wasn't a lawyer, nor was he a lawman, but he did "lay down the law at home." He was also the judge and the jury. He didn't hesitate to use his belt when necessary, and most of the times it was

Standing: L to R:Tom, Jack, Charlie, Bob, Bill, and Ben
Seated L to R: Emma Jean and Mother Davis

necessary. I can't say that he tempered justice with mercy, nor can I say that the punishment always fit the crime, but I can say he always got our attention, especially when he devised a new way to discipline me and my brothers, which was to make us wear a dress. If Johnny Cash thought being a "boy named Sue" was bad, he should have tried wearing his sister's dress.

It was only after we got a little older that he dispensed with using the belt, and started making us wear one of our sister's dresses when we misbehaved. We brothers will admit that the "dress" was very effective, and we concluded that it was all our sister's fault, because she provided the ammunition. I would have preferred that he beat me with a tire tool than to send me back up to the ball park to play "for no less than thirty minutes." Wearing a dress was humiliating for a boy, even if it was a pretty dress. It was no challenge to get into thirty fights in those thirty minutes. My older brother, Bill, was no stranger to fighting, so wearing a dress didn't bother him. He was big and strong for his age, and the dress was just as good a reason as any to get into a good fight.

Perhaps our dad was just trying to teach us boys something about human nature, or how to react under extreme, adverse conditions; or better yet, maybe he was toughening us up for a possible career in politics. We did learn a lot. For example, I learned that my so called friends were less concerned about why I was wearing a dress than they were about what I was wearing under the dress.

I often wonder where my dad got the idea of the "dress" as a form of punishment, since he was really a loving and kind father, yet very strict. He was an elected county official and remained in office for thirty-two years, which should prove that he was liked, well respected and not too weird. We boys didn't love him any less for making us wear a dress, and although we didn't realize it at the time, we had the distinction of being the first, and perhaps the only known "cross dressers" in East Pensacola Heights.

Illustration by Steve Blair

21

Fay

Fay and Charlie on the beach of Escambia Bay

I don't believe my mother knew she would be giving birth to twins on that early morning of July 9, 1932, when my sister Fay and I were born. That's another one of those questions I forgot to ask her. I did ask which one of us was born first, but now, after all these years, I've forgotten her answer. If I had any inclinations of being a gentleman, perhaps I might have said, "Fay, you go first." It really didn't matter which of us led the charge, as it had absolutely

Capt. & Mrs. William Ed Brown,
Papa & Mama Brown
Courtesy of Tommy Brown

nothing to do with the price of eggs on St. John's Street in Brent, the community about five miles north of Pensacola, where our parents, three brothers and a sister lived. Anxiously awaiting us was our "Aunt Willie" (Willie Creighton Johnson), who did all the doctoring and baby delivering in our family, and our grandmother, "Mama Brown" (Emma Creighton Johnson Brown). I always laughed when my mother would recall that "Mama Brown" said at the time, "Flossie, they look like two little white rats."

Fay and I were born during the height of "The Great Depression." Herbert Hoover was president, and would soon be replaced by Franklin D. Roosevelt. Although Hoover had been assuring the country that "Prosperity was just around the corner," there wasn't much hope for changes anytime soon for the folks in Northwest Florida. Many people were out of work, including my dad. Two more mouths to feed and clothe must have taken the sheen off this double-blessed event, because Dad had been taking any kind of job he could get. Fortunately for my family, just two weeks before Fay and I were born, Dad won his first political race at age thirty-three. He defeated the incumbent in a run -off election for the Escambia County Supervisor of Elections position. He didn't go into office until the following January, but there was hope in the Davis family, that things would soon get better, and they did. The new elected position paid $125.00 per month, which doesn't seem like much money today, but in 1933 that was a darn good income, considering that the depression was in full bloom. According to my brother, Ben, who was about twelve years old at the time, "With his first paycheck, Mother and Dad went to Sidney Shams Grocery Store

Davis Gets Two To Register If He's In Office In 1953

Happiness can come in double-barreled loads, so believes Ben L. Davis, young Brent resident.

Just two weeks ago, June 28, Davis was successful in his campaign for supervisor of registration. He received the Democratic nomination, which is equivalent to election.

Saturday, Mr. Davis and his wife were presented with a set of twins. One is a boy and the other a girl.

The Davises have named the latest arrivals, Charles Eugene and Fay Alice.

Charlie and Fay' s birth announcement,
Courtesy of The Pensacola News Journal, 7/12/32

to shop, and also bought groceries for several other families who were in the same shape our family was in." The $125.00 check would purchase a lot of groceries in 1932. For example, The Pensacola Journal advertised the following prices in the July 9, 1932 issue: (The day Fay and I were born)

Electric Maid Bake Shop:	
Orange Cake	$.15
Cinnamon Rolls 1 doz.	$.15
Peoples Fruit Company:	
Bananas 1 doz.	$.20
New Potatoes 10lbs.	$.15
Bray's Quality Market:	
Ground Pork Sausage lb.	$.10
5 Lb. Box Bacon	$.45
Dressed Hens 1lb.	$.20
Dainty Delicatessen:	
Chicken & Okra Gumbo qt.	$.30
Georgia Peaches...basket	$.40

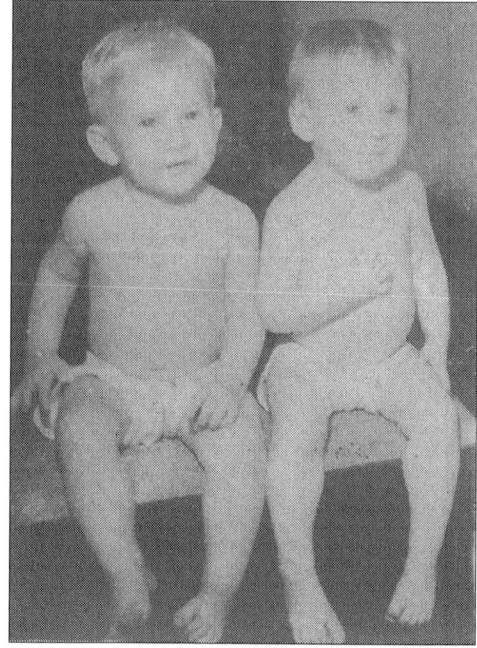
Charlie and Fay

"Twins might be twice the fun," Mother would often say, "but they were more than twice the work," she quickly added. Fortunately, she was an excellent seamstress, and as far as I know, she used the same electric Singer Sewing Machine until a few months prior to her death at age ninety-three. She made most of our clothes back then, and much of the material she used came from feed sacks. That's right, feed sacks. Many families had cows in the twenties and thirties when my siblings and I were young and sacks of cow's feed were often selected not just for their contents, but for the quality of the sack material or the patterns on the material. Sack material, or "sack cloth" was usually of the best quality available. That's one way cow feed was marketed. We boys wore good looking shirts, and my sister had beautiful dresses, all home made. I still have some of the baby clothes, mother made for me and Fay. She couldn't make just one, she had to make two, always a matching set. Today, we have hanging on the wall of our living room, a shadowbox frame, in which my wife, Sandra, placed the small, red, wool coat and matching cap, the lone survivor of the pair Mother made for us when we were less than two years old, more than seventy-four years ago. It's difficult at times to fully understand the real reason why I get such a deep melancholy feeling when I explain the circumstances surrounding the cute little coat and hat to visitors. Its appearance on the wall demands an explanation beyond my mother's obvious talent that went into its construction. A full explanation evokes a sadness my family experienced, and an admiration I have always held for my parents for their handling of one of the most devastating experiences for a parent.

This experience occurred during our dad's first term in office. The economy was still in shambles, as the "Great Depression" was still ongoing, but our family's comfort level had improved considerably. Unfortunately, Fay developed what Mother and Dad assumed was the "croup," but early the following morning they became alarmed when her condition worsened, and the doctor was summoned. She was diagnosed with pneumonia, and sadly, she died on January 15, 1935, when we were two-and-one-half years old. In recent years, I've read a lot about how the death of a child affects a marriage, and its effect on the family as a whole. I am very proud of the way my parents reacted after Fay's death. From what I've read, the weight of loosing a child sometimes tears a family apart, but more often draws them closer together. The latter was the situation with our family, thanks to the love that my parents had to share with us kids. I was too young to realize the trauma Fay's death had on the family, but as I grew up, I became aware that parents never get over the loss of a child. My mother certainly didn't. She kept a box of Fay's toys, dolls and clothes for years in her closet. I know she had guilt feelings and blamed herself, but from what I've read, that was a natural reaction to losing a child. She later gave my daughter, Lolly one of the Fay's dolls when she was a small child.

Today, at age seventy-seven, I can't recall the things I used to remember about Fay, but I continue to have guilt feelings about the fact that she died instead of me. I knew we were real close, because Mother used to tell me how if one of us got something, like a cookie or a piece of candy, we would each request that the other receive one also. I wish I could recall more about our being together.

It's true that I can hardly remember her, but I miss her often.

Pensacola News Journal 1/17/35

FAY ALINE DAVIS

Fay Aline Davis, age 3, died Wednesday morning at her home at Brent.

She is survived by her parents, Mr. and Mrs. Bennie Davis, four brothers, one sister, and her grandparents, Mrs. A. W. Davis and Mr. and Mrs. Ed Brown.

Funeral services will be held this afternoon at 2 o'clock from the home of Ed Brown on Palafox highway, with Rev. I. I. Roberts officiating.

Pallbearers will be: Harold Creighton, John Perry Johnson, Jack and Charles Cauley, Ernest Johnson and Clark Wiggins.

Burial will be in Whitmire cemetery.

Fisher-Pou in charge.

22

A Fish Called Mullet

If fish really is brain food, then we folks who like to fish for and eat mullet should be intelligent, we should be intellectuals, we should be the "intelligencia" of the Gulf Coast, because we've been eating a fish called mullet all our lives. If you live in Northwest Florida or South Alabama, and you don't love mullet, then it's quite common for folks around here to consider you weird, or sick, or that there simply must be something wrong with you. There have been several publications in recent years by psychologists and other medical professionals citing the health benefits of Omega-3, which is derived from fish oil. One of the benefits, they profess, is that Omega-3 aids in preventing depression. This must be true, because you don't run into too many depressed rednecks along the Gulf Coast, unless, of course, it's that time of the year when the mullet are hard to find. The Mullet is considered an oily fish, so it must be loaded with Omega-3. The great thing about mullet, is that it's delicious, no matter how you cook it; they're fished for in our bays, bayous, rivers and the Gulf of Mexico; and since the "net bans," went into effect in 1995, there have been enough mullet for both commercial and recreational fishermen. For some folks, to be called a "Mullet Fisherman" is a badge of honor.

Mullet are caught with castnets, which are thrown by individuals. Up until 1995, most commercial fishermen and some recreational fishermen employed the use of "gill nets" or "trammel nets" to catch mullet. The nets ranged from one hundred feet to several hundred feet in length. Often, some commercial fishermen would illegally join their nets together, resulting in a net thousands of feet long. Not only were the fishermen using longer nets, they also began to construct nets wider, or deeper, so the fish could be caught in deep waters while spawning. Consequently, the public and the recreational fishermen began to put pressure on the state agencies to ban the nets altogether, or to at least ban fishing for mullet during the "Roe Season." It was believed that the mullet was being over fished and that the mullet population had dropped drastically. So, after several years of heated debate between the commercial fishermen and the recreational fishermen, the state of Florida finally passed a law, banning the use of gillnets by either commercial or recreational fishermen. As a result of the ban, the mullet count has definitely improved. Mullet are still fished for commercially, but with castnets. The price of mullet, which used to be comparatively cheaper than most other food fish, increased considerably since the net ban.

Buck Wiseman and Bob Joseph fishing for mullet with castnet in East Bay, Gulf Breeze

Most mullet fishermen hold a part of the lead line of the castnet in their teeth, which they automatically release as they throw the net...or, they should, otherwise it's quite a jolt to the teeth. If the teeth aren't real, then what began as a fishing trip, could end up a diving trip for dentures. The real danger is when the fisherman is unaware that a bit of the net, the twine, or the monofilament can get around a tooth, and the weight of the net

Bob Joseph casts a perfect spread, fishing in East Bay

can do a better job of pulling a tooth than the old method of a string and a doorknob. This happened to me several years ago, while fishing with my friend, Ben Early. One of my front teeth wasn't pulled all the way out, but it was straightened out to where it didn't belong. I appreciated our friend, Dr. Charlie Crooke, taking me in without an appointment to put my front tooth back in place, but he didn't have to laugh during the whole procedure.

The mullet is unique in that it has a gizzard. Many people eat the gizzard, but I am not yet that brave or hungry. Several years ago, some guy wrote a letter to the editor of the Pensacola News-Journal, stating that it was his belief that the mullet was a bird and not a fish, because birds have gizzards...not fish. It was very funny and well done, and I wish I had a copy of the entire letter to share with you. He was obviously a mullet fisherman, because he had a good sense of humor, which is a requirement of all good mullet fishermen. You have to maintain a good sense of humor, and it helps to be a little bit goofy at times, because all sorts of things can happen, besides losing your teeth and falling out of the boat. For example, you might plop that lead line in your mouth after it was exposed to what we've always called a "stinging nettle" a specie of jellyfish that stings upon contact. It's a bit uncomfortable, causing your lips to sting and swell. Or perhaps what you thought was a large school of mullet, before you made the perfect spread of your net, turned out to be choppers (pinfish), alewives (LY's) or catfish, and you caught them all. Then you spend the rest of the trip trying to get them out of the net. Most times though, you can catch enough mullet to take home and enjoy. You just have to remember that a mullet is a sucker, and usually won't bite a hook, so it's up to the fisherman to outsmart the fish. May the best sucker win!

Catching mullet is a great sport, whether it's from a boat, a dock, a bridge, along the shore or from waist deep water. Sometimes people even catch mullet with a hook and line, using bread that's been squeezed back to the dough stage. Also mullet can sometimes be caught by using a small hook and pieces of earth worms or wiggle worms. They can also be hooked by "snatching" them. You know you've got a fight on your hands when you manage to hook a mullet. Another way is to gig them, but you have to be faster than the mullet, and believe me, a mullet is fast. The real benefit from all the work involved in catching mullet, is that you get to eat them. I will eat mullet any way it's prepared, except raw. Some of the ways mullet are prepared for eating are, deep frying, pan frying, broiling, baking, smoking and canning. Canning is a great way to preserve the fish for a long period of time. It's amazing how close canned mullet taste like canned tuna. It's an easy process to can mullet fillets, and then you can have "mullet on demand," without having to go out to catch them. Several years back, the State of Florida was encouraging commercial fishermen and investors to consider canning mullet as a new enterprise and an expansion for Florida's fishing industry. The marketing arm of the state agency pushing the idea of canning mullet decided that it would be better from a marketing standpoint to call mullet by its Spanish name of "Lisa." Referring to our beloved mullet as Lisa was considered blasphemy, and didn't go over too well with us "Rednecks," and "Fish-heads" of Northwest , Florida. The state soon abandoned the idea, but not because of the opposition to the name change. "Canned Lisa" died a sudden death when research showed that the shelf life of canned mullet, alias, "Lisa," was too short to make the product profitable. It was one of those ideas that wouldn't float from a business standpoint, even though a mullet by any other name is still a mullet. However, canning mullet for personal use is a great idea.

Mullet fishermen look forward to "Roe Season," the latter part of each year, usually beginning in September or October, when the "Black Mullet" begin to develop eggs, or roe, in preparation of the spawning season. Thousands and perhaps millions of mullet can be caught in the bays, bayous and rivers before they migrate later to the Gulf of Mexico to spawn. The "Silver Mullet," a smaller specie, but just as delicious, follows the same spawning routine, beginning around March of each year. The "Yellow Roe" from the female mullet is considered a delicacy by many Florida residents, and is usually prepared by frying or smoking.

The roe is indeed delicious, especially if served with grits, but should be eaten sparingly, or your day or evening could be ruined. Otherwise don't stray too far from the "Loo."

Above: L to R:
Bob Joseph's castnet spread.
Charlie Davis with catch

Left:
Buck Wiseman and Bob Joseph

Below:
Charlie Davis' castnet spread

23

The Flossie A

My brother, Jack, had the following quotation framed and on the wall of his houseboat, the "Rambling Rose:"

> *Believe me, my young friend, there is nothing--absolutely nothing--half so much worth doing as simply messing about in boats."*
>
> *The Wind In The Willows*
> Kenneth Grahame

The author, one of the foremost writers of the animal fantasy genre penned these words, as spoken by the water rat to the mole. I don't know much about moles, but we had many water rats, human water rats that is, in East Pensacola Heights. Most people who lived in the "Heights" loved the water, loved fishing and loved "messing about in boats." My siblings and I were lucky, because we were exposed to boats at an early age, all kinds and sizes. My paternal grandfather, Arthur W.

Davis, sailed the seven seas for years, before settling down to a law practice in Pensacola, and my maternal grandfather, Capt. William Ed Brown, was the elected Harbor Master in Pensacola for many years. When I was twelve years old, my brother Bill gave me a rowboat, and my brother Bob kept us supplied with kayaks. We kids and our friends spent many happy hours in and on Bayou Texar and Pensacola and Escambia Bays, but my most memorable experience with messing about with boats was with our family boat, the *Flossie A* back in the mid forties.

Well, I'm not sure that "worth" is a fitting description of all the good and bad times we had with the *Flossie A,* but we had some great times fishing in the Gulf of Mexico, shrimping in Pensacola and Escambia Bays, or just cruising the bays and bayous in the area. She was large enough to accommodate the whole family, and then some, which was great fun. But, owning a large boat is "like keeping a herd of elephants in your back yard; they have to be tended often, or things can quickly go wrong." Boats are going to break down, or spring a leak, or refuse to run; it's the unwritten law of boat ownership that applied in the 1940's as well as today. As you continue to read, you will learn that what eventually happened to the *Flossie A* was unfortunately a bad experience, and at the time, seemed to overshadow all the good experiences. Yet, today I mostly remember the good times.

My paternal grandfather, Arthur W. Davis
Courtesy of Emma Jean Davis Redding

How many twelve year old kids get the chance to help rebuild a large boat, and then spend days and nights, sometimes several days at a time on the water, often out of sight of land? I was lucky and fortunate to have been involved with helping my older brothers and my Dad refit a badly damaged boat for our use. We obviously never believed any of those old mariner's tales about bad omens, and what we should "beware of" and what we should "delight

My maternal grandfather, Capt. William Ed Brown
Courtesy of Emma Jean Davis Redding

in." We did, however, learn the truth of two overused clichés: First, "The two happiest days of a boat owner's life was the day the boat was bought and the day the boat was sold," and secondly, "A boat is a hole in the water, into which you pour money."

The *Flossie A* began life as a beautiful thirty-eight foot pleasure craft with a wooden hull and powered by a Chrysler Marine engine. She was one of the classic *Playmates,* manufactured by the Wheeler Yacht Company in the 1930's, and advertised as "America's Most Popular Family Cruiser." The bunks, galley and head were forward in the raised bow, and the spacious cabin housed the wheel and controls, with a 360 degree visibility, and more than ample space for entertainment and eating. Like all first class yachts of that era, she was all spit and polish, with much brass, chrome and beautiful mahogany throughout. She was probably the pride of the U. S. Navy at Pensacola Naval Air Station, and we have no way of knowing, but she might have previously served as a "Captain's Gig," or an "Admiral's Barge." In 1944, she was being used locally by the Navy for recreational purposes. Unfortunately, she caught on fire while berthed in a local marina on Bayou Chico, and was subsequently considered a total loss by the Navy. Sadly, a young sailor, a member of the crew, died as a result of burns suffered in the fire. The beautiful yacht ended her Naval service, with extensive fire and smoke damage, resting on the bottom in the shallow waters of Bayou Chico, a visible reminder of the hazard involved with gas fumes in a boat's bilge.

My dad, Ben L. Davis, Sr. Courtesy of Bob and Marilyn Davis

My dad and his friend, Judge Harvey Page, were interested in purchasing the boat from the naval authorities, and apparently made an offer which was accepted. When they both inspected what they were about to purchase, Judge Page made a wise decision, when he said, "Ben, I believe I'll just let you buy the whole thing." So, Dad and my two oldest brothers, Ben and Bill, became the proud owners of a thirty-eight foot, badly burned hull, resting on the bottom of Bayou Chico. First, they had her raised and towed to Pitt's Slip, located next to the Port of Pensacola, where Joe Taylor pulled her up on his marine *waves,* a commercial boat lift. Mr. Charlie Berry, a Boatwright, constructed a new transom, as the major fire damage to the hull was in the stern section. While on the *waves,* we gave her a new coat of bottom paint, and then had her towed to Doug Walker's boathouse in East Pensacola Heights, just a block from our house. Over the next few months, Ben and Bill converted the once beautiful yacht to a commercial fishing boat, resembling the lobster and crabbing boats of the Northeast. She was a fine looking fishing boat. They maintained the raised bow, which suffered the least amount of damage, and left the bunks, the head, and the galley in the original design. The rest of the boat was an open design with a permanent, hard canopy that extended all the way to the stern deck. Next, they constructed a large icebox, capable of holding several hundred pounds of iced down fish, which was situated in the center, under the canopy, leaving plenty of room for fishing along each side. She was a comfortable boat, and looked good in the water. We named her the *Flossie A,* after my mother, although she protested. It was late 1945, and we were finally ready to go snapper fishing in the Gulf of Mexico.

Brother Ben

Brother Bill

When preparing for the maiden voyage, the whole family and many of our friends, were as excited as a bunch of kids on Christmas Eve. She was loaded with ice, bait, food and all the tackle we would need, plus other necessities such as peanut butter, jelly and moon pies. The plan was to stay out for several days, or until we had caught all the fish we could ice down. On the day of the maiden voyage, we left Walker's Boathouse in the late afternoon, passed under the old Gadsden Street Bridge that crossed over Bayou Texar, navigated the narrow, shallow channel leading us under the old railroad trestle near 17th. Avenue, and finally into the narrow pass that leads into Pensacola Bay. Unfortunately, we didn't get much further. We ran aground in the pass. By late evening, at low tide, the pride of the Davis family was high and dry, just a few hundred feet from the old Florida Highway Patrol Station at the north end of Pensacola Bay Bridge.

Perhaps, Mother was correct when she jokingly warned against naming the boat after her. "It will bring bad luck on that boat," she said. The *Flossie A* did seem to have more than it's share of bad luck, in spite of the good times. The purpose behind all the hard work of refitting her as a commercial fishing boat was to make money fishing the snapper banks in the Gulf of Mexico. Both Ben and Bill had recently been discharged from their military service, and each had a young family to support. Both loved to fish, so the idea of having a good time and making money appealed to them. Actually, messing about in a boat on the weekends is what really appealed to them since both had their old jobs back at the "Navy Yard," as Pensacola Naval Air Station was commonly referred to back in those days.

The second attempt at the maiden voyage was a success, and over the next several months the *Flossie A* and her crew of family and friends from East Pensacola Heights made many trips to the *Timber Holes,* the *Gully*, the *Trifling Grounds*, the *Edge* and many other well known locations in the Gulf of Mexico. Those *Snapper Banks* were often hard to locate, and a lot of guessing and assuming was used when following the verbal charts handed down by many old, seasoned snapper boat captains. Commercial fishermen back then didn't have the advantage of modern day electronics such as a Loran, depth finders and GPS equipment. The most modern device used at the time, other than a marine compass, was a lead weight tied to a snapper line. The bottom of the lead weight was hollowed out and stuffed with soap, and the line was marked for fathom readings. Sand would stick to the soap, so we could tell what the bottom was like as well as the depth. These soundings had to be repeated over and over and sometimes it seemed we spent more than half the trip looking for the fishing grounds.

Weather was always the prime concern of both commercial and sports fishermen, and still is today, even with all the modern electronics on board most boats, and the continuous updates from weather stations. In the forties, the one device that serious, local fishermen looked to, to determine whether or not they would venture out into the Gulf of Mexico, was *Maggie's Drawers,* a red flag at the end of Palafox Pier. Actually I don't remember a pier at the end of Palafox Street, although that's how most people referred to the location at the end of Palafox Street. As I recall, there were docks along the west side of Palafox Street, where many of the *Fishing Smacks,* and other commercial boats tied up. The body of water at that particular location was known as the *Baylen Street Slip* or *Basin.* I don't know who, or what agency, was responsible for raising the red warning flag when bad weather was predicted, but it was of real importance to serious fishermen at the time. It would be interesting to know the origin of the term, *Maggie's Drawers,* but it would be more interesting to know who, and what kind of lady "Maggie" was, and if she really wore red drawers.

Nor did we have the advantage of the bicycle reels or electric reels used today in both sports and commercial fishing. Sixty years ago, when we were snapper fishing, or deep sea fishing from the *Flossie A,* we used hand lines, as did all other commercial fishing boats in the area. I feel safe in saying that probably the most miserable experience for those who were real commercial fisherman back in the days prior to the bicycle reels, was using the hand line, or *Snapper Line,* as it was called. All commercial boats had a ready supply of spools of snapper line on board. The red snapper, once hooked, had to be brought to the boat fast because of the type hooks used. Sometimes, there would be several fish hooked at the same time, and by the time the fish were brought to the boat, the fisherman's hands would be hurting, even when gloves were used. After several days, our hands were so sore we could hardly touch anything because of the pain. There were all kinds of salves and remedies on board, but nothing would make the pain go away. The old timers around the fish houses swore that the best remedy was to pee on your hands. Frankly, I can't tell you from experience if that remedy works, but I was tempted to try it.

At some point in the *Flossie A's* short career, she was operated as a charter, or party boat. Ben and Bill would take people out into the gulf to fish for the day. If the weather was bad, they would fish the bays.

Mr. and Mrs. Allen Williams
Courtesy of Mary Williams

This didn't last long, because when the fish were not biting, people got irritated, and the captain got the blame. The next phase of commercialization for the *Flossie A* was shrimping. By that time I had my paper route and couldn't go with them as much as I wanted to, but the times I did go, I can very well remember that being real sleepy goes right along with shrimping. We would shrimp all night long, and then dock at the fish houses at the foot of "B" Street to unload and weigh the shrimp. At that time Allen Williams and Clyde Richburg owned American Seafood Co., which was just a small building at the water's edge with a short dock. They later split up, and Clyde retained ownership of American Seafood Co., and Allen formed Allen C. Williams Seafood Co., just a few hundred feet south, and on the same body of water. Another small building in the same area was Joe Patti's Seafood. Nobody would have dreamed just how large their businesses would become.

The fish houses paid more for shrimp when the heads were removed, so we would take the time to "head" the shrimp. A shrimp has a horn, or a sharp prong on the top of its head, which will stick you, if not handled correctly. The juices and acid from the prong caused my hands to peel, and I looked as though I had a rare disease. I could still fold my papers, but I went around A. V. Clubbs Junior High with

Mr. and Mrs. Joe Patti
Courtesy of the Joe Pattie Seafood Company

my hands in my pockets, so other students couldn't see them. Perhaps I should have peed on them. Maybe that would have helped.

It was about an hour's trip by boat from the fish houses at the foot of "B" Street to Walkers Boathouse on Bayou Texar, where the *Flossie A* was docked. I have good memories of those trips, and the many trips back and forth across the bay, past the Naval Air Station, to the Gulf of Mexico, because there was always something exciting and interesting to see. Pensacola Bay was always crowded back in the forties, with all types of boats and ships under way, and numerous merchant ships tied together and anchored out in the middle of the bay. I specifically remember one of the picturesque *Fishing Smacks* under way, with its jib sail up, having left either Saunders or Warren Fish Company, probably on its way to fish the snapper banks off Campeche, Mexico. The port of Pensacola was alive with activity, and I could see customers entering and leaving the Harborview Restaurant situated at the "foot" of Palafox Pier. It was during one of these trips when we were heading back to Bayou Texar, that a Navy PBY was practicing landings out on the bay, and concerned us because at one point it looked like it wasn't going to get off the water in time to clear the *Flossie A,* which it did, fortunately. On other occasions, we observed the railroad cars being pushed to the end of Muskogee Wharf so the contents of coal could be unloaded into barges below. I was very fortunate to have witnessed, as a teenager, a little bit

Shirley Brown
Courtesy of Bill and Shirley Fay Bryant

of what was going on around Pensacola's waterfront over sixty-five years ago. I was also very lucky and fortunate to have older brothers who allowed me to tag along on many of their trips. It was exciting.

At some point in 1946, my uncle, Shirley Brown, owner of Brown Marine Services, had contracted to provide ferry service for crewmen aboard ships docked in Mobile Bay. He offered Ben and Bill an opportunity to participate by using the *Flossie A* as a ferry boat. So, she became involved in the maritime industry. Ben and Bill obtained their captain's license, and relocated the *Flossie A* to Mobile. This was considered an opportunity to make a lot of money, and they did just that, the first week or so that they operated. Things were going great, until a crewman moved the *Flossie A* to a marina on the Mobile River to be gassed up. Unaware that a larger gas tank was installed when she was refitted, requiring a relocation of the gas cap. The attendant pumped five hundred gallons of gas thru the old gas cap, which was left in place, directly into the bilge. The sparks from the starter ignited the fumes and the *Flossie A* ended up in almost as bad a condition as she was when we first met her. That was the end of the ferry boat business, and the end of the Davis family's affair with the *Flossie A.* She was later traded for thirty-three acres of prime wetlands on Lillian Highway, near Perdido Bay. We're not quite sure who got the worse deal out of that trade, but as far as I know it's still thirty-three acres of wetlands. A short time later, somebody wanted that thirty-three acres more than Ben, Bill and Dad did, so they accommodated him. We don't know what eventually happened to the *Flossie A,* but I suspect she either became a good fishing reef or firewood. It was great while she lasted, especially for me. I have such good memories. Maybe we should have listened to my Mother, or even better, perhaps everyone should have followed Judge Harvey Page's lead.

Messing around with the *Flossie A* must have infected Ben and Bill with some type of boat virus, because Bill, a Licensed Sanitarian with the Escambia County Health Department, had several commercial fishing boats up to the time of his death at age eighty; and Ben, now age eighty-eight, and a retired Realtor, has owned several small shrimp boats. His latest shrimp boat was destroyed by hurricane Ivan, but he's making do with his pontoon boat. They were living proof that *"there is nothing, absolutely nothing, half so much worth doing as simply messing about in boats."*

Above: American Seafood. Below: Joe Patti's Seafood. Both are part of a mural on the wall of Oscar's Restaurant
Courtesy of Oscar's Restaurant

24

Horses And Other Animals In East Pensacola Heights

There were a lot of horses, cows and other animals in the Heights back in the forties while I was growing up. We had a cow named "Bossie" and a goat named "Nanny." The milking of both these critters became Mother's responsibility because Dad claimed the cow didn't like him, and that might have been true, because there were occasions when ole Bossie kicked over both him and the bucket. The truth was, or at least Mother teasingly accused Dad of intentionally pinching Bossie's teats just to make her mad. As for the goat, we kids would occasionally try to milk her, just to show off in front

Jack and Nanny

Dad hitching up Frank at our "farm" on Olive Rd.

of the neighborhood kids, but ole Nanny didn't take to that too kindly, and we had the bruises to prove it. She could butt like a bull. We learned to avoid her since she was about as user friendly as Dad's push lawnmower. As for horses, we didn't have one, but we did have a white mule named Frank. My dad sold him to a man, who promptly returned him and demanded his money back because the mule had bad breath. Several of our friends had horses, plus there were two riding academies in the Heights that did a big business, especially with the military guys.

Not too many of the streets in East Pensacola Heights were paved back during the war years, so it was an ideal place for horseback riding, and the two stables that rented horses to the public did a big business.

Buck Buchanan, a well known professional boxer, owned the Bar-None Riding Academy. His two daughters, Neenie and Nell, were avid riders. At the southern end of the Heights, the Bonifay family owned Bonifay Oil Company, and Bonifay Stables and rented saddle horses to the public. Kathryn Bonifay was more involved with the stables than were her brothers, Earl, Harry, E. F. and Pat. It was exciting to ride my bicycle over to Bonifay Oil Company, where the stables were also located, because there was always something exciting going on. Actually, excitement followed the Bonifay brothers, especially when it

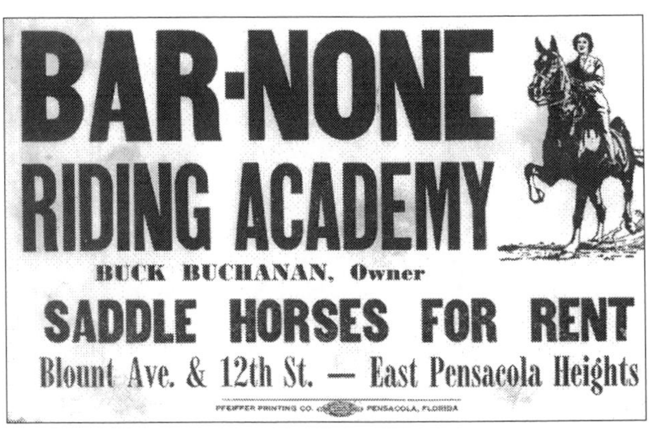

BAR-NONE
RIDING ACADEMY
BUCK BUCHANAN, Owner
SADDLE HORSES FOR RENT
Blount Ave. & 12th St. — East Pensacola Heights
PFEIFFER PRINTING CO. PENSACOLA, FLORIDA

Courtesy of Earline Buchanan Woods Family

FLEET OF E.C. BONIFAY OIL CO. TRUCKS LATE 1941. LT. TO RT. HARRY BONIFAY, EC. BONIFAY, EARL BONIFAY, CLARENCE KELL, HILTON CROSBY, UNKNOWN, UNKNOWN.

Courtesy of the Clinton Bonifay Family

came to boats, water skiing and other sports. Earl, at one time, was one of the top boxers at Pensacola Beach. It was normal to see sailors, soldiers and marines, as well as the general public enjoying horseback riding in East Pensacola Heights during the years of World War II.

Courtesy of the Clinton Bonifay Family

I envied my friends who had horses, and I always wanted one for myself. My dad was smart enough to know that once you bought one, you also had to feed it and care for it. He already had seven kids to feed, plus "Bossy," the milk cow, "Nanny", the goat, "Rosie," our dog, brother Bob's ducks; our chicken yard, and that mule with halitosis. I hadn't realized until recently that we really did have a menagerie there on Bayou Boulevard. At some point Mother and Dad got rid of the cow, and we began getting our milk delivered by Creighton's Dairy. Dad gave the goat away because one of the neighbors complained about her "Baa-ing." Bob traded his ducks for something that didn't eat, but I don't remember what happened to ole "Frank," the white mule. However, I do know he wasn't around too long.

That left only the chickens, but we still didn't get a horse, which is probably a good thing because, it would become a question of who did the horse really belong to among the five kids still at home. Better yet, who was going to feed it every day. It wasn't a problem feeding the chickens, because Mother did that when she gathered the eggs. The only real problem with the chickens was the rooster, who wanted to make sure everybody knew he was king of the roost. He looked like that rooster on top of Roy Philpot's "Chicken In The Rough" restaurant, and was almost as big. My youngest brother, Tom, was five or six years old, and for some reason that rooster took a real dislike toward him, so Tom would stand outside the pen while Mother gathered the eggs. On one of those egg gathering trips, Tom kept his usual distance, but apparently he had tolerated about all the disrespect from that rooster he could stand, so he decided to pee on him through the fence. Tom's decision was admirable, but like the old story about the buffalo that attacked the locomotive, we could admire his spunk, but we couldn't say much about his judgment. The rooster took one look at the source of the small stream of water directed at him, and grabbed it. Fortunately, Mother heard the screaming and came to Tom's rescue before any permanent damage was done.

Tom about the age of his "encounter" with the rooster

Tom and the rooster
Illustration by Steve Blair

I don't know for sure, but I suspect Tom didn't get too close to the chicken yard fence after that episode.

When driving around East Pensacola Heights today, it's hard for me to believe that hogs used to run loose in the neighborhood when I was a kid, but they did. Many residents had pigs, but they were usually kept in a pen. Occasionally they would get out and roam around the neighborhood for days before the owner would round them up and return them to their pens. My dad paid a couple guys to sod part of our yard with grass. They must have dug the grass from around some oak trees, because that night, hogs got into our yard and turned over every piece of sod, looking for acorns. "Green Side Up," didn't mean a thing to those critters. George Pfeiffer, owner of Pfeiffer's grocery store, kept several huge hogs in a pen behind the grocery store. The big challenge for us kids was to be "double-dogged-dared" to ride one of his biggest hogs. I suppose some kids, if humiliated enough, will do anything; like do a canon-ball off the bayou bridge, or ride your bicycle backwards down the Cervantes Street hill in front of the Mirador apartments. Riding George Pfeiffer's hogs was a cake walk for some guys. My one and only attempt satisfied my desire to ride hogs for the rest of my life. It wasn't the hogs, and it wasn't the hog poop and slop that was so humiliating and painful. We could always run and jump into Bayou Texar and wash off. Riding his hogs was always a painful experience, because the large pen was built on top of roots from all the oak trees on his property. By the time the hogs finished rolling and dragging us around, we would be pretty skinned up.

Then came the worst part: Pine Oil! When anyone in our family got skinned up, my mother's remedy was pine oil, which hurt more than the injury. That's why, as I have written elsewhere, we referred to her as "Flossie, the Goddess Of Pine oil."

The Browder family had two horses. Well, actually they had a horse and a half, with one big horse and a Shetland pony named "Jeff." Johnny, Jerry and June Browder kept their horses at their home on Scenic Highway, overlooking Escambia Bay. Their real address was 700 Bay Boulevard, which adjoined the old Scenic Terrace nightclub. The family also owned a farm over in Baldwin County, Alabama on Highway 90, near the beautiful Magnolia River. Mr. Browder employed a family to run the farm, but when the soy beans were ready for combining, Johnny and Jerry, still teenagers, went over to help. Johnny invited me along one summer and I spend several days with them doing real farm labor. I probably wasn't much help, but I got a good idea back in the late forties just how hard kids on a farm had to work.

L to R: Johnny Browder, Terry Williams and unidentified young lady
Courtesy of June Browder Merritt and Jerry Browder

What impressed me the most about that visit to the Browder's farm was that teenagers, like Johnny, Jerry and the son of the family running the farm, operated the huge combine machines and all the other equipment as well as any adult would. They also had horses, cows and all the other critters that normally live on a farm in the south, including hound dogs. In the late afternoons, we would go swimming at Magnolia Springs, located not too far from their farm, where it was great to cool off after being in the hot sun all day. We also went coon hunting at nights in the woods along the creeks that ran through and near their farm. We were not the least bit impressed that we had the energy to work all day, swim for a couple hours, hunt half the night, and then be ready early the next morning to do it all over again. I believe the site on which that farm was located is now a subdivision, not too far from downtown Foley, Alabama.

Back row, L to R: Tom Brown, Jr., Ed "Peter Rabbit" Lee, Eugene Cardenas. Front row, L to R: Ed "Bubba" Brown and Lavern "Nappy" Goodrich
Courtesy of Lavern Goodrich

Cliff Chancellor was probably the most knowledgeable horseman living in the Heights back in the forties. He had several horses, which he kept in a corral behind his father-in-laws house, (Olie Johnson), at the corner of Brainard Street and Pickens Avenue. His corral was a popular hangout for kids who had horses, as well as those of us who dreamed of having a horse. Eugene Cardenas, Ray Goodrich, George "Junior,"and Trent VanMatre and Ansel "Sonny" Stowe also owned horses, which they kept in their yard at home. Averette "BoBo" Wyse and his dad had several horses, which they kept in their home corral, just one block west of Cliff's corral. With so many horses in the Heights, it was not uncommon to have horse races on occasions. A favorite spot for these impromptu races was unpaved Perry Avenue that borders the ball park.

Ray Goodrich later became a professional jockey because of his experiences racing against

Ansel "Sonny" Stowe
Courtesy of Fannie Stowe Davis

George "Junior" Van Matre
Courtesy of Joan Daniel

Charlie on Averette "Buck" Wyse's horse, Judy.

Averette "Buck" Wyse and his horse, Judy. Courtesy of Averette Wyse

Left:

Ray Goodrich and Eddie Lee
Courtesy of Doris Goodrich

Right:

Averette "Buck" Wyse on one of his horses

Top L to R: Max, Sr., and Wilma Horne. Front L to R: Max, Jr., "Buster," Emily, and Jane
Courtesy of Max Horne, Jr.

his friends in East Pensacola Heights, and as an amateur jockey riding at a popular racetrack, located just off Mobile Highway, about where a Wal-Mart Store is located today. He later followed his dream and became a professional jockey, riding at tracks all over the country.

There were others in the Heights that had horses and other kinds of animals, but Max Horne, Jr. was the only person that I know of who had a monkey. Max, Sr. had built what could be considered a miniature zoo. As for fowls, almost everybody had a few chickens. Mrs. J. Whiting Hyer, Sr., whose family home is still standing beautiful as ever on Bayou Texar, would have won the prize for having the largest number of feathered friends. She had a large gaggle of geese, which flew all over the neighborhood, plus she had an equal number of guinea fowl, a West African bird related to the pheasant. It was not uncommon to find both flocks of birds in our yard, and it seemed like they were often trying to

Mrs. J. Whiting Hyer and her flocks
Courtesy of Ed and Jean Wallace

outdo each other in the amount of noise they could make. Mrs. Hyer was a sweet lady, and a good neighbor. She had one idiosyncrasy, however, that amused many of her friends and neighbors, which was her penchant for wearing men's pants while attending to her large wooded estate,

Mrs. Hyer as a young woman
Courtesy of Ed and Jean Wallace

Mr. and Mrs. Hyer
Courtesy of Ed and Jean Wallace

known to the local residents as, Hyer's Point. As would be expected, when shopping in town or at social functions, she would be fashionably attired. Today, it would be politically correct to say she was comfortable with her sexuality.

Any year was a great year to live in East Pensacola Heights, but the late thirties through the late sixties were the years I lived there, and I cherish the memories of the places and the people who lived on that wonderful peninsula during those years. It was like living way out in the country somewhere, but, the distance to the city was only a short bridge away.

The "city folks," who lived across the bayou from the "Heights," probably considered all of us a bunch of country bumpkins, and they might have been correct, because living in the "Heights" was like living on "Old MacDonald's Farm" and in a quaint fishing village at the same time. It was a great place to live. I understand how Isak Dinesen must have felt when she wrote in her classic novel, Out Of Africa, "Here I am, where I ought to be."

This plaque hangs on the wall in the Author's home on East Bay.

Harry Bonifay on one of his horses
Courtesy of Clinton Bonifay Family

E. F. on Earl's horse Tony
Courtesy of Clinton Bonifay Family

Earl and Clinton
Bonifay

Courtesy of the
Clinton Bonifay
Family

Clinton Bonifay skiing on Bayou Texar
Courtesy of the Clinton Bonifay Family

Parks, Pete, and Earl Bonifay.
Parks holds the Guiness Book of Record's title of youngest skier at the age of 6 months.
Today, Parks Bonifay is considered the greatest wakeboard freerider in the world.

25

Jack and the Rambling Rose

Jack Davis

My younger brother, Jack, like the rest of us loved boats. He had his share of them, including a houseboat he built himself, while living in Stuart, Florida. As written in another essay, he had the following quote framed, and on the wall of his houseboat, the *Rambling Rose:*

"Believe me, my young friend, there is nothing—absolutely nothing—half so much worth doing as simply messing about in boats."

Kenneth Grahame, *The Wind in the Willows*

Jack had a love affair with boats long before he served two years on board the battleship, *USS New Jersey* back in the mid 1950s, but being at sea for long periods of time didn't hamper his interest in smaller boats. We brothers grew up with boats, especially kayaks and rowboats in Bayou Texar; then, larger boats with motors for use at the *Swamp House,* our family cabin on Escambia River; and then on to our family's commercial fishing boat, the *Flossie A*, and others, for trips into the Gulf of Mexico.

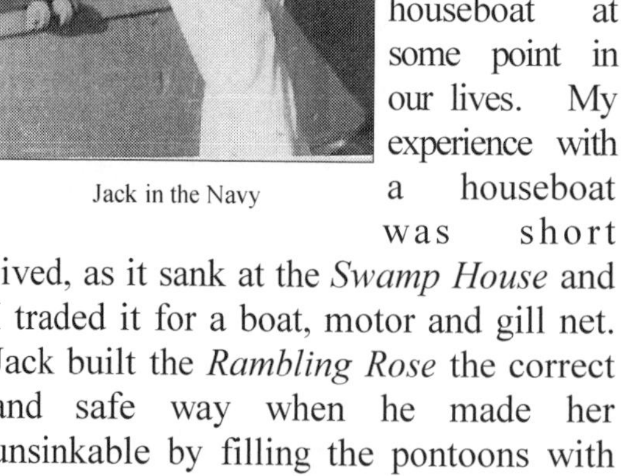

Jack in the Navy

We six brothers were infected with some kind of boat disease. My brother, Ben, called it "bilge disease." Each of us has owned a houseboat at some point in our lives. My experience with a houseboat was short lived, as it sank at the *Swamp House* and I traded it for a boat, motor and gill net. Jack built the *Rambling Rose* the correct and safe way when he made her unsinkable by filling the pontoons with closed cell foam, the type that won't absorb water. He and his family lived on a canal in Stuart, Florida, an area of Florida that is a fisherman's paradise.

Jack and a mess of flounder
Courtesy of Jack Davis Family

Jack' s Rambling Rose
Courtesy of the Jack Davis Family

Which reminds me, I forgot to mention that Jack was a fishing fanatic, which is just another reason he loved boats, and decided he needed a houseboat. When Jack moved down to Stuart he was the manager of a mortgage company, and by the time he decided to move back to Pensacola, he was the vice President of a local bank. Like I wrote elsewhere in this book, some people are anxious to move away from Pensacola, but most will eventually find their way back. When Jack and Rose Marie and their kids, Ron, Valerie, Ken and Brian moved back to Pensacola, he had the *Rambling Rose* hauled by truck to Pensacola, and for several years Jack kept the houseboat at the *Swamp House*, where many of us enjoyed fishing and hunting with him from the comfort of the *Rambling Rose.*

It's not too difficult to describe Jack's personality, and if I had to choose one word that might describe him, I would choose *impetuous,* because his personality, attitude and demeanor were subject to change in a heartbeat. Our dad enjoyed telling a story about taking Jack fishing with him when Jack was a young kid. He said, "It was like fishing with Donald Duck." We can envision Donald Duck pitching one of his fits when thing go bad, and that's how Dad saw Jack every time he missed catching a fish he had hooked. Our brother Ben tells the story about the time he and Jack were mullet fishing with a gill net near Fort.

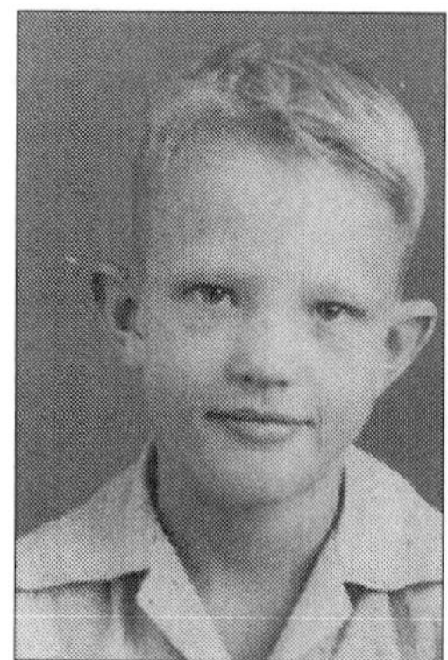
Jack Davis at A. K. Suter School

Morgan in Alabama, when Jack, irritated with Ben's reluctance to set the net, told Ben, "Just take me to the beach, and I'll walk home; you're too hard headed to fish with."

Beneath his short temper and abruptness, Jack really had a big heart and a soft underside, but he didn't want anybody to know about it. He did a good job of keeping that aspect of his makeup secret. To more than offset his tempestuous nature was his sense of humor. There are too many incidents to write about, and some I can't write about. I'll always remember what Jack did to his Mother-in-law; Mrs. Kennedy, shortly after his oldest son was born. He dressed a spider monkey in baby clothes, including a baby cap and blanket, and knocked on her door unannounced. She was so excited, but when Jack pulled the baby blanket back, and all she could see was the monkey's face, she almost passed out. Another incident with his in-laws had to do with his father-in-law who wanted to take a picture of Jack as he flew low over their home in the Ferry Pass area, outside the city limits. Mr. Kennedy, a serious photography enthusiast, gave him detailed instructions on how he wanted him fly by, so he could get the best shot. Jack had only recently been certified for his pilot's license, and approached at a much lower altitude than he should have, which scared the family's horse, which ran over Mr. Kennedy and damaged his camera equipment. These and other incidents are why Jack was persona non grata at the Kennedy home.

Brother Ben with Jack and son Brian after a great day fishing
Courtesy of the Jack Davis Family

Although I've named this essay after Jack's houseboat, and so far that's about all I've written about, I must tell you that owning a houseboat doesn't do anything toward classifying or identifying brother Jack. In fact, it's quite difficult to classify Jack, and I mean that in a positive way. Jack was a man of many talents and ideas, and he usually accomplished what he had in mind or set out to do. He was like all my other hardheaded brothers, if you tell them they can't do something, they will find a way. He was a good businessman, and good at managing his money. He provided well for his family, and had a nice home and the usual number of toys that successful men his age accumulate, such as cars, trucks, boats, a trailer at a fish camp in Mississippi, etc. He was a Realtor for several years and had several land development projects, but changed gears completely when he purchased

Jack at the wheel of his houseboat

The Jack Davis Family, L to R: Jack, daughter, Valeria, sons, Ronnie,. Brian and Kenny, and wife Rose Marie

an established business, B & M Generator and Alternator Service, which he operated successfully until his death at age forty-seven in 1983. His son, Ron, now owns and operates the business along with his brothers, Ken and Bryan.

I wrote above that it was difficult to classify Jack and I wrote that because of his many positive ideas and plans for the future. I know that if he had survived his disease there's no limit to what he might have accomplished. There's no question that he was devoted to his family. He fought their fights and healed their wounds, and at the same time he was running a successful business, getting his share of fishing in, developing real estate, and cultivating a beautiful rose garden. I'm sure he had several other projects and responsibilities under way, but unfortunately, at the same time he was running a losing battle with an insidious disease, at an age when most men are in their prime. Jack lost that battle twenty–six years ago. It was bad timing, as death usually is, because in the ensuing years since he died, medical science has made tremendous progress, especially in liver transplants.

We miss Jack. All of us do. He gave us a lot to laugh about, and anytime our family gets together, and we often do, we are reminded of some of the funny things Jack did or didn't do. He's still making us laugh.

L to R: Ken, Ron, Brian, Rose Marie, and Valeria

Above: Two of Jack's sons Kenny and Brian showing off their catch in front of their houseboat. Rose Marie in the background on the deck.

Below: Sons, Brian and Ronnie, eating their catch and having fun in the houseboat. Rose Marie watches through the window.

26

A Letter to Genie

November 15, 2001

Miss Genie Davis
Fairhope, Alabama

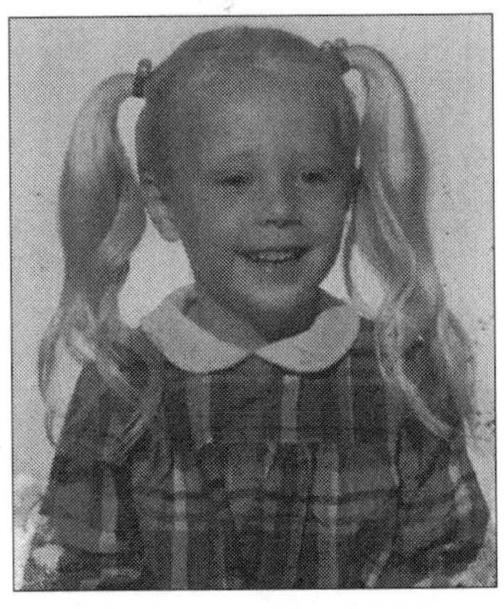
Genie

Hi, Genie! Thought you might like to know my thoughts about a certain phone call I received last night. I began writing this, thinking I might make it one of my monthly articles, but decided it was too personal. So, this is just for you.

It was November 14, 2001, one of those dates I will always remember, like December 7, 1941 or September 11, 2001; but this date is more personal. It was a normal midweek night. Sandra was preparing dinner, and I was switching news channels back and forth, trying to get the latest news on the war in Afghanistan. I heard the telephone ring, and then I heard Sandra say, "Sure, he's right here." Frankly, it was not a good time for someone to be calling, because CNN was showing the good guys advancing into Kabul, which the bad guys had abandoned. It would have been okay with me if she had said something like, "I'm sorry but he's in the bathroom," or "He's washing the dog." She steadfastly refuses to lie for me, plus, we don't have a dog. As I approached the kitchen, Sandra said, half whispering, "It's Eric so-in-so, a member of one of the professional organizations I belong to. I don't know why he's calling you."

"Me either," I muttered, as I picked up the telephone with an automatic "Hello!" unlike my normal friendly, positive way of answering the telephone. The voice on the other end identified himself with, "Hi, Charlie, this is Eric." I think I said, "Hi, Eric, how are you doing?" Frankly, I didn't know "Eric" from "Adam's House Cat." I have met a lot of people thru Sandra at the college and at the many functions I have attended with her, but unfortunately, I'm not good at remembering names. However, his voice did have a familiar, friendly sound to it. Then he said, "Charlie, I want to run something by you to see how you feel about it," or words to that effect. At that point, I was certain that he had the wrong "Charlie," or he was trying to sell me something. I responded with, "Okay." He then said, "I want to ask Genie to marry me, and I would like to have your blessings!" Whoa Nellie!!

Genie at Woodham High School

Suddenly it was a different world. It was Eric alright, an Eric I knew. This Eric was my daughter's beau, and I knew she cared for him a lot. I liked him. We all liked him. Then, I lost it. I had a lump in my throat as big as a tennis ball. I managed to say, "Eric, I didn't realize it was you on the telephone." He said something nice and understanding at that point, but I can't remember what. He then said the magic words, "I love Genie very much, Charlie, and I want to marry her," which increased my lump to the size of a soccer ball. It seemed like a long time before I got my brain and my mouth coordinated enough to say, barely above a whisper, "You've got it!"

Eric was very patient while I partially regained my composure. I apologized to him for my unexpected reaction, and as I recall, we both laughed. I did tell him that I had remarked several times to Sandra that I would be very pleased if he and Genie decided to get married someday. So, I'm pleased! Very pleased! Eric showed real character by asking for my blessing and I appreciate him honoring me with that respect. When I got off the telephone, Sandra came over and hugged me. She had heard only my part of the conversation, but she knew what it was all about; but she wanted me to tell her everything, word for word. I began, but turned into one hundred and ninety pounds of squeaky words and blubbering. I was shocked at my own immediate reaction, and I knew Eric was also. After my show of strength under fire, he might request some sort of certificate of mental stability from the family "shrink." Well, rots of ruck!!

Love ya, Genie, and I'm real happy for you and Eric. You two are a great looking couple. We anticipate several little "rug rats." Tell Eric we will be proud to have him as part of the family. By the way, Genie, we will try to keep some of the relatives hidden prior to the wedding.

Love and best wishes for a great future together.

P.S. Eric didn't mention anything about a dowry. Did he forget?

Genie and Eric's Wedding pictures , February 9, 2002
Courtesy of Mr. & Mrs. Eric Beall

The Bealls of Fairhope, Alabama
Courtesy of Mr. & Mrs. Eric Beall

27

Local Politics

Local politics and the political scene have always been interesting in Northwest Florida, especially in Escambia County. In some instances, frightening might be a better description. Because of my dad's involvement in local politics, my family members have each taken a real interest in the goings on in local politics. The citizens of Escambia County were kind and generous to my dad by electing and re-electing him to office eight times. He won his first election in 1932; at age thirty three, to the office of Supervisor of Elections, by defeating the incumbent, Arthur J. Johnson, Sr. He was re-elected three more times, spending a total of sixteen years in that

BEN L. DAVIS IS CANDIDATE

Seeks Office Of Supervisor Of Registration

Ben L. Davis, candidate for the office of supervisor of registration, was born in Escambia county 33 years ago, being one of four children of the late Arthur W. Davis, attorney and United States commissioner.

Davis was educated in the public schools of Escambia county and has lived in this county all of his life with the exception of 19 months which he spent in the United States army during the World war. Fifteen

Courtesy of the
Pensacola News Journal

position. In 1948 he was elected as the Escambia County Tax Collector, and again, he was re-elected three more times. He retired in 1964, amazed and humbled, that the citizens of Escambia County were kind enough to keep him in office for thirty two years. He died five years later at age seventy.

Until recent years, winning the Democratic primary election, or the Democratic primary run-off election, was tantamount to being elected to office, because their was no Republican opponent. The first Republican slate of candidates in Escambia County was in the May 8, 1966 primary election, when Claude Kirk ran for Governor. I remember my dad talking about new residents in Escambia County who had moved from a two-party state, where they were registered as Republicans, getting very upset and threatening a lawsuit because they could not register as Republicans in Escambia County. I don't know if it's true, or how it came about, or when it happened, but I have been informed by several people who should know, that my dad did in fact end up in court, as the Supervisor of Elections, regarding the absence of a two party

Courtesy of the Pensacola News Journal

VOTE FOR
BEN
L.
DAVIS
For
SUPERVISOR
of
REGISTRATION
On June 28

I have conducted a clean campaign for the office for which I m seeking and have never slung ny mud at my worthy opponnt. Your vote and support was ppreciated in the first primary nd will be more so when you go the polls on Tuesday.

I promise to all a courteous, fficient and accurate administation if elected.

(Paid Political Advertisement)

Courtesy of the Pensacola News Journal

Former Governor Claude Kirk Courtesy of the State Archives of Florida

I wish to thank my many friends and supporters for the splendid vote given me on June 28, 1932.

My promise to all, courteous, efficient and accurate service.

BEN L. DAVIS

(Paid Political Advertisement)

system in Escambia County. This was long before Claude Kirk, a Republican, ran for Governor of Florida.

As explained in another chapter, my dad was elected as the Supervisor of Elections just eleven days before I was born, so I've always felt like I was "born into politics." My siblings and I certainly were exposed to politics at close range for the thirty-two years our dad was in office. You can't be that close to something as fascinating, interesting and volatile as the local political system, over such a long period of time, and not feel like you are part of it. As Tip O'Neal, the late Congressman and Speaker of the House once said, "All politics is local." In our great system of electing those individuals, whom we want to represent us locally, statewide, nationally or internationally, he or she must periodically be judged by the constituents at the voting booth. Politicians are very sensitive to public opinion, because they know those opinions are best expressed at the "ballot box."

My dad had opposition every four years during the sixteen years he was the Supervisor of Elections for Escambia County. Of his sixteen years as County Tax Collector, he was unopposed his last twelve years. Escambia County was typical of the old time politics during those thirty-two years my dad was in politics. The 1960 election year was the last year he had to qualify for re-election for the Tax Collector's race. Although he was unopposed, he still attended all the political rallies conducted around the county, and also spoke to the crowds, thanking them, "For returning me to the office of Escambia County Tax Collector unopposed." He was not anything like the stereotypical politician, because he didn't relish speaking before large crowds, but when he had to speak at the rallies, he made it short and to the point. When I was a student at Clubbs Junior High, Mrs. Shell, my Civics teacher, suggested I

BEN L. DAVIS
. . . for tax collector

Davis Announces For Tax Collector

Incumbent Asks Re-Election at Polls

Ben L. Davis, 700 Bayou Blvd., Sast Pensacola Heights, announced Saturday as a candidate for tax ollector of Escambia County at he May 6 Democratic primary.

Davis has served as tax collector he last four years. Before that he erved as county registration oficer for 16 years.

Davis was born in Mobile County, labama, but moved to Escambia County when he was 4 years old. Ie attended local schools, graduating from Pensacoal High School. Ie attended business college and hen entered the United States rmy, serving overseas for 18 months during World War I. He as discharged in September, 1919.

He was employed by L and N ailroad in the clerical and transortation departments for 12 years efore becoming county registraon officer.

He is married and has six sons d one daughter. He is a member the Masons, American Legion, eterans of Foreign Wars, Lions lub and Elks.

Courtesy of the Pensacola News Journal

ask Dad to speak to our class about the County Tax Collector's responsibilities. I thought that was a great idea, but I knew before I asked him what his answer would be. That just wasn't his style. He never spoke negatively about his opponents, and he always thanked the crowd, and he always ended with, "God Bless you, and good night." His political speeches probably never went over sixty seconds. He avoided being controversial, and he didn't wait until election year to start campaigning. He campaigned year round, every year, by just being himself and doing a good job at what he was elected to do.

Old time politics was a lot more fun back in the thirties through the sixties. The various rallies held around the county were mild, compared to television commercials used in today's campaigns. Don't get me wrong, there were usually a few of the races where the candidates were mad, either with their opponents, or about something else. I well remember a fight in the square downtown between supporters of my grandfather, Captain

William E. Brown, the incumbent Harbor Master, and his challenger, Captain Bennie Edmundson. There was a lot of heated rhetoric between those two because my grandfather previously unseated Captain Edmondson, who repeatedly ran for his old job every four years until he eventually won it back. He remained the elected Harbor Master for many years, until the job was no longer an elected position.

The political rallies that were held throughout the county were a necessity prior to the advent of television. They were usually sponsored by a local civic group, school, church or community and the rallies were the best means for some candidates to meet voters in local precincts. It was also a great opportunity for the candidates and voters to sample some delicious food for sale by the sponsoring organizations. It was a great civic service that the sponsoring groups provided, but it was also a money raising project. I went to all of them after I was old enough, and I don't remember any bad food. The food that I remember best was the fish chowder that was prepared at the rallies held at the Community House in East Pensacola Heights. Three ladies, Mrs. Delehanty, Mrs. Bradley, and Mrs. Cardenas were legends in the "Heights" for their fish chowder and gumbo. They helped raise a lot of money for projects at Annie K. Suter School. I really miss that part of local politics, but it's a thing of the past that won't be back. It's a shame. I regret that my children and grandchildren won't experience local politics as I did during my dad's eight terms in office, from 1932 until 1964.

It's written somewhere that "The fruit doesn't fall far from the tree," and I've had that quote directed at me many times in the past. As much as I love local politics, I have never entertained the idea of running for a political job as a primary source of income. Just for the hell of it, I ran for the Freshmen Senate at Florida State University in 1953, got in the runoff, and was severely and summarily trounced. Later, in the 1980's, not yet convinced that I was politically unattractive, I was a candidate to be a delegate at the Democratic National Convention, and was so badly defeated, that I'm convinced that neither my wife nor my mother voted for me. The outcome had nothing to do with my switching party affiliation a few years later.

My brother, Bill, decided to throw his hat in the political ring in 1964, after my dad retired. He didn't think small. He qualified to run for Escambia County Sheriff, as William A. "Bill" Davis, against the incumbent, William E. "Bill" Davis. This was a bit confusing to everybody concerned, so his name appeared on the ballot as W. A. "Bill" Davis, which didn't help much, because "W.A." lost in a big way. It was a great experience for me and my brothers, because we worked hard in an effort to help him win the election. Although we brothers were not the candidate, we worked through the political process as though we were. It was a satisfying experience, even though we lost big time, because we were a very active part of a process that makes this country so great. We saw just how the ballot box and the election process worked, first hand. We were disappointed because of his loss, but I for one wouldn't take anything for the experience. Our efforts were not wasted, as "W.A" ran for County Commissioner two years later and defeated the incumbent, W. H. "Bully" Abbott, a fine and decent man. Several other family members have since thrown their hats in the political arena, and although they didn't win their race, they valued the experience of participating in the democratic process. It has been several years now since a member of my family has sought public office through the ballot. To paraphrase, "The Davis Clan has left the building."

Ben L. Davis

Candidate For

SUPERVISOR OF REGISTRATION

Escambia County

I hereby express my appreciation to my many friends, who gave me their support during the June 7th primary.

Your vote in the Second Primary on June 28th will be greatly appreciated.

(Paid Political Adv.)

Courtesy of the
Pensacola News Journal

BEN L. DAVIS
. . . Tax Collector

Ben Davis Seek County Tax Job

Feb 13-48

Announces For Collector's Post

Ben L. Davis, 700 Bayou boulevard, East Pensacola Heights, formally announced his candidacy Tuesday for the position of county tax collector at the Democratic primaries May 4. Davis is now county registration officer.

Davis was a candidate for registration officer for the first time and elected in 1932. He has been re-elected four times. As a result he is now beginning his 16th year as county registration officer.

Davis is a native of Escambia county. He attended the local schools and after graduating from high school entered the Army in 1917. He served 15 months overseas being stationed in France and Germany. Receiving his discharge in 1919 he returned to Pensacola and accepted employment with the L. and N. railroad.

THERE EIGHT YEARS

After being employed for eight years with the L. and N. he entered business college and following the completion of the course became county registration officer.

Davis is a Mason, and a member of the Veterans of Foreign Wars and the American Legion. He is married and has seven children. Four of the children live at home. The other three are married and reside in Pensacola.

"I feel that after serving the county for 15 years as registration officer I am qualified to be promoted by the voters of the county

RE-ELECT
Capt. Ed Brown
— FOR —
HARBORMASTER
OVER 20 YEARS AS DEPUTY HARBORMASTER
EXPERIENCED . . QUALIFIED
YOUR VOTE AND SUPPORT APPRECIATED

CAPT. W. E. (ED) BROWN
FOR HARBORMASTER

FRIENDS OF THE WATERFRONT SUPPORT

Capt. W. E. (Ed) Brown, candidate for re-election as harbormaster at the Democratic primaries Tuesday, has been connected with the office for more than 40 years. He has served both as deputy and harbormaster during this period.

He is further qualified to hold this important post connected with the business of Pensacola port in that for more than 45 years he has held a master's and first class pilot' license, both of which are issued by the federal government.

He, over a period of years, personally piloted vessels of all sizes from the stream to the dock in Pensacola harbor. In view of the intense public interest today in further development of Pensacola port we feel that Capt. Ed Brown is the best qualified for this position. We recommend him on the basis of his record of co-operation and efficiency, and he has promised us he will continue that type of service.

(Political advertisement paid by friends on the waterfront.)

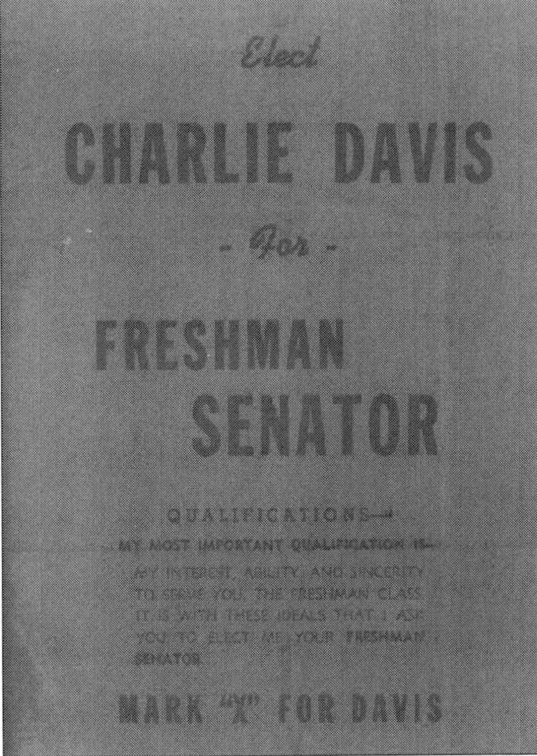

W. A. (Bill) DAVIS and his brothers - a cross-section of Escambia County

W. A. (BILL) DAVIS

BEN

BOB

CHARLIE

JACK

TOM

Civic Clubs and Organizations

- Charter President, West Pensacola Optimists
- Masonic Lodge No. 15
- Scottish Rite
- Morocco Temple
- Pensacola Shrine Club
- Elks
- National Association of Sanitarians
- Registered Member of the Florida Association of Sanitarians
- Secretary-Treasurer of the Scenic Hills Toastmasters

BEN L. DAVIS, JR. — Realtor and Building Contractor
BOB DAVIS — Union Construction Worker
CHARLES E. DAVIS — Insurance Agent
JACK DAVIS — Chemical Operator, American Cyanamid Company
TOM DAVIS — Former Deputy Tax Collector, now Employee of Local Mortgage Firm.

We Earnestly Solicit Your Vote & Support for ***W. A.*** (Bill) ***DAVIS***

ELECT

W. A. (Bill) DAVIS

SHERIFF

PROVEN

ADMINISTRATIVE ABILITY

YOUR VOTE AND SUPPORT

APPRECIATED

W. A. Davis Asks Commission Job

W. A. (Bill) DAVIS - *family man, experienced public servant, veteran, and active civic worker*

W. A. (Bill) **DAVIS** - family man, shown left with his wife (the former Fannie Stowe of Pensacola) and sons.

W. A. (Bill) **DAVIS** - family man, from a family that for generations has dedicated itself to public service. Shown right with his father, Ben L. Davis, for 16 years Supervisor of Registration and for past 16 years County Tax Collector. Bill Davis' grandfather, Arthur W. Davis, was a Pensacola attorney, County Commissioner, and U. S. Commissioner.

W. A. (Bill) **DAVIS** - experienced public servant, for the past 11 years has been County Sanitation Supervisor. As administrative head of this department has gained invaluable experience in operating on a budget. In field work has demonstrated ability in generating enthusiasm among fellow workers and exercising good judgment in the delegation of authority and responsibility.

W. A. (Bill) **DAVIS . . .** responsible civic worker — one of the organizers of the Escambia Search and Rescue Unit, Davis is currently a Commander in the Unit and serves on the Board of Directors. He was raised in the Baptist Church.

W. A. (Bill) **DAVIS . . .** combat veteran — served in the Air Force in Europe during World War II, completing 55 combat missions.

W. A. (Bill) DAVIS, *the kind of man YOU would like to have as Your Sheriff*

CANDIDATE — Dickie Davis has announced his candidacy for the office of Escambia County Property Appraiser. Davis, 33, a former deputy sheriff, is a native of Pensacola and a graduate of Pensacola High School. He attends Pensacola Junior College. Davis, mkaing his first entry into the political arena, is the fourth generation of a family that has held elected office in Escambia County. He is the great grandson of A. W. Davis, who was a federal judge, the grandson of Ben L. Davis, former tax collector and supervisor of registration and the son of W. A. Davis, who served as chairman of the board of county commissioners. Married, Davis is the father of two daughers.

Author's collection of political memorabili

28

Lolly and the Blowfish

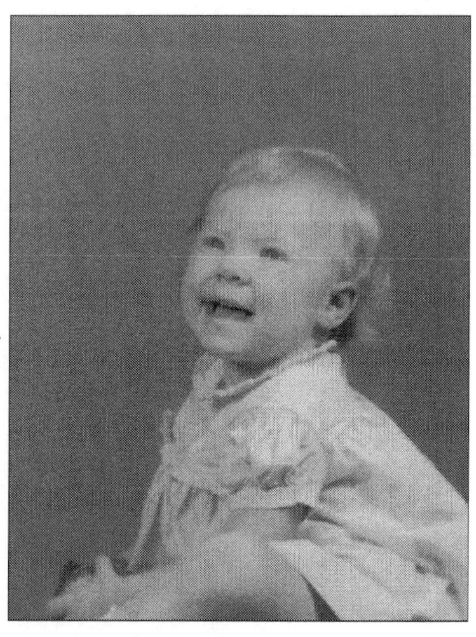

Lolly Davis Rogers

My daughter, Lolly, was about the cutest little red-headed kid I've ever seen. There were other cute little red-headed kids in my large, extended family, but Lolly was my contribution to the "Society of red-headed Davis kids." When Lolly was a little kid, many people commented on how much she reminded them of the vivacious, "Buffy" in the long running television Series, *Family Affair.*

Lolly was born while I was in my senior year at Florida State University, and although we named

Lolly and Daddy

her Charlotte, we called her Lolly after one of her mother's high school friends in Tallahassee, Florida. This story about Lolly and the blowfish took place in the early 1960s and is about a picnic with my two oldest children, when Lolly was about three years old and Chuck was almost five years old. I lived on Pensacola Beach at the time, and I had the kids for a week as their mother and I were divorced. As we crossed over Santa Rosa Sound by boat from Santa Rosa Island to the beaches near Gulf Breeze, Florida, the kids were excited about being in the boat and going for a picnic. Teco, the dachshund I bought for them several months earlier, didn't appear to share their enthusiasm during the trip over, but was back to normal once the bow of the boat struck the sandy beach. We arrived at our destination, an area where Camp Big Heart, the Boy Scout Camp was once located. Our picnic spot overlooked the sound which is part of the intercoastal waterway that stretches from Pensacola Bay to Choctawhatchee Bay. Our chosen spot was and still is part of a long strip of pristine beachfront, with beautiful white sand, bordered by ancient oaks and magnolia trees. In recent years, the area was made part of the Gulf Islands National Seashore under management by the National Parks Service. Our view to the south was Pensacola Beach, Santa Rosa Island and the Gulf of Mexico.

Chuck and Lolly

It was a beautiful fall day, and although the leaves on the sycamore trees had begun to show their colors, the water was still warm. The weather was as comfortable as a summer day, just not as hot. The water along the shore was so clear that we had no difficulty seeing the many different species of small fish and crabs close to the shore. I brought along my castnet, which no self respecting redneck fisherman would be caught without while anywhere near a bayou, bay, sound or the Gulf of Mexico. I also brought a scoop net for catching crabs, and after I unloaded the boat, the three of us waded along the shore in ankle deep water. I scooped up all kinds of beautiful pieces of broken shells, hermit crabs and little blue crabs so small they escaped through the mesh of the scoop net. It was a wonderful way to spend time with my two small children, and it was such a delight for me to observe their excitement and interest in all the new discoveries that nature provided.

As we continued to wade along the shallow waters of the beach, we surprised a large blue crab that was dining on a dead fish that had floated onto the beach, and as I was directing their attention to the barnacle encrusted crab and its dinner, Teco decided to investigate. The sudden appearance of Teco scared the crab and it released its prey and swam toward deeper water. Lolly did what she always did in similar situations, she stomped her feet and fussed at Teco, an admonishment that was totally ignored, as he continued to bark. I caught the fleeing blue crab in the scoop net as it approached the seaweed, where it would have been more difficult to see. It was a male blue crab, and by any standard, he was large, had both claws intact, and he was ready to fight, and who could blame him, since his meal was interrupted and now he's in a pickle. I cautioned the kids about the dangers of the crab's two pinchers, and dug out a pool in the soft beach sand and deposited the crab in it so they could observe his actions. They were fascinated and excited, and gave the crab a name, which I can't remember. Teco was also fascinated with the large crab, but was smart enough to keep his distance.

A Puffer fish like Lolly's.

After awhile the excitement of the crab wore off, and it was as if they were saying to me, what are we going to do now, Daddy? So, I decided to use my castnet to catch some other critters from the sea for them to observe. On the first throw, I caught a blowfish about eight or ten inches long. The blowfish is an interesting critter. It's sometimes called a puffer fish and a balloon fish. It has an interesting defense mechanism when threatened, as it will blow itself up with water until it resembles a round ball. It becomes much larger and ominous. When caught and removed from the water as I did, it will blow itself up with air like a balloon. It became a round ball immediately after I removed it from my castnet. Everybody was excited, as this was something new and weird. The fish turned itself into a ball. They wanted to keep it, of course. So, I put it in the pool with the crab, and the little round fish simply floated at first, and then expelled its air, and began to swim around the edges of the little pool. Suddenly, the unexpected happened. The old encrusted blue crab, who was buried, out of sight, in the soft white sand, grabbed the blowfish with both claws. The blowfish instantly began to fill up with water, and about the same time Lolly began crying and screaming at the crab. She was upset, even after I separated the crab and the blowfish. I decided to give the crab his freedom, and it took a while to convince Lolly that the little blowfish was okay. So she became attached to the little blowfish, since it had been so mistreated. She became its protector.

Lolly

Later, after we enjoyed a picnic in the shade of the large live oaks, I decided it was about time to head back across the sound to the cottage I was renting, so I began getting our food and equipment together to put into the boat. I explained to Lolly that we would have to let the little blowfish go so it could go back to its home in the water. She didn't like that idea one bit, because she wanted to take it home with us. I continued to load the boat, and about that time Lolly screamed and began crying. As I ran to her, I saw that her finger was bleeding. I asked the obvious question, "What happened?" She shouted out in a loud, clear voice, "That damn fish!" She was mad. She had attempted to pick up the blowfish because she wanted to take it home with us, and it bit her. She was going to load it into the boat. She didn't want to leave it.

The blowfish bite was a pretty bad bite, and I know it must have hurt. I consoled her, and bandaged the little finger with napkins and rubber bands, as I had no first aid kit with me. I finished packing everything into the boat, except Chuck and Lolly. I gently picked up the little blowfish, and beckoned them to follow me, and as we three and Teco stood at the water's edge, I placed the little puffed up fish in the water. It immediately expelled the air and began its swim to freedom. I just knew Lolly would be heartbroken, so I hugged her, waiting for her to start crying, but she didn't, she just stood there looking at the little fish swim out of sight, and walked over to the boat, waiting for me to help her get aboard.

As you can determine for yourself, Lolly was a feisty little girl, and in many ways we could say she's still feisty, although she's changed a bit since that picnic over forty-five years ago. Today, Lolly is a tall, pretty redheaded school teacher on an island near Seattle, Washington. She's a single mom with two beautiful daughters, Kelsea and Lorelei, both attending college in Oregon. Yep, they are pretty redheads also.

L to R: Lolly, daughter, Lorelei, cousin Julie, and daughter, Kelsea.

29

The “Mic-Sue”

As an insurance agent in the early 1960’s, I provided marine insurance coverage on a commercial sports fishing boat named the “Mic-Sue,” which unknowingly put me in an indirect relationship with organized crime. It also earned me a personal visit from the F.B.I.

Insurance companies were reluctant to insure individually owned commercial fishing boats. Aside from being one of the most dangerous occupations in the world, success is often at the mercy of Mother Nature. Most commercial fishermen are honest, hard working folks, but the occasional dishonest ones cause the underwriters to be tough on all applicants. Many fishing boat owners, especially newcomers to the business, are usually “hocked to the gunnels,” and when fishing is down, for whatever reason, and the bank notes are not met, the insured boats have a tendency to sink, burn or disappear, which was commonly referred to as “Selling It To The Yankees.” That made it difficult for the honest boat owners to secure insurance.

I became aware of the "Mic-Sue," when two men, seeking coverage on her, walked into my office. One, a tall, muscular, handsome looking guy, identified himself as the "Captain." The other man, who looked more like a bouncer at the Dipsy Doodle, was identified as a crewman aboard the "Mic-Sue" Both were dressed in starched khaki pants and shirt, and the shirt bore the likeness of sports fishing boat, and the name "Mic-Sue" embroidered in bright colored thread. Each wore spit-polished, plain toed, brown shoes. The captain's hat, with "scrambled eggs" emblazoned in gold, was cocked on the side of his large head, like a seasoned fighter pilot of World War II. They looked more like a couple character actors out of a Hemingway inspired movie, than the typical charter boat crew we were accustomed to seeing. I was surprised when the captain explained that they would be taking chartered trips from Panama City, Florida, out into the Gulf of Mexico to fish for Blue Marlin. In the 1960's, most fishermen had not discovered that blue marlin could be caught this far north, on daily trips into the gulf.

A re-creation of the Mic-Sue

After many phone calls, applications and letters, I secured coverage on the "Mic-Sue," but by that time she and her two well dressed crew members had disappeared. Other boat owners in Panama City told me the "Mic-Sue" and her mysterious crew had vanished, maybe to the bottom of the sea or back to Miami. I never heard from them again. **I** did hear from three, equally well dressed F.B.I. agents, who suddenly appeared at my office. The F.B.I. trio inquired about the "Mic-Sue" and her crew, but it was obvious that they already knew everything I knew, but they obtained copies of everything in my file. They wouldn't reveal much, but I did learn that the "Mic-Sue" was owned by Mickey Cohen, the convicted mobster, who at the time was in prison. His girlfriend (Moll?) was named Susan, thus the name "Mic-Sue."

All this happened almost fifty years ago. I cancelled the insurance at the time, and I trust that the statute of limitations has expired if a claim arises. However, I have been looking over my shoulder, halfway expecting a much older, wet, but well dressed "captain," and perhaps a couple well dressed "mob attorneys" at my door, inquiring about his copy of the policy. *IT COULD HAPPEN!!*

Mr. Mickey Cohen

30

The Monster of Bayou Texar

Most people are aware of the mystery surrounding the "Loch Ness Monster, " and many of us have read the sagas of giant sea monsters preying on sailors in ancient times. The appearance of a monster or some unexplainable phenomenon seems to always happen somewhere else, far away from where we are. However, on a summer day in the early 1940's a real monster suddenly appeared in Bayou Texar, scaring the devil out of four young boys, who ranged in age from ten to twelve years. It was the first time they, or anyone around Walker's Boat House had seen anything like the huge scaly creature that was larger than any of the boys. It suddenly appeared, splashing water everywhere as it churned the shallow bayou water beneath the boys as they watched in horror from the stern of Wilmer Walker's boat, docked at its usual spot at Walker's Boathouse. Most kids their ages would have headed for the hills, but their curiosity got the best of them, and what they decided to do, caused a lot of excitement around East Pensacola Heights for a few days.

The four friends, Tom Brown, Billy Harris, Bill Early and Junior Gomez, had met "Mister Wilmer" at the dock, as he returned from an all night shrimping trip on Pensacola Bay. As expected, he hired them to "head" the several hundred pounds of freshly caught shrimp at the going rate of "a-penny-a-pound." The job consisted of removing the heads from the shrimp, washing the shrimp with fresh water and then "icing 'em down" in the boathouse, where they were sold for either the table or for fish bait. As they removed the heads from the shrimp, they tossed them overboard at the stern of the boat into the bayou, which

Top:
Back row: Tom Brown, Jr., Ed "Peter Rabbit" Lee, Eugene Cardenas.
Front row: Ed "Bubba" Brown and Lavern "Nappy" Goodrich at the Goodrich family tourist court in Gulf Breeze.
Courtesy of Lavern Goodrich

Left:
Bill Early and his little brother, Ben
Courtesy of Ben Early

Anthony "Junior" Gomez and Anthony "Tony" Gomez, Sr.
Courtesy of Virginia Gomez Newsom

attracted a lot of small fish and crabs. This was probably one of the reasons we could always catch crabs around Walker's Boathouse when you couldn't catch them anywhere else. We used crab traps, the easy way, or we scooped them, by tying a fish head or a chicken neck to the end of a string, which we pulled in slowly and "scooped" the unsuspecting crabs before they got away.

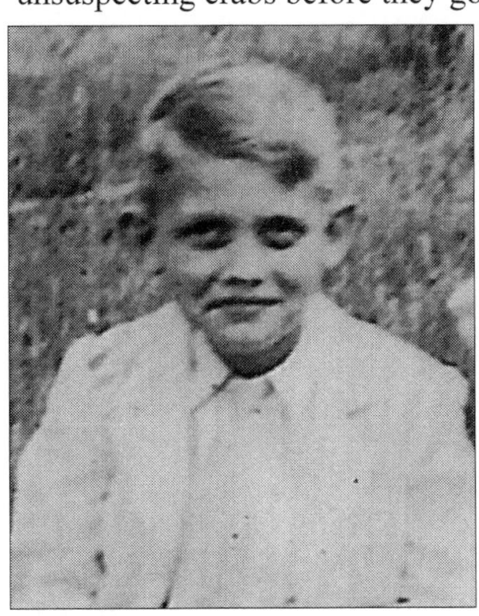

Billy Harris
Courtesy of Virginia Gomez Newsom

The discarded shrimp heads obviously attracted this huge creature, with big eyes, huge diamond shaped scales, a long wide snout and rows of sharp looking teeth. They had never seen anything in the same water they normally swam in big enough to make such a ruckus, except a porpoise, or a grown guy who had been stuck by a catfish, and this was neither of those. It had muddied up the water around the docks, as it rolled and circled in the water, consuming the shrimp heads. The four guys had two major concerns. First, was being hurt by, or because of the "strange thing" in the water that was bumping the bottom of the boat;

Mr. Wilmer Walker's boat is the smaller cabin boat tied at the dock.
Courtesy of Thomas Brown, Jr.

and secondly, not earning the money they would make "heading" the shrimp. The money was important, because it would buy a lot of ice cream, cookies and comic books. So, they decided to catch the darn thing anyway, and took a short sabbatical from their job, and went hunting for the right bait and tackle.

They found everything they needed in Wilmer's boat. For some reason, he had rigged a snapper line with a large hook and a wire leader, and they found a "spot" or "croaker," which they used for bait. The baited hook was thrown a few yards from the boat, and the other end of the line was tied to the boat's railing, and then they waited. They had not seen the monster for a while and didn't know if it was still around, so they returned to the task of "heading" the shrimp. Within minutes, the line started going out, slow at first, and then very fast, in a direction away from the boat, toward the open bayou. They grabbed the line to try and slow the monster down, so the line wouldn't snap. The hook was obviously set, and the fight was on. At first they couldn't hold the line, and it continued to lead out, but all four of them held on tightly. The monster rose to the top of the water, and it was then that they saw just how large it was. At first, it looked like a large log floating on top of the water, but with a spurt of energy, it "came alive," and the four boys couldn't hold it any longer. The line stretched tight, but held. When it appeared the monster was getting tired, they untied the end from the boat and went to the beach, and to their surprise, they pulled him all the way in. Avoiding the sharp teeth, they pulled it onto dry land by using the gaff from Wilmer's boat. The excitement drew a large crowd. Drivers traveling by on Bayou Boulevard stopped their cars to watch the action.

The monster was identified as a giant alligator gar, and measured eight feet in length. The largest on record, measured ten feet long and weighed three hundred pounds. It was a miracle that those four kids landed such a large specimen. The boys were proud of their catch, and wanted to display it, so they borrowed a rope, and hung it from the large oak tree in front of the boathouse. It remained there several days, and was the main topic for discussion around the neighborhood.

Tom, Bill, Billy and Junior completed their job, and with the money they earned, evenly divided and safely in their pockets, they walked up to Pfeiffer's Grocery Store, a couple blocks away. The popular choices back in those days were ice cream, "moon pies" cokes or R.C. Colas, and of course, for dessert "Black Cow" suckers. It had been a great summer morning, which some would say was typical of the excitement kids experienced while growing up in East Pensacola Heights.

The Marina Oyster Barn Restaurant, today.

Walker's boathouse, 1962. Note the oak tree where the "monster" was displayed.
Courtesy of The Marina Oyster Barn Restaurant

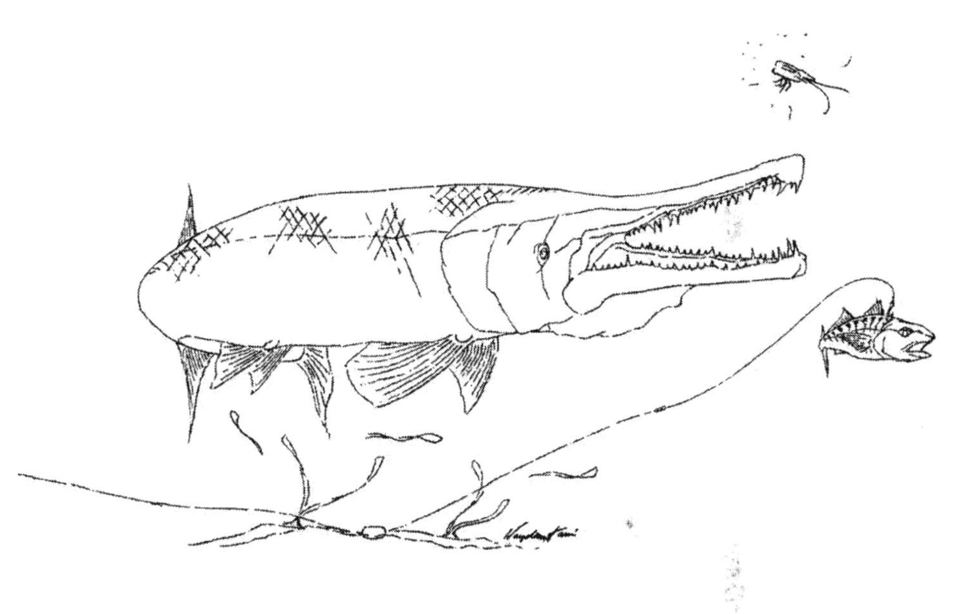

"The Monster of Bayou Texar"
Illustration by Hayden Davis

31

Mother's One Hundredth Birthday

If my mother had lived a few years longer, she would be one hundred years old on the twenty fourth of November, 2002. She often said, "If you live to be a hundred, life is still pretty short." Well, ninety-three ain't all that bad, and she was still driving her 1963 Buick LaSabre at age ninety-two. The beat up garage doors were proof that only her aim was getting bad. Fortunately, the neighbors looked out for her..... literally!! She believed that "you can do anything in this world that you want to do if you want to do it bad enough," and that the "old days" were not necessarily the "good old days."

Ms. Flossie Davis

She was a storehouse of local history and shared wonderful stories about growing up in West Florida, where she attended the first six grades in a one room school house on Olive Road.

Flossie Johnson

As a small child her family moved to Mississippi and back in covered wagons. Later, as a young girl, her family moved to Panama City, Florida by tugboat and barges. They moved everything, including the livestock, and we enjoyed most hearing the story about the cows getting seasick. The family moved back home, and as a young lady, she enjoyed riding the trolleys to Sander's Beach, Kupfrian Park and Bayview Park for picnics; and attending parties at the Barkley house and dances at the then new San Carlos Hotel. She married my dad soon after he returned home from Europe following World War I. Five sons and one daughter later they built a home in East Pensacola Heights, just a few months before my youngest brother, Tom, was born.

My mom liked everybody, and the things that she didn't like were oak leaves, birds in her fig trees and her own first name, which was "Flossie." "Sounds too much

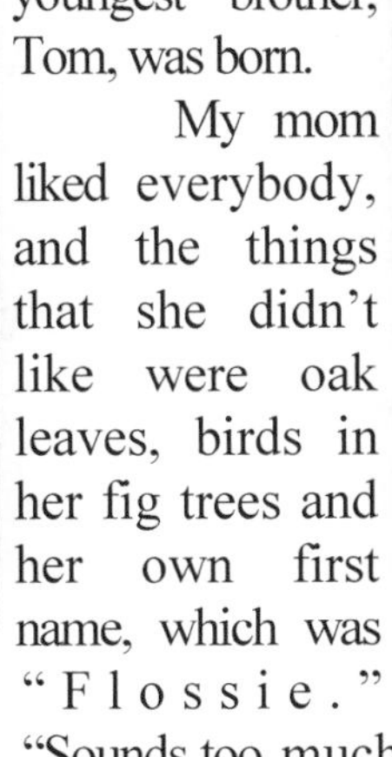

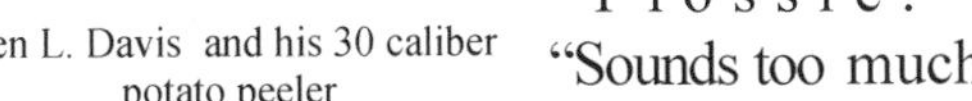

Ben L. Davis and his 30 caliber potato peeler

Ben L. Davis in uniform

Mr. & Mrs. Ben L. Davis, Mother and Dad

like a cow's name," she often said. In 1945, my dad and my two older brothers, Ben and Bill, bought a boat and named it the "Flossie A." She protested, "That name will bring bad luck on that boat." As usual, she was right. The "Flossie A" ran aground on her maiden voyage out of Bayou Texar, nearly sank in the Gulf of Mexico, and she finally blew up, burned and sank in the Mobile River.

Mother and the fig tree

As for the oak leaves, we lived on Bayou Boulevard under a blanket of oak trees, and she would attack those oak leaves with a vengeance. We had two large fig trees, and she resolved her battle with the birds by covering the trees with old castnets. Pine oil was her great cure all for scratches, cuts, fleas, and most everything else. We kids and our dogs grew up smelling like pine oil. We affectionately referred to her as "Flossie, the Goddess of Pine Oil."

After we kids were "grown and gone" she continued to cook large meals, and she insisted we have lunch at her house, which we referred to as "Miss Flossie's Boarding House." After dad died, she became a world traveler. We have pictures of her, in her seventies and eighties, riding elephants in Asia, shooting rapids in New Zealand, and getting in and out of tour boats and small airplanes all over the world. She lived life to it's fullest.

Mother on an elephant in Thailand

Mother and Sally Emory in the Philippines

Mother and Sally Emory deboarding a ship

Mother and traveling companions boarding a plane somewhere.

When she died in 1994, it was appropriately on Mother's Day, with all the family gathered around her. St Paul must have had her in mind when he wrote, *"I have fought the good fight, I have finished the race, I have kept the faith."* She certainly did!

Sally Emory, Mother , and Harry Parazine at the Coliseum in Rome

Happy Birthday, Mom!

32

A Mule Named Frank

In 1942, my parents purchased a house and ten acres on Olive Road, and rented our home in East Pensacola Heights to a military family. At that time Olive Road was thought of as being way out in the country, and Olive Baptist Church was a tiny shotgun building. Our small, white house had two bedrooms and a path, a barn, and about five of the acres were in pecan trees. We were like city slickers moving to the farm. Well, you can't be on a farm without livestock, so my uncle, Eddie Creighton, gave us a

Emma Jean Davis Redding at our country house

heifer from his dairy, and my dad purchased a white mule named, Frank, from a horse trader named, Joe Antone. I might forget a lot of things that happened on our "farm" on Olive Road, but I won't ever forget

the experiences, which were mostly good, that we kids had with that hard-headed, one-way, white mule.

Dad purchased a plow with ol' Frank, because a mule and a plow just naturally go together. Everybody knew that, everybody but Frank, that is. Everybody knows you must plow the ground around pecan trees, but what I'm not sure about is who my dad had in mind to do the plowing. My two oldest brothers, Ben and Bill were in the army, fighting a war. Dad was the County Supervisor of Elections, and everybody knew he couldn't plow when he had to be down at the Court House. As for my mother doing the plowing, everybody knew not to even go there. The same went for my sixteen year old sister, Emma Jean, who probably could have done

Dad and Frank, the mule on Olive Road

Flossie Davis

the job better than anybody else, if she had to. My brother, Bob, was fourteen, but he convinced our parents to let him stay in town with Mr. and Mrs. Roy Philpot, and everybody knows you can't plow when you're curb hopping at "Philpot's." I was age ten, and even I knew my two younger brothers, Jack and Tom couldn't do the plowing. So, I became the designated driver of that plow and mule. I was the pushee and Frank was the pullee. There was a

Emma Jean Davis

Jack, Bob, Tom and Charlie

Charlie as pushee"and Frank as "pullee"

lot more pushing than there was pulling. It does something to a kid when he's repeatedly outsmarted by a mule.

The one inconvenience we never adjusted to, was the outdoor privy, the little building with the typical half moon cut into the sides. We kids were not opposed to an "outhouse," but we were strangers to the little "two holer" situated way back behind the house, even though a few families in East Pensacola Heights still had them in 1942. We had country kinfolks in Brent, Ferry Pass and Cantonment, who also had to walk the path for relief. I've always thought it was queer that some folks wouldn't dare think of trotting out to the outhouse without shoes or boots, a stick, or a shotgun or "Ole Blue" for added protection against unknown critters; but once there, they will expose their derriere and all the appurtenant private parts to a zoo of critters without too much concern. When you gotta go, you gotta go, no matter the time of day or night, or the weather conditions. Fortunately, an alternative to having to visit the privy in rain, sleet, snow, hail and gloom of night, was invented by some ingenious person long before indoor plumbing. I know what they called the small, round, porcelain device back then, but today it is irreverently, and perhaps affectionately, referred to as a *chamber pot* or *thunder mug.* As kids and young adults, we gladly used that bedside potty in the middle of the night, but, today, as a senior citizen, I would walk through a forest fire before using one of those things.

Frank and the outdoor privy

As a former contractor, I know how people are always thinking about remodeling, or at least making some changes in their home, and my mother was no exception. She decided to move the outhouse closer to the house. Ole Frank didn't know it, but my mother had his day all planned that summer morning, and as soon as my dad left for work, she began marshalling the workers. Her work force consisted of me, my sister-in-law, Fanny, and, of course, our four footed friend, Frank. Neither of us volunteered for that dangerous project, we were conscripted, a term we were all familiar with in the early forties. Frank was cantankerous from the gitgo. I put blinders on him but he had a long neck, and he was always looking backwards. It was like he was thinking, "You ain't hooking me up to that thing, Hoss!" Well, it wasn't easy, but we did get that hardheaded mule hitched up to the outhouse, and with "one-mule-power" we moved it about ten inches, and all hell broke loose. Ol' Frank must have thought the outhouse was falling on top of him, because he was spooked, and lit out across the yard toward the barn, dragging me and the outhouse, with Mother and Fanny running behind us. He stopped at the scuppernong arbor, as though he had changed his mind about the whole thing. Was he pulling our leg about being spooked? Was he testing us, or did he have a change of heart? "Who knows what evil lurks in the mind of a stubborn mule?"

Mom deconstructing the privy one wall at a time.

Frank won the battle and we dismantled the privy and relocated it in parts, ourselves.

There is a lot of wisdom behind the idea of using a two-by-four to get a mule's attention, but I'm glad I never resorted to such an extreme measure. The only thing more effective is a hornet's nest, which doesn't help the plowing, but it's interesting to watch. Second to that is when two little brothers jump out of a pecan tree onto the back of an unsuspecting, hitched up, plowing mule. It's possible that my partner, Frank, just used that as an excuse to head to the barn. If so, it worked! My lasting memory of that incident was that scared

Jack, Tom, and Charlie in the country

mule, heading for the barn, running as fast as he could go, with Jack and Tom holding onto the horse collar, the traces, and each other for dear life, and the plow bouncing up and down. I often wonder, when recalling that incident, who was the most frightened, Jack, Tom, that mule, or me?

Well, I think we all had about as much fun as we could stand being on the farm, so Mother and Dad sold the property, and we moved back to East Pensacola Heights. Dad sold our old pal, Frank, to an individual, and not too long after we moved back into our house, the man called and said he wanted his money back, and please come get the mule. My dad asked him what the problem was, and he replied that the mule had halitosis. My cousin, Ellis Davis, and I rode Frank all the way from Ferry Pass to East Pensacola Heights, and that mule spent the entire trip scraping our legs against fence posts and trees, trying to get us off his back. We looked like we had been dragged through a briar patch.

Cousin, Ellis Davis
Courtesy of George Bokas

If ol' Frank wound up in a glue factory, I'll guarantee you, that batch of glue refused to stick.

33

My Charm

We've all heard the phrase, "The third time's a charm." Well, it's true! I have living proof…under my roof. Of course, this quote usually shows up when it's discovered that someone is married, or getting married for the third time. It's not clear how that saying got started, but in my limited research, I discovered that some believe it's possible that it originated from an old English Law that states that anyone who survives three attempts at hanging would be set free by the courts. Now, I'm certainly not comparing marriage to a hanging, or anything of that nature, because I obviously believe in marriage; I must, since I've been married three times. It wasn't that I didn't take the first two

Sandra with flowers congratulating her on receiving her doctorate.

seriously, because I did. It wasn't that I didn't want my marriages to succeed, because I did. A divorce is traumatic and everybody loses, especially the children. I don't remember who wrote the sage words, "Out of every adversity there is an equal and opposite benefit," but it sure proved true in my case, because I have the most wonderful four children in the world. In addition, my third time around partner, Sandra, is a real charm, or better than that, she's a jewel. I'm a lucky son-of-a-gun, and I know it. I keep telling her, "If you leave me, Honey, I'm going with you." Now, this is not one of those mushy, gooey type stories that will suddenly turn into a romance novel. I just want people to know that I'm proud of my wife, and I want to write about her, and include these writings in this book…against her wishes.

You should know that it's not just my opinion, but the opinion of many others that I married a "brat." That's right; she is a brat, a "military brat," that is. "Military Brat" is not considered to be a derogatory term,

A Lockney Family portrait. L to R: Sandra, Pandora, Candace, father, Bill, son Randolph and, mother, Grace

Sandra as Homecoming Queen in 1957

and may in fact be seen as a term of endearment, and is a term used to describe a person whose parent or parents have served full-time in the armed forces during the person's childhood. That description fits Sandra and her siblings. Her dad, LTC William J. Lockney, was a U.S. Air Force pilot in WWII, Korea and Vietnam, and she and her family lived all over the world. Sandra said, "By the time I graduated from Kaiserslautern High School in Germany, I had attended twenty-four schools." She attended the University of Maryland in Munich, Germany, but later transferred to Arizona State in Tempe, Arizona, where she and her dad graduated together in 1962. In 1970, Sandra earned a masters degree from Catholic University in Washington, D.C. After we were married in 1986, she continued her studies, and earned her Doctorate from Florida State University in 1990. Okay, so she's a lot smarter than I am. Now, let's continue with the rest of the story.

I wrote about Sandra's adventures in Vietnam elsewhere in this book, but I didn't write much about her work in South Korea with the U. S. Army Special Services as a civilian employee. She actually had two tours in South Korea, and lived in places with funny names like Yongsan and Taegua. She was often mistaken for a Korean woman because of her size (she's a runt), features and long black hair, especially when she wore long Korean dresses. She loved the excitement and challenge of living in a foreign country, which is probably why she decided to return to Germany in 1972.

Sandra on the right in Korean dress visiting with Korean friends

Sandra was fluent in the German language, and worked for a German

Sandra fished for trout in Germany, mid 1970s

corporation. Living in Germany allowed her to travel throughout Europe, and enjoy skiing in Switzerland and Austria and trout fishing in German streams. Traveling around the world just seemed to be her thing. It all started when she and her siblings traveled with their mom to Germany aboard ship as military dependents. That was also her first experience with being seasick which happened before they left New York Harbor! Her family was able to travel around Europe extensively, since they lived in Germany and Luxembourg. Her high school senior class, of which she was the Homecoming Queen, went to Paris on their senior class trip. Due to the sudden death of her father while stationed at Eglin Air Force Base, Sandra returned from Germany in 1974, and decided to remain in Fort Walton Beach, to be near her mom and siblings.

Sandra skied in Germany, Austria and Switzerland

In Fort Walton Beach she became a Real Estate salesperson and did well, eventually becoming a Real Estate Broker and a member of the Board of Realtors. In 1980, disenchanted with the real estate business, she decided to put her Master's in Library Science to work, and became a Librarian at Pensacola Junior College. In 2008, twenty eight years later, she retired as Dr. Sandra Lockney Davis, District Director of Library Services.

Sandra as a Real Estate Broker/ Salesman in Ft. Walton Beach , 1976-80

I've always encouraged Sandra to write about some of her life experiences, and now that she's retired perhaps she will. She's shared with

Sandra and her dad spent Christmas 1970 in Korea. He was stationed in Vietnam at the time.

me so many interesting, exciting and unbelievable stories about her travels and living all over the world that definitely should be put into writing, because people would enjoy reading about them. I hope she will write about many of her experiences, especially about her tour in Vietnam during the North Vietnamese and Viet Cong Tet Offensive, and the experiences she had flying all over Vietnam.

I've never known anyone who plans a trip in such detail as Sandra does. It doesn't matter if we're traveling to Grants Pass, Oregon or to Dee Wah Ditty, she will have accumulated tons of information, some of which will be useful. She also has a talent for vacationing on the cheap. For example, after graduating from Arizona State, she and a girlfriend by the name of Gloria planned a trip through Europe. First, Sandra learned that the Lutheran Church had reserved a round trip air package to Europe at half price for members of the Lutheran Church. Sandra and Gloria were not Lutherans, so they joined the World Lutheran Federation at a cost of ten dollars each, which qualified them for the discount. Gloria had a friend who was a Catholic priest, who every year ordered a new Volkswagen from the factory in West Germany. He would fly to West Germany, pick up the V.W. and secretly visit the underground Catholic churches in East Germany, and later return home after shipping the VW to the United States. He would then sell the car for a profit, which he used to pay for his trip. He was unable to make the trip that particular year, but ordered the car as he had always done. He suggested they pick up the car, use it on their month's trip throughout Europe, and then deliver it to Hamburg, West Germany for shipment to the United States, which they happily agreed to. You can't get much cheaper than that.

Sandra chose to be a professional woman, and her professional life was very rewarding and successful. By choosing occupations that had her traveling all over the world when she was young, left no time for marriage and children. She would have been a great mom, just as she has been a great step-mom, even though my children didn't live with us. She's a wonderful grandmother, and as I recall, when the grandkids were young, especially the out of town ones, and we would visit, it seemed that they always ran to her first.

Sandra's hobbies are many and unbelievably diverse. Among them are: learning new computer software, electronic gadgets and traversing the virtual world of Second Life. Another of her many hobbies, and talents, is crocheting. Over the years, she's made Afghans for just about everybody in the family, half the faculty and staff at Pensacola Junior College, neighbors, members of our church, our no-name cat, and for our grand-dog, Sushi, for when we dog sit. She's now switched to making ponchos. Soon, there will be so many ponchos around; the neighbors will be getting nervous. I wish she could crochet a boat.

Another thing I would like to share about Sandra. It's her cooking. She doesn't realize what a great cook she is. She's an excellent cook and she will prepare some great dishes. The problem is, she will always change it the next time she serves the same dish. It's like being married to a chemist, as she's always adding different ingredients, trying to make it better when it's already great. I call the variations a "Lockney" which is her maiden name. Each time we sit down to eat, I will ask if this is a "usual" or is this a "Lockney"? She will prepare some delicious recipes and won't know what to call them. If it's too difficult to classify, we simply call them a "Lockney" and give it a number.

Living with Sandra is like living with an animal trainer. Several years ago we discovered some feral kittens in our garage one of which was totally blind; it had no eyeballs. I wanted to destroy it, but it became part of our family for the next thirteen years. "Ms. K" was an amazing animal who feared nothing and didn't know she was handicapped. I also brought home a dead opossum, with a baby in the pouch. The baby, "Opie," became part of our family for the next four years which is the life span of an opossum. I'm scared to bring anything else home.

My son, Frank, said, "Dad, if it wasn't for Sandra, you'd be living in the *Sunshine Trailer Park*, eatin' Twinkies."

So, that's my gal, Sandra, "my charm," who did more work on this book than I did. I wrote it, but she put it together. Thanks, Hon!

Sandra's sister, Pandora and husband , Chris Beal, who hunt and fish all over the world

Sandra's brother, Bill (Randolph)

Our Wedding, May 24, 1986

Sandra's afghans. Inset: Ms. K

34

The Neighborhood Bully

Every neighborhood has its bully, and East Pensacola Heights had more than it's share back in the 1940's and 1950's. The "designated bully" for the southwest quadrant of the "Heights" was definitely Freddie Cleaveland. He seized the title at an early age and held it for several years. If an election had been held for the title, he would have won by acclamation. Some kids probably become bullies due to emotional problems or other reasons, but for Freddie it was simply recreational. The amazing thing is that this "Hellion of the Heights" grew up to be one of the nicest and most well liked guys in Pensacola.

Freddie Cleaveland
Courtesy of Helen Simmons

Barne Morain
Courtesy of Ray Wheat

Barne Morain lived a couple blocks from Freddie's house, and he once explained how each morning he would have to devise a new plan to get to school without suffering the wrath of Freddie. The experiences he related were more like the cartoons in Tom and Jerry or the Roadrunner and the Coyote.

I've heard reports from other residents of the "Heights," how Freddie would purposely ride his bicycle over their feet at the ballpark and other similar pranks, but it seems that Freddie really got everybody's attention whenever he would go swimming at Black's wharf. His favorite form of punishment, which he particularly enjoyed inflicting on the girls, was to swim underwater and pinch the gal's legs and elsewhere. Most of the swimmers, boys and girls, stayed out of the water when Freddie was around. He didn't just pinch, he bruised. My sister, Emma Jean, informed me a few years ago, when a version of this article was first published in Dockside Magazine, that she was a victim of his underwater pinches, so she caught him and held his head underwater until he screamed for help. I've heard other reports of Freddie getting his due from the opposite sex. "Sis" Oliver Beal, daughter of John Oliver, owner of Nob Hill, not only cured him of his penchant for pinching, but he rarely came around Black's wharf after she got through with him. "''Sis" didn't have a little brother, but Emma Jean did, so I'm convinced that Freddie decided to take his wrath out on me.

Emma Jean Davis Redding
Courtesy of Emma Jean Redding

Sis Oliver Beal
Courtesy of Chris and Pandora Beal

Once, while riding by the Cleaveland's house on my bicycle, I stopped to watch Freddie and his brother Harold practice shooting with their new bows and arrows they had received for Christmas. It was a bad decision. I was four years younger than Freddie, and the next thing I knew, I was tied to a large oak tree in front of their house, and he was pretending he was an Indian, shooting the arrows close to me without actually hitting me. The tips on their arrows were not rubber suction cups, they were metal points. Harold disappeared and shortly afterwards, Mrs. Cleaveland appeared on the scene. She brought the firing squad to a halt, made Freddie untie me and allowed me to escape.

Norman Redding riding by Russell's Drugstore
Courtesy of Emma Jean Redding

When I was nine or ten, I was about to enter Russell's Drugstore, just as Freddie was coming out. He was eating a "double-dipped" ice cream cone, and decided to entertain himself by refusing to let me enter the store. This went on for several minutes until I accidentally knocked the ice cream cone from his hand. He stared at the upside down cone on the pavement, and then went nuts. In an instant, he had me over his shoulder, and started up a ladder a workman had positioned against the building. If that kind gentleman, who was repairing the roof of Russell's Drugstore, had not stopped him, I might have been killed, albeit it probably would have been accidental and Freddie would have been in prison instead of having been the owner of the Coffee Cup Restaurant for many years.

Today, so many years later, I could sit for hours and listen to Bob Davis and Bob LaBounty tell funny stories about Fred Cleaveland. He obviously changed from the kind of kid who would throw the ball back at Coach Ernie Priest at Pensacola High School into the kind of adult we enjoyed being around. At a dove shoot up in Georgia several years ago, he was the delight of the trip, keeping us entertained with his antics and stories.

There are many people in Pensacola who were proud to call Fred Cleveland their friend, and I was one of them.

Freddie Cleaveland's Coffee Cup

Bob Davis

Bobby LaBounty
Courtesy of George Bokas

35

Old Joe, Little Johnny, and Pfeiffer's Grocery Store

When I was a kid in East Pensacola Heights, in the early forties, there were several neighborhood grocery stores. The one closest to our house was Pfeiffer's Grocery Store, which was located on Scenic Highway, just one block from the old bridge across Bayou Texar. George Pfeiffer's store was different from the others in many ways, and there were always some colorful and interesting characters hanging around his store.

Pfeiffer's Store was a combination gas station and grocery store. It had a covered drive-thru area across the front, where we paperboys were allowed to fold our papers. In addition to gas and oil, he sold kerosene, beer and wine. Volume wise, he probably sold as much beer as he did gasoline, which is the reason why there were always so many interesting characters around his store. Inside the crowded store were several chairs and benches, arranged around a pot-bellied stove, where customers could drink beer and listen to his pet parrot use all the known "cuss words." Also, under the covered drive-thru was a bench for customers.

One character, who was always around Pfeiffer's store was Joe Youd. His scraggly grey beard and mustache covered most of his face, and the ever-present pipe and unkempt hair distorted the rest. He was a small person, and wore an old, oversized overcoat year round, that reached almost to the ground. If he wasn't wearing it, he was carrying it. He didn't talk much, except when he was drunk, and then he would sing and dance. He was a happy drunk. Nobody knew where Joe lived. Since he was often seen under the bayou bridge, we sometimes referred to him as "Billy Goat Gruff."

Another character was Johnny Brosnaham. He looked like he just stepped out of a "Brooks Brothers" clothing store, as he was always impeccably dressed, usually sporting a three piece suit, a bejeweled tie clasp, and shined shoes. He was a very small, thin man, clean shaven, and he wore his monocle attached to his vest. He was "old," but he was a sport. He hooked his carved walking cane to his arm as he sat on the bench at the store.

One day while I was folding my afternoon papers, Joe and Johnny were sitting on the bench together. Joe suddenly burped so loud it either scared Johnny, or he was just simply appalled. He admonished Joe in his own, very polite way. Joe burped again, and Johnny again voiced his displeasure. Joe responded by bending forward, his head almost to the ground, and raising his baggy butt upwards, he "burped" from his posterior. He apparently was very proud of himself, because he gleefully danced a little jig, laughing the whole time. Johnny was not amused, and he promptly put down his beer, put on his hat and started walking in the direction of his home. Joe instantly seized the abandoned beer off the bench, and chug-a-lugged it before Johnny was out of sight.

I continued folding my papers as Joe, still singing and laughing, walked down toward the bridge, his overcoat pockets bulging with mysterious items; and Johnny, elegantly walking in the opposite direction, disappeared from view.

36

The Old Pensacola Zoo

In 1963 a group of dedicated men and women founded the Northwest Florida Zoological Society, Inc. The objective of the society was to establish a zoo in Pensacola, and I had the honor of being the president during its first two years. Later, the Pensacola Zoo became a reality with Pat Quinn as its Director. Pat was destined to be a zoo director. I have many fond memories of all the hard working members of the Zoological Society, but what I remember most are the amusing things that happened when we were preparing a large display of zoo animals at the Interstate Fair to promote the idea of a zoo in Pensacola.

We made arrangements to borrow a large number of animals from the Audubon Park Zoo in New Orleans. Pat, Dr. Charlie Kraselsky and I borrowed an "eighteen wheeler" from Benton's Dairy and drove to New Orleans and loaded it up with all kinds of exotic animals, large and small. We quickly learned a lot about State and Federal laws regarding the

Many animals are on exhibit at Pensacola's new zoo.

PENSACOLA ZOO

Off 9th Avenue near Workman Junior High School is a one-acre site -- the Pensacola Zoo.

The collection of animals and fowls consists of red and grey foxes, a multicolored peacock, a huge anteater, a badger and a llama from South America, a wild Mexican boar, parrots, reptiles, a turtle estimated to be 500 years old, an elephant, many reptiles, camels, a pair of roseate spoonbills, two beautiful flamingos, monkeys and various other interesting exhibits.

The zoo plan is patterned after one in Fresno, Calif. Long-range plans call for an exhibition-type zoo where animals are free to wander without being confined to cages, and their home confined to their natural habitat. A moat will separate the animals from visitors and a special area is provided where some of the more docile animals may be petted by children.

transportation of animals across state lines. The State of Mississippi would not allow us to continue with the peccaries (Javelins) or the African zebu, so the state held them in quarantine, and we reloaded them on the return trip. We took turns riding in the trailer to make sure the animals were okay in their pens and cages, which made me aware of the aroma that Noah and his family must have experienced in the ark.

At the fairgrounds, the animals were like kids, they didn't want to stay in one spot. The woolly monkey got loose and toured the fairgrounds on his own, the European red deer bolted his pen, and the little African goat got out of his pen the first night and ate all the paper tags that had taken hours to prepare. The guanaco, a wild specie of the llama, skinned the top of his head, and was taken to a local veterinary clinic for treatment. The next day, Pat and I loaded it into Roy Tummler's company van. En route to the fairgrounds, it jumped into the front seat with me and Pat. The Ford van was not designed to accommodate two men and a llama in the front seat. We were in heavy

Roy Tummler

traffic, and he refused to move, so we allowed him to stay, since his kind has a bad habit of spitting on people when irritated. The look on the deputy's face as we three rode through the gate at the fairgrounds was priceless.

On another occasion, we used Pat's car to transport a borrowed Burro, also called a Jackass, to the fairgrounds. We removed the back seat, and his oversized head stuck out the window on the passenger side, and his long bushy tail and rump bulged out the window on the other side. The little burro seemed to double in size after we got him into Pat's small car. Other than his bad breath, it all went well until we approached a traffic light. Four well dressed, elderly ladies in the car on our left were highly amused at what they saw, which was the rear end of a donkey. On our right, several young kids were walking along the side of the road. All of us reached the intersection at the same time. The Jack's stomach started heaving, like he was about to throw up; the beginning stage of several loud hee-haws, which sounded like a sawmill gone awry. It scared the kids, they screamed, and ran in all directions. The ladies in the car had rolled down their windows to get a better look. Each time he reached the "haw" part of his "hee-haw," he passed gas in a very audible fashion. All their windows went up at one time. We all laughed so hard we sat through several light changes.

The exhibit at the fairgrounds was a great success, and the animals ended up with fewer cuts and bruises than the Zoological Society members. We were successful in getting the recalcitrant wooly monkey back in his cage, but not before he rumpled up one nice church lady's wide brim hat, which he snatched while hanging upside down from the rafters.

There were many more amusing and interesting incidents with animals that happened to us in the process of establishing the Pensacola Zoo, but there just simply isn't enough room in this publication to share all of them with you. Likewise, there were many amusing incidents with individuals who were excited about the possibility of a zoo in Pensacola, and were doing all they could to help. From the very beginning, people were calling to donate animals of all species and sizes, long before we were able to accommodate them. On one occasion, J. B. Hopkins, a local attorney, dropped off a boa constrictor at my office while I was out. I had no choice but to take it home. I put the box containing the snake, which was about four feet long, in my laundry room. A member of the

Zoological Society, who was into snakes in a big way, agreed to keep the boa and would pick it up in a few days. Unfortunately, I neglected to inform Kathryn, the maid/baby sitter about the contents in the box. She normally arrived for work around 7:00 a.m., and once she opened the box, she was on her way home about 7:05 a.m.

In another incident, I received a call at my office from a gentleman who had an alligator he wanted to donate to the zoo. I explained to him that it was premature for us to accept animals. What I understood him to say was that he caught the alligator while fishing from the Muscogee Wharf. I also understood him to say that it was a foot long when he caught it, and that kids in the neighborhood were teasing the animal. I reluctantly agreed to pick up the gator later that day. When I arrived at the address he gave, only his wife was home, but she was aware of my conversation with her husband earlier, and she informed me that the gator was "out back in the dog pen." I entered the unlocked pen, which was overgrown with weeds, and opened the small cardboard box I had brought along to place him in. Suddenly, all the tall weeds seemed to move at the same time, and a deep-throated hissing sound shook the ground, and it would be an understatement to say I underestimated the size of this *Alligator Mississipiensis.* I went back through the gate almost as fast as Kathryn went through my laundry room door. What I didn't understand the man to say earlier was that he caught the little one foot alligator twenty-one years before. What he didn't say was that the little alligator was then fourteen feet long. I contacted Ross Allen at The Ross Allen Institute at Silver Springs in Ocala, Florida and I learned later that they purchased the fourteen-foot-long monster.

Pat Quinn
Courtesy of Donna and Pat Quinn

The Pensacola Zoo eventually failed, but Pat moved on to greater things, and became associated with several of the country's large zoos. Fortunately for us he returned to the area to help found the Zoo in Gulf Breeze. As the Zoo Director, he was able to entertain and educate people through the exciting world of animals. He is currently the Director Emeritus of the Gulf Breeze Zoo.

LJB Is a Snake

J. B. Hopkins, local attorney, says goodbye to his pet boa constrictor. The snake, better known as LJB, has resided at Hopkins' office for the past four months. Hopkins gave the snake to the Pensacola Zoological Society because he felt it needed more freedom and a warmer place to live.
(Pensacola News photo by Elsie Ellis)

Courtesy of Stella Hopkins and The Pensacola News-Journal, Wednesday, October 7, 1964

37

The Oldest Brother

Ben L. Davis
Courtesy of Margaret Miller

My oldest brother, Ben, said, "If there's such a thing as reincarnation, I want to come back as a little brother." As one of his five younger brothers, I did, on occasions, borrow his shoes, his clothes, his car, his boat, his fishing tackle, his hunting gear, his money, his credit, his "Michigan Frog Grabber" and only God and Ben know what else. So, what's your point, Ben?" Did he ever complain? Yes he did, so I stopped borrowing his shoes when they would no longer fit. It must be tough being the oldest brother, but this eighty-eight year old retired Realtor, developer and builder did it in style, like he did everything else, he did it his way, and did it well.

During the early years of World War II, I came home from duck hunting in Bayou Texar to find Ben, home on furlough. He met me at the door, looking pretty sharp in his army uniform. He did the one thing I wasn't expecting, he shook my hand and said, "How you doing, Hoss?" It was the first time anybody ever shook my hand. At twelve, I was neither child nor adult, but brother Ben gave me the benefit of doubt. That's the way he is. It's an example of his style.

Ben L. Davis, Jr. in his U. S. Army uniform

As a real estate developer, he was a principal in several subdivisions in our area, including Oakfield Acres and Twelve Oaks. He also developed and owned The Swamp House Fish Camp on Escambia River. One night, after a couple "toddies," Ben mentioned to our brother, Jack, that "after I'm dead and gone, nobody will remember me, because nothing's been named after me." The next morning, when Ben awoke, he discovered that during the night, Jack had installed a large floating sign in the center of the small lake in front of his house. The sign read, "Lake Ben L. Davis, Jr."

"FATHER AND SON REGISTER. Typical among the fathers and sons who registered under the third presidential proclamation as manpower for another World War are Ben L. Davis, Sr. (above, right) Escambia county supervisor of registration, a veteran of World War I, who saw service throughout France and in Coblenz, Germany, and his 20 years old son, Ben L. Davis, Jr., (above, left), a civil service employee at the Naval Air Station." Courtesy of Pensacola New Journal

You can tell a lot about a man by how he treats his pets. Ben and his family of several girls and half again as many boys had a dog named "Travis," a small, black and white mix-breed, with a big dog attitude. Ole Travis would disappear on occasions as he went hunting for girl dogs, but he always returned home. During one of his excursions, Jack called to tell Ben, "there's a dead dog on the road, and it looks just like Travis. Ben went to the location and sadly wrapped poor Travis in a blanket and brought him home to a sad family and buried him..

A few days later, Ben's daughter, Margaret said, "Dad, I thought you buried Travis?"

"I did", replied Ben.

"Well, you had better bury him again," she said, "he's standing out there on the patio."

The real Travis, unaware of his recent death, had arrived home safe and sound.

In retirement, Ben has been a perfect model for "The Old Man And The Sea." He's worn out several castnets, caught tons of shrimp with his shrimp boat, grown vegetables for half of the Gulf Coast, and continues to help reduce the deer population in Mississippi. He and his wife, Jean, live in their new home on East Bay in the Holly-Navarre area, in a subdivision he and others developed.

Ben and wife, Jean

The Ben L. Davis Family
Back Row L to R: Larry, Marie, Moni, Vickie, and Greg
Front Row L to R: Margaret, Ben and, wife Jean

Mr. and Mrs. Ben L. Davis, Jr.
Courtesy of Margaret Miller

38

On Being A Paperboy

Why, in the 1940's, did some of us young guys willingly get up about 4:30 A.M. every morning and ride our bicycles for an hour or two, and do the same thing every afternoon, except Sundays? To throw our newspapers, of course! We were paperboys for the Pensacola News-Journal, and we followed the same

Carl's Bakery

procedure every day, "come hell or high water." At that time, the News Journal published a morning and evening issue, and after folding our papers at Carl's Bakery, Pfeiffer's Grocery Store, Fud's Sandwich Shop and other business locations, we delivered the papers on our assigned route. Paperboys on bicycles are a thing of the past. We were replaced by adults in automobiles. There were many advantages and only a few disadvantages to being a paperboy. "Throwing" our paper routes was mostly routine, but occasionally the unexpected would happen.

Robert "Pee Wee" Mackey
Courtesy of Robert Mackey

Having a paper route was about the best job available for a student, and getting a route was not easy, because the demand for the position was high. Guys worked their way into a fulltime position by being a "substitute," or being a little brother to a paperboy. My District Manager was Robert "Pee Wee" Mackey, and he decided who got the routes. The other District Manager was Ray Bagley. We collected money from our subscribers on Fridays and Saturdays, and turned the money in to "Pee Wee" by noon on Saturday. He was only a few years older than most of us, and had already spent several years as a paperboy. We were lucky to have "Pee Wee" for our manager, because he was just as nice a person back

Paperboys: Harold Neal, Ted Bobe, and Tom "Greek" Psaltis
Courtesy of Tom Psaltis

Paul Daniel and Crick Reynolds
Courtesy of Crick Reynolds

then as he is today. He's retired from the U. S. Postal Service, and he and his wife, Norma, live in Myrtle Grove.

It was not easy getting out of a warm bed at 4:30 A.M. on a cold, wet morning, but it had to be done if the papers were to be delivered that morning. I played games with my alarm clock by hiding it under the bed or in a dresser drawer. By the time I found it, after it "went off," I would be awake..., and so would everybody else in the house. My dad always checked to make sure I was up. He never got much sleep, because later my brothers, Jack and Tom, also became paperboys.

Being a paperboy taught us the importance of being responsible at an early age. We learned the importance of work ethics, and how to manage and save our own money. I recently got together with some of the guys that were paperboys around the same time I was, and each one lauded the positive influence their experience as paperboys had on their lives. Some had saved enough money from their paper routes to pay their way through college, and others said their earnings were important in helping the family meet their financial needs.

Tom "Greek" Psaltis had a route that was particularly difficult to collect, but he managed to collect enough money by noon on Saturdays so he could pay his bill. Tom said he made about thirty-five dollars per week, and saved enough money while a paperboy to pay his two years college expenses at Pensacola Junior College, and his first two years at Florida State University. Tom retired from a very important position at Eglin Air Force Base, and he and his family live in Gulf Breeze.

Emanuel Villar
Courtesy of Emanuel Villar

Don Allen "Crick" Reynolds said he earned about thirty dollars each week. He attended Florida State University on a football scholarship. After graduation, he spent several years in sales, and later retired from Pensacola Junior College.

Some former paper carriers later chose a career in the Military. Emanuel Villar became a U. S. Navy fighter pilot, and after retirement, built his dream home in East Pensacola Heights. Michael Ferguson graduated from the U. S. Military Academy, later retiring as a Brigadier General. He currently practices law in Pensacola, and also serves as a Civilian Aide to the Secretary of the Army.

Paul Daniel continued to work hard, and had a very successful career as a life insurance professional. He earned the Chartered Life Underwriters designation, and retired as the Manager of Metropolitan Life Insurance Company. It was a sad shock to all of us, who knew Paul when he lost his life in an auto accident in December, 2004.

Robert Pyle chose the medical profession and practiced medicine locally. He twice served as President of the Santa Rosa County Medical Society, and owned and operated The Fertility Clinic of Northwest Florida. Another paperboy, Frank Buchanan, chose Dentistry, and had a very successful practice and career.

Dr. Robert Pyle
Courtesy of Judith Johnson
Gulf Breeze Hospital

Many of us had paper routes during some of the four years that World War II was going on; a time when people were anxious to get the latest news about what was happening in the war zones. I had my paper route during the latter part of World War II. The only real sources for the latest news in the 1940's was the newspaper and the radio, and it wasn't uncommon to find our subscribers waiting at the gate for the newspaper in the early morning hours as well as late in the afternoon for the evening issue. There was no twenty-four hour, seven days a week T. V. news coverage, as we have today. We paperboys recognized the familiar voices of the great commentators of the war years, such as Eric Severeid, Edward R.

Paul Daniel, Robert "Pee Wee" Mackey, Unidentified, and Harold Neal. Courtesy of Joan Daniel

Murrow, H. V. Kaltenborn and other well known war correspondents because many of our customers kept their radio tuned, often very loud, for the latest news morning, noon, and night.

One of my customers, a prominent Pensacola businessman, would drive up to Pfeiffer's Grocery Store, long before daylight to pick up his paper while I was still folding the morning Journal. He lived across the street from my family's home on bayou Boulevard, and his house was at the end of the route. He didn't want to wait the hour or two it would take me to get the paper to his house. As a favor to him, I decided to start out each morning by riding my bike to the end of the route, and deliver his paper first, and then ride back to the start of my route. I was glad to do this for him, since I felt I owed him a favor because he and his wife would let me use their rowboat, probably many more times than they wanted to. I also had an ulterior motive. The Pensacola News-Journal provided us Christmas cards, (at a price, of course) that included our individual picture, which we gave out personally while making our weekly collections a few days before Christmas. The card was a sneaky way to remind them to give us a little extra money for a Christmas present. I assumed he would remember my

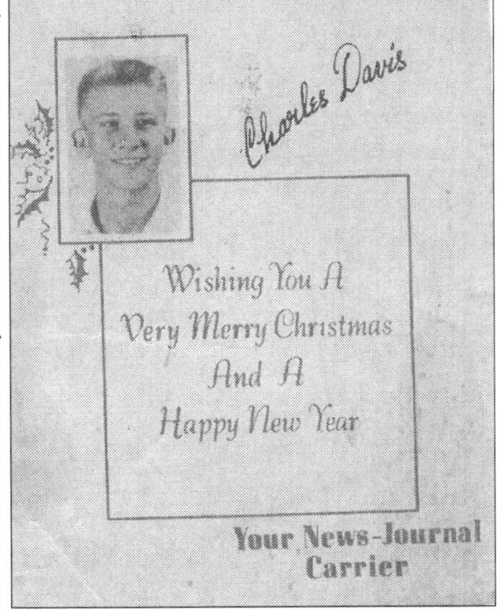

Charlie's Paperboy Christmas Card Courtesy of Fanny Davis

early morning favors, especially while everyone was in the Christmas spirit. I was wrong.

There are many other former paperboys I knew, who worked for the Pensacola News Journal while teenagers, and went on to successful careers. I apologize for not mentioning them and their accomplishments, but they know who they are and I salute them. Some that I remember who are not mentioned above are:

Bill Anderson	Ray Donnelly	Jimmy Mackey
Buddy Anderson	Pat Donnelly	Billy Miller
Gene Bridges	Daniel Flowers	Harold Renfroe
Clark Busbee	Freddie Flowers	Eugene Segers
Charles Carroll	Eddie Gebera	Abner Sheffield
Howard Carroll	Bill Hayes	Jack Smith
Ralph Chandler	Henry Hines	Richard Smith
Bill Crooke	Ken Johnson	Kirby Sorrells
Tommy Crooke	Lester Lintz	Raymond Weekley
Jack Davis	Danny Lodge	Dick Wheeler
Tom Davis	Lance Lodge	

The responsibilities of being a paperboy didn't allow much time to socialize or play sports during the day. We were occasionally bitten by a surprised or unfriendly dog, fussed at by an irate subscriber when the paper was wet or late, nearly run down several times by careless drivers, had difficulty collecting from some customers, surprised by newly installed clothes lines, and sometimes were late getting to school because the papers were dropped off late. We were always sleepy, which went with the job. Yet, it was the best job available, and I realize today that I folded papers along side some of the best citizens this area ever had. Some have gone on to their great rewards, and others are still serving our community in worthwhile endeavors.

I value my experiences as a paperboy, and the lifelong friendships I established with other paperboys and customers. Although I do understand the reasons why most newspapers have switched to having adults deliver the newspapers in vehicles, it's still unfortunate that ambitious young boys don't have the same opportunity today that some of us had when we were boys.

The current newspaper carriers have their own problems, as well as some of the same one's we had sixty years ago. Our carrier is Robert Miller, and he's very efficient, and as we learned recently, he also has a tender heart. A little bird recently built a nest in our paper slot under our mailbox. At first, I tried to discourage her by removing the straw each morning, but after a week or more, I gave up and she completed her task, with straw hanging out both ends of the "tube." I "wished her luck," because I knew she and her little family would be in jeopardy each morning as Robert slammed the paper in the slot. But, I was wrong. Little did I know that he had been keeping an eye on the little bird's progress also. He began placing our paper, secured in a plastic bag, on top of the mailbox. The first morning of his abrupt change in delivery, he put a note in the plastic bag, which read, "Wren nest in tube," and signed, "R. Miller."

Robert Miller, our current newspaper carrier, an avid fisherman
Courtesy of Robert Miller

Above: Former paperboys at lunch at the Marina Oyster Barn. L to R: Tom Davis, Charlie, Davis, Bennett Orr, Ray Donnelly, Charlie McLemore and his wife, Nan

Below: Former paperboys at lunch at Hall's Restaurant. L. to R: Tom Psaltis, Paul Daniel, Robert "Pee Wee" Mackey, and George VanMatre
Courtesy of Joan Daniel

Tribute to Pat Donnelly
Courtesy of Bernice Donnelly Gilmore

Bill Crooke, then and now
Courtesy of Tommy Crooke

Brigadier General and Mrs. Michael Ferguson
Courtesy of BG Michael Ferguson, Ret.

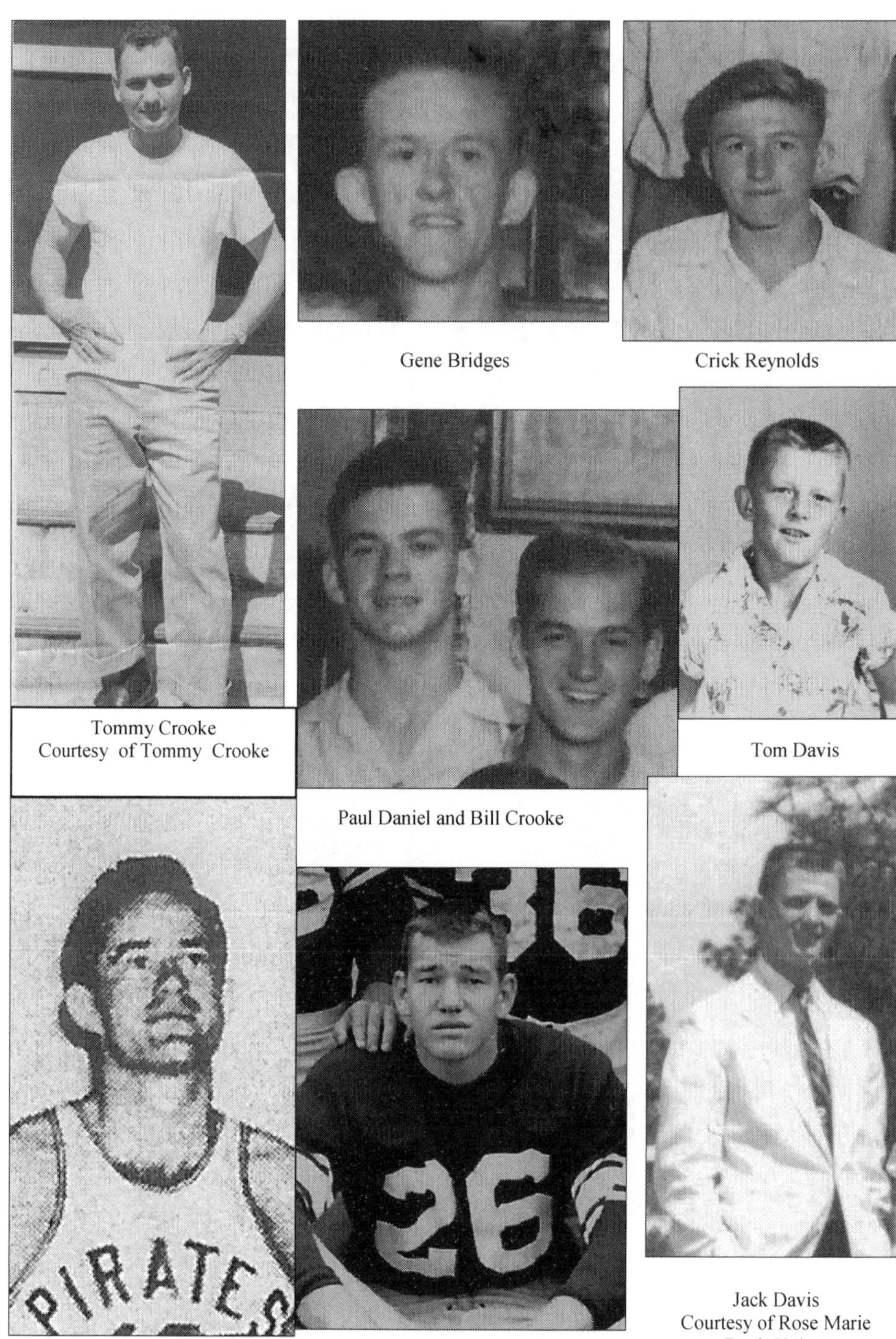

Tommy Crooke
Courtesy of Tommy Crooke

Gene Bridges

Crick Reynolds

Paul Daniel and Bill Crooke

Tom Davis

Tommy Bridges

Bill Hayes

Jack Davis
Courtesy of Rose Marie Davis Kaiser

39

Paper Bowl Champs, The Fighting Alumni

1950 Paper Bowl Champs
Members of the Pensacola Fighting Alumni semi-pro football team flank coach Bill Jones after winning the Pensacola Paper Bowl championship with a 7 - 6 victory over undefeated Jacksonville, Alabama State. (Names of players are listed on last page of this article) Courtesy of David Burch

On December 2, 1950, the Pensacola Alumni, Semi-Pro team, defeated Jacksonville State College, 7 to 6, in the third annual Paper Bowl Game, played before a full house at Pensacola High School's Tiger Stadium. A parade preceded the game, featuring the Paper Bowl Queen, Diane Dashiell (Crona) of Pensacola High School, and her court, Ann Martin (King) of Catholic High School and Dolores Falk (Miller) of Tate High School. Also, present in the parade were local high school teams and their coaches and representatives of the Pensacola Navy's Goshawks football team.

1950 Paper Bowl Queen and Court. Queen Diane Dahiell Crona (center) who represented Pensacola High School . In her court were, Ann Martin King (right), who represented Catholic High School and Dolores Falk Miller, (left) who represented Tate High School. Military escort unidentified
Courtesy of David Burch

The Paper Bowl was a smashing success, due to the combined efforts of several leading citizens who were members of the Pensacola Paper Bowl Association, which was officially organized in November, 1950. Officers of the Association were, A. C. Pace, General

Manager, Pratt Martin, G. T. Wegner, Tom S. Kennedy and Justin Weddell. Board Members were, J. H. Allen, J. C. Pace, Wally Dashiell, A. C. Johnson, William Ray, H. J. McRoberts, Raymond Dyson, Henry Hilton-Green, Walter Harbison, Crawford Rainwater, Kenneth Fulgum, Eugene Smith, Calvin Todd and J. Holliday Veal. These leading business and professional men and others were also responsible for the 1948 and 1949 Paper Bowl games. They started, what many hoped would be an annual tradition that would provide exciting games for football fans, and funds for local charities. Unfortunately, in late 1950, the Korean War suddenly turned more ominous when China unexpectedly entered the fray. Many more young men would be exchanging their football uniforms for military uniforms, and future Paper Bowl games were put on hold.

The Pensacola Alumni team, also known as the Cardinals, was owned and coached by Bill Jones, a Milton Native, a football standout at Perkinston Junior College, and a former coach at Catholic High School. Coach Jones was also the Escambia County Supervisor of Elections, and subsequently was elected to the office of County Tax Assessor. He was a living example of courage, which he demonstrated to us every night at practice, and during each game. Being confined to a wheelchair, due to a football injury while in college, didn't slow him down one bit. If anything, it seemed to make him more determined to succeed, and succeed he did. He showed equal respect for each of us, whether we were "bench warmers" or star players, and he had our respect and admiration in return. Coach Bill Jones died in 1992.

The Alumni Team was made up of local players, most of whom had played football in high school, but a few had played in college. Sam Goldman played with the Washington Redskins and the Chicago Cardinals, and Fred Haushalter, who later became the Superintendent of Education for Escambia County, played for Livingston State Teacher's College. Ray Wheat and Bill Davis played for Perkinston Junior College. Most players were employed locally or in business for themselves. Some, like me, were undecided about career or college goals due to the war situation. Leading up to the Paper Bowl game, the "Fighting Alumni" team had a string of twenty-eight undefeated games. In the 1950 football season, Coach Bill Jones' team had defeated Chipola Junior College, Mobile Alumni, Florida State University's B Team, Biloxi, Miss. and Metairie Athletic Club.

Unfortunately, in 1950, just weeks before the Paper Bowl game, the Korean War suddenly escalated when Communist China, unexpectedly entered the conflict. By the end of 1951, a large number of the Alumni players had exchanged their uniforms from football to military uniforms. Although the team continued into the next season, future Paper Bowl games were put on hold. The local Naval Reserve unit at Ellison Field was activated in October, and several hundred of us were ordered to duty stations. Many of us reported to the Naval Training Center at Bainbridge, Maryland for Boot Camp. It was like old home week with so many of us from Pensacola being there at the same time. Bodie McCrory was a sports writer for the Pensacola News-Journal. He covered many of the Alumni games, and wrote some great stories about the team. He and I reported to Boot Camp together, and over the next three months, we learned a lot about discipline, the U. S. Navy and how miserably cold it can get in Maryland.

On December 2, 1950, most Pensacolians were preparing for the Christmas season, a time of joy and thanksgiving. However, there was a pall over our nation. Our young men and women were dying in Korea, and there was widespread fear that the Korean War might be the beginning of World War III. It had only been five years since the end of World War II, but in spite of these fears, people were trying to live as normal a life as was possible, and attending the much publicized Paper Bowl game allowed some to put their worries aside.

David Burch
All three photos courtesy of David Burch

Top Right: Bill Davis, former Paper Bowl Camp and Sheriff of Escambia County

David Burch and Doug Peacock

Above: Pensacola Alumni team, circa 1949-1950 with Coach Bill Jones
Courtesy of Ray Wheat
Below: Pensacola Alumni team, circa 1950-51 with Coach Bill Jones
Courtesy of David Burch

Above: Pensacola Alumni team circa 1948-49, with Coach Bill Jones
Below: Pensacola Alumni team circa 1952, with Coach Sam Goldman
Courtesy of Ray Wheat

Pensacola Alumni team reunion at the Scenic Terrace, early 1960s
Courtesy of Ray Wheat

Names of the players from the picture on first page of this article

1950 Paper Bowl Champs
Players identifiable by numbers are:
Bill Davis(10), Frankie Grasso (14), Al Davidson (36), Gerald Sermons (42), Dick Barker (15), D. Penton (36), Charles Arnold (18), Jim Bradley (27), Art Sobota (25), Carlton Melvin (26), Johnny Catches (48), David Burch (33), Leon Watson (31), and Rocky Masterfries (51). Other players in the picture are: Roy Tummler, Johnny Browder, Charlie Davis, Bobby Nellums, Dan Dobbins, Fred (Big Red) Haushalter, Shorty Haynes, Nick Varazo, John Jolley, Red Hutto, Cecil Bell,, Wayne "Log" Chestnut, Barney Morain, Crick Reynolds, Ralph Atwell, Doug Peacock and Ray Wheat.

40

Pensacola Team In 1949 Little League World Series

In the summer of 1949, while the nation prayed that Margaret Mitchell, author of *Gone With The Wind*, would win her struggle to survive a hit and run accident in Atlanta, Georgia, Pensacola residents were also praying that the state champions from Pensacola would win their struggle to capture the 1949 Little League World Series in Williamsport, Pennsylvania.

Front row: Jesse Barrow, Sonny Able, Jasper Falzone, and Eddie Listander. Coach Pappy Williamson. Second row: David Cobb, Paul Holden, Chester Dungan, and Gene Dorch. Third row: Bill Womack, Jerry Hudson, Jerry Miller, Frank Willis, and Bill Powers. Not pictured: Philip McSwain and Coach Phillip Miller
Courtesy of Frank and Mary Willis

The Optimist Club Little League All-Stars had advanced to the state tournament in St. Petersburg. Of the ten teams, they were considered the dark horse, but when the rain soaked tournament ended there was joy in Pensacola, because the mighty Optimist Club Little Leaguers had won the State Championship. The Pensacola News-Journal headlines for Sunday morning, August 14, 1949 was, "Pensacola Little Leaguers Capture State Title." Doubters, fans, and sports writers were dazzled by the dynamic pitching abilities of Jerry Hudson and Chester Dungan. Hudson pitched three shutouts in the tournament, allowing only three hits, and pitched one no-hitter. Heavy hitters in the tournament were Jerry Miller and Jasper Falzone. The local all-stars, expertly coached by Pappy Williamson and Phillip Miller, consisted of twelve year old kids who won four straight games to claim the state title, and earned the right to play for the national title.

Team members of the Optimist Club Little League All-Stars, who brought pride to Pensacola sixty years ago were:

Sonny Able	Jerry Hudson
Jesse Barrow	Eddie Listander
David Cobb	Jerry Miller
Chester Dungan	Philip McSwain
Gene Dorch	Bill Powers
Jasper Falzone	Frank Willis
Paul Holden	Bill Womack
Pappy Williamson, Mgr.	Phillip Miller, Coach

On Sunday night, August 21, 1949, fourteen boys, their manager and coach, representing the best Pensacola and Florida had to offer in Little League baseball, boarded a train in Pensacola, and traveled to Williamsport, arriving there on Tuesday afternoon. They took along a case of grits for fear that the local staple would not be on the menu in Pennsylvania. Wesley Chalk, sports editor of the Pensacola News-Journal, accompanied the team to personally cover the tournament. There were three separate parades during the week, and many notables, including Connie Mack, attended the games.

The Team meets the Mayor of Williamsport
Courtesy of Frank and Mary Willis

The event had all the excitement of Major League World Series games. Umpires from the National league handled all the games, and Pennsylvania's Governor, James H. Duff, tossed out the first ball. Of the eight teams in the tournament, Pensacola had the honor of leading off the first game, which was against Lock Haven, Pennsylvania, winners of the 1948 National Championship. Pensacola beat them, 3 to 0, allowing no hits. Advancing to the semi-finals, the next opponent was a tough team from Bridgeport, Connecticut. The Pensacola lads won the semi-finals in overtime, 9 to 8. The winning run was scored by David Cobb. It was the most exciting game of the series. The lead changed hands several times, and each of the boys from Florida played an important part in winning the game, which moved the Pensacola All-Stars into the finals.

Jerry Hudson shaking hands with opponent and Mayor
Courtesy of Frank and Mary Willis

The headlines in the August 27, 1949, Saturday morning issue of the Pensacola News-Journal informed the hometown folks that their team had made it to the finals. The front page also included pictures of some of the team members. While the families and fans at home were reading about the great win their team had on Friday, the All-Stars were on the field, playing the team from Hammonton, New Jersey for the final game, the championship game. It was the third trip to the national tournament for the team from New Jersey. Excerpts from Wesley Chalk's front page article, which appeared in the Sunday morning Pensacola News-Journal on August 28th. tells it like it was:

> The Florida champions were great in victory and they were great in defeat on Saturday as they bowed to Hammonton, N. J., in the world series of the Little league tournament there Saturday afternoon 5 to 0. Pensacola hustled and tried, but it wasn't there. It appeared that the 9 to 8, eight inning game of Friday took more out of the youngsters than their elders really knew. The loss of Jerry Hudson, ill with a fever, probably had a demoralizing influence on the little fellows.
>
> Although the boys received medals, wristwatches and trophies, they broke down and cried. It was a heart rending scene, and they sneaked off the field and into the cars, shaking off the well wishes of the fans who had cheered them on each occasion.

It cannot be said that there was no joy in Pensacola because of the loss to the New Jersey team. The citizens of Pensacola were excited and proud of their young ball players and their manager and coaches. Pensacola's Optimist Club's Little League All-Stars were the number two team in the nation. There were many reasons to celebrate, and the hometown welcomed their famous young citizens in style when they returned. The team arrived on Tuesday, August 30th., after an exciting trip home. In Washington, D.C., they were met by Florida Senators Claude Pepper and Spessard Holland, and properly entertained and recognized. Upon arrival at the L.& N Depot, the kids were shocked at the number of people there to greet them. Sitting atop one of the city's new fire trucks, they were loudly applauded by the crowds along the parade route. Mayor C. P. Mason, greeted the team and the coaches in a ceremony at Palafox and Garden Streets, where many speeches were made in their behalf. It was an impressive recognition of their accomplishments.

Excerpts from the Pensacola News-Journal editorial on August 31, 1949, are as follows:

Nothing perhaps, in many years has so stirred the imagination of the people as the victories of the first team which Pensacola has entered in the state and national contests.

They met defeat in the last contest, but it does not take one iota from the credit which is due them and due those who have made the Little League possible. The contests make for keen competition and good playing. They also make for good sportsmanship. A good looser is better than a poor winner. Perhaps it is well that the top rung of the ladder was not reached by these boys in their first attempt. Pensacola Little Leaguers still have the national championship to shoot for.

World Series team
Courtesy of Frank and Mary Willis

Unfortunately, and sadly, Margaret Mitchell also lost her struggle to win that same week back in 1949, but the above editorial proved to be correct. In 1950 and again in 1951 other Pensacola Little League teams also made it to the national championship tournament. Perhaps, with more prayers and the spirit of the 1949 Optimist Club All-Stars, a team from Pensacola will someday win the National Championship.

Frank and Mary Willis
Courtesy of Frank and Mary Willis

Frank Willis was a star outfielder at Rollins College, and was most valuable player of the 1957 Small College World Series. The Pensacola native worked in the Escambia County school system for 34 1/2 years, including 25 as a principal and two years as Woodham High's baseball coach (1965-67). He retired in 1993.

From an article in The Pensacola News Journal, dated Sunday, August 22, 1999
Courtesy of The Pensacola News Journal

41

The P.J.C. Float

I transferred from Florida State University to Pensacola Junior College for the school year 1955-1956. At that time, P.J.C. was in the old Pensacola High School building, at the top of the hill on Palafox Street. I really enjoyed those two semesters, and I made good grades. The courses were not any easier than they would have been at F.S.U., but the atmosphere at a small college, as opposed to a large university like Florida State was refreshing. I will always cherish the memories of that year at P.J.C. I took a heavy load both semesters, worked part-time, and still found time to be on the debate team and to participate in other activities. However, being involved with designing and entering a "P.J.C. Float" in the 1956 Fiesta of Five Flags Parade, almost caused me and a couple other guys to be kicked off campus.

There had been some discussion among the students about having a float in the Fiesta parade, but it didn't get beyond the dining hall. So, with the parade a few days away, a small group of us, with the interest of the college at heart, of course, decided it would be a nice thing if we did have a float in the parade. We, the "committee of three" had an intense, late night meeting at Jerry's Drive-In. By the time Ray Wessel, the owner, kicked us out, we, with the help of some patrons, had designed a float that we thought best represented the spirit of the unofficial school motto, *"Illigitimus Noncarbirundum."*

The next day, we borrowed some kid's little red wagon. Then, I borrowed my sister-in-law's dog, a fine specimen of the "Heinz-57 Variety." The only thing outstanding about that mama dog, which looked like a cross between a Chihuahua and a Blue Tick Hound, was that she had more puppies than she had nipples. She never sat or laid down, even when nursing her puppies.

Someone contributed a nice rabbit cage, which we secured onto the top of the wagon. Although it was a little crowded, the mother dog and all of her puppies fit in very nicely. Across the bottom of the cage, we installed a paper skirt, which covered the wagon's wheels, on which we scrawled, in large letters, "Pensacola Junior College." When the parade began, my two colleagues and I quickly moved our float in between two huge floats. The moment the parade began, the mother dog started barking, and never stopped during the entire parade. As she stood and barked, half the puppies nursed, while the other half stared at the crowd.

We each took our turn pulling the wagon, or throwing dog biscuits to the crowd. They seemed to appreciate us, and we were surprised at the laughs and applauses we received, even though our float was a little bit different. On top of the cage we placed a hand printed sign, which read, in bold letters, "THIS IS OUR FLOAT, AIN'T IT A BITCH ?"

The following Monday morning at school, we received mixed reviews. The rumor was that we were in trouble, and we were expecting to be invited to Dr. Henry Ashmore's office, so he could explain how the college would miss us, but could manage without us in the future. Fortunately, the call never came, which proves, what I have always believed, that even college presidents enjoy a good laugh.

Illustration by Steve Blair

42

The Preacher's Wife

Norman & Emma Jean Redding
Courtesy of Mrs. Norman Redding

Emma Jean Redding of Starke, Florida , is our only sister. She had the disadvantage of growing up among six brothers, which is why she's tough as nails, has the energy of ten women, and always has several projects going on at the same time. Her husband, Norman, died a few years ago, after serving twenty-five years as a Chaplain at Raiford Prison, ten of those as the death row Chaplain. Emma Jean graduated from Pensacola High School in 1944, and she and Norman married in 1945, while World War II was still raging. In 1952, they were off to Howard College in Birmingham, and in 1958, Norman graduated from the Baptist

Seminary in New Orleans. For the next forty plus years she was a preacher's wife.

At age eighty-three, "Cindy," the moniker our dad put on her, doesn't know what it means to slow down. Where in the devil did she get all that energy? My bet is that she learned some of it as a young preacher's wife, as Norman pastored several small churches in rural communities in Louisiana and South Alabama. It took a while for the skinny, red headed gal from East Pensacola Heights to get used to being paid in hogs, chickens, hams, eggs and other goodies, but she said, her freezer was always filled with good food. One small church he pastored, paid him a percentage of the amount collected each Sunday, so Emma Jean said, "Norman's sermons always emphasized the importance of tithing."

Emma Jean "Cindy" Davis Redding

There are several dozen people in the small town of Starke, Florida who look forward to Tuesday evenings. That's when Emma Jean shows off her culinary talents with a display of delicious food and desserts that would make the owners of Barnhill's Country Buffet envious. Who all shows up for this weekly ritual? Well, the regulars are her kids and their kids and friends, folks from her church, and many other good friends. Also, every now and then, a brother or a nephew from Pensacola shows up, when we just happen to be in the neighborhood. Occasionally a stranger shows up out of curiosity and becomes a regular, like the two nice young men from the Mormon Church who first showed up on their bicycles.

So, you might ask, "How in the devil did that get started?" Well, the devil didn't make her do it, that's for sure. Like I said before, she learned it from being a preacher's wife all those years. You know what they say about preachers and how they love to eat...and they had all that food in the freezer. So, Emma Jean just started cooking, and now she doesn't know how to stop.

During a conversation with Cindy recently, she said she felt like she had been muzzled most of her life, because being the daughter of a local elected official, she had to be careful about what she said or did in public; and as the wife of a preacher she said, "I was expected to be seen a lot, but not heard from too much." She retired several years ago from the Bradford County School System, and recently said, half joking and half laughing, I'm going to say what I want to say and do what I want to do without worrying about voters, parishioners or the students' parents." So, I guess she is making up for lost time. Just don't get in her way. It could be dangerous.

The Davis Family
Back Row, L to R: Bob, Charlie, Tom, Bill
Front Row, L to R: Emma Jean, Mother, Ben, Jr.

Norman and Emma Jean Redding's family
L to R: Back row Lori, Jamie, Christie, Carl, Butch, Shelley, Andy, Front row: L to R: Amanda, Norman, Emma Jean, & Mary
Courtesy of Mrs. Emma Jean Redding

43

Pulled Overboard by a Shark

Ben Early and Jerry Browder are excellent fishermen, and both grew up in East Pensacola Heights. I believe I can write with confidence that they have, individually or together, caught more than their fair share of fish over the years. Now, I'm not so sure about sharks. They probably have fished for sharks on occasion, because like all good fishermen, they would

Benny Early and Jerry Browder

Everette Gabel, 1952
Courtesy of Harry and Nadine Kastanakis

consider anything that will bite a hook as fair game. I would like to share a story that was related to me by Ben over forty-five years ago, when he, Everette Gabel and I shared a beach house on Pensacola Beach. It's about an incident that happened out in the middle of Pensacola Bay at least ten or fifteen years earlier, so we're talking maybe fifty-five or sixty years ago. I recently confirmed the story with both Ben and Jerry. Some of you might get the idea that I'm writing about the famous ice cream makers, but if so, you can forget that. I'm writing about two adventurous guys with the same names, who in their youth, decided to try something different with one of mother nature's ancient killers, a curious shark that was larger than either one of them. This story will bring to mind the old saying, "You can admire their spunk, but you have to question their judgment."

It wasn't uncommon in the fifties to find Ben and Jerry shrimping in Pensacola or Escambia Bays, especially in the summer months, and no school to be concerned with. They had access to Bill Early's shrimp boat, the *Lula Belle,* which Bill docked at Coursen's Boat House, formerly Doug Walker's Boat House on Bayou Texar. They had an agreement with Ray and Bill Wessel at Jerry's Drive-In to supply them with fresh shrimp. They had other customers as well, such as Big Lee's Grocery in East Pensacola Heights. They were out shrimping on that particular day, pulling a commercial shrimp net in Pensacola Bay, and they had been watching a couple sharks, each about six feet long, that had been following the boat. They were concerned about the two sharks, since sharks have a tendency to destroy shrimp nets in their effort to get at the shrimp and fish that collect at the end of the funnel-shaped net, called the "bag." It's not clear whose bright idea it was to attempt to dissuade the sharks in the manner they chose, so we can assume it was a joint decision.

They put the boat in a long wide turn in front of the Muscogee Wharf to keep the net from getting tangled up, and when completed, they were heading south, parallel to the old Pensacola Bay Bridge. The two sharks made the turn with them as if on cue. The plan was to gaff one of the sharks as it swam along side the boat. Both Ben and Jerry were obviously aware that it took a bit more planning to gaff a six foot shark than it took to gaff a good size grouper, redfish or a large sloop-rigged catfish, so they agreed on the procedure. Ben would do the gaffing. A gaff is a large barbless hook attached to one end of a handle. A leather strap or thong is attached to the other end through a hole in the handle, which is then looped around the user's wrist so it won't slip out while being used. Their gaff was about six feet long, which allowed Ben to reach the shark as he leaned over the side of the boat. To entice the shark, they baited the gaff with a croaker, a small fish caught in an earlier "drag" of the shrimp net. Jerry's responsibility was to wrap one arm around Ben's legs and his other arm around a stanchion or post that was part of the shrimp boat apparatus. It was a great plan as plans go. Who would doubt or question the success of such a plan?

With the boat continuing to drag the large shrimp net in a straight line, Ben and Jerry set the trap, or the gaff. With the fish firmly attached to the gaff, and Jerry firmly attached to Ben's legs, the bait was lowered as deep as Ben could extend it as he leaned way over the side of the boat. According to Ben, it didn't take long. The shark grabbed the bait, and Ben set the hook…and all hell broke loose. They didn't anticipate the explosion that occurred. The shark didn't follow the script and it thrashed about so violently that water was being splashed everywhere, and the water around the boat turned into foam. Another thing that neither of them anticipated was their own instant reaction. Each must have realized the ridiculousness of their situation simultaneously. They didn't panic; they laughed, and the more the shark thrashed about and showered them, the harder they laughed. What's wrong with this picture? There's a mad -as-hell killer on one end of the stick, and two laughing teenagers on the other end. Whoever it was who said laughter is the best cure, probably didn't have this scenario in mind.

You don't have to be a scientist or a medical professional to know that it's possible to lose muscle control when we get tickled or laugh out of control. This must have happened to Jerry as he lost his grip on Ben's legs, and since Ben was already leaning over the side of the boat, the irate shark had the last laugh as Ben was pulled overboard into a hostile, murky environment where the shark had a definite advantage. Ben is a good swimmer, especially since he has six toes on each foot, but he was still no match for that shark, or any shark, as they are born into the sea, swimming. Ben had to learn to swim, and only one of them could breathe under water. What ensued probably took less than a couple minutes, but must have seemed like a lifetime to Ben.

As Ben was being pulled down through the water, he attempted to free himself from the gaff's handle as the leather thong was looped tightly around his wrist, and the hook end was firmly implanted in the shark's mouth. At that point, the hazards he faced, included the shark, other sharks, drowning and getting caught up in the shrimp net. As the conjoined pair neared the bottom of the bay, Ben managed to free himself, and rapidly swam up in the direction of the boat to avoid the net. The boat was still running in forward gear, and continuing to drag the shrimp net. Suddenly, Ben faced a greater hazard, one he had not considered in his haste to escape the sharks, the net and the possibility of drowning. The bay water was, as mentioned, murky, and hindered visibility under water, and just as he reached the boat he almost swam directly into the spinning prop, which would have been more fatal than all the sharks in the area. Finally, he surfaced along side the boat, and with Jerry's help he managed to get back aboard the shrimp boat. Neither one was laughing.

Other than that, guys, how was the trip?

44

The Rebel Cap Episode

In 1951, I was in boot camp at the U. S. Navy Training Center in Bainbridge Maryland. Our Navy Reserve unit at Ellison Field, Pensacola, Florida had been activated, and it was like old home week at Bainbridge, because several hundred of us from Pensacola were ordered to boot camp at the same time. Many of the Ellison Field unit wound up in the same company at Bainbridge, but Bodie McCrory and I were the only two from Pensacola in our company. The barracks accommodated two companies on our floor, for a total of one hundred and twenty-eight men. The boys from the north outnumbered us southern boys about three to one. Naturally, the major topic, or argument, was the Civil War. We were all young, and full of P & V, and really didn't know enough history about the "War of Yankee Aggression" to make a real point. That didn't stop us, and the rhetoric almost reached a flash point a few times. We would have probably

Charlie in his Navy uniform

gotten through the entire twelve weeks of boot camp without a fight, if my brother, Jack, had not sent me that rebel cap. Who would have thought that one little grey cap could cause such a ruckus, involve the company commander, the shore patrol, regimental headquarters, and the base commander?

I was happy to get the package from Jack, which I received at mail call, after a morning of marching to and from classes in the snow, and an afternoon of firefighting training. We all smelled like smoke, oil and grime, and most of us were running around in our underwear, waiting for our turn in the shower. I was hoping the package contained wool socks, as 1951 was a bad winter, even for the folks in Maryland. It was too light to be food, but since it was from Jack, it could have been anything, so I was not too surprised to get the rebel cap. That's something every southern boy needs when he's in the middle of a beehive of Yankees, especially when most of them looked like they came from coal mines and steel mills, which they did. I proved I wasn't too bright when I donned the cap, and paraded around the quarterdeck, where others were still getting their mail. All the southern boys wanted to wear it, and of course the Yankee boys wanted to take it, so I almost lost it in the first thirty seconds. It was one big pile on, and my cap and I were in there somewhere. After a bloody nose, a few scratches, and the loss of a new pair of baggy Navy drawers I was wearing, I managed to get my cap back. I kept a tight grip on the rumpled cap, and quickly stored it away in my locker. I didn't mind

My brother, Jack Davis

the bloody nose, or losing my drawers, but I was more than a little upset with a big, jovial Jewish guy from the Bronx, who for some dumb reason, kept stomping on my bare feet with his newly issued brogans. Who knew things like that would happen? Jack knew, that's who! I later found my drawers in the trash can with about two dozen cigarette holes burned in them.

Charlie in uniform

The following day, a short time before we were to assemble outside and march off to the chow hall, a few of us from the south unwisely decided to have a little fun, and entertain the troops. I wore my rebel cap, a couple others used trash cans for drums, and we marched down the middle of the barracks, singing and whistling "Dixie." That's all those miners and mill workers needed. One guy literally dove from his top bunk and snatched my cap, nearly taking my head with it. Bunks and mattresses were strewn in all directions, as Jack's cap moved from hand to hand. Fortunately, everyone seemed to know we were pushing our luck, since our barracks housed the chiefs' Regimental Office. We had already experienced a couple 3:00 a.m. wakeup calls to sweep and swab the barracks. Fortunately, cooler heads prevailed, and I got my cap back. Like the others, I was scratched up, dirty and sweaty, and I had to hurry and get cleaned up before chow. So, in my underwear, which I managed to keep this time, I walked toward the head, possessing only a towel and my ditty -bag, and, still wearing the cap. Just before I reached the door to the head, I saw the Chief, and of course, the Chief saw me.

Most Navy chiefs' have been around, and they have seen just about everything. They are the old salts of the Navy. They are the ones who see to it that things work properly. They run the Navy. With the start of the Korean War, the Navy brass called thousands of retired chiefs' back to active duty. Many of them, in their late forties and fifties, became company commanders, equivalent to drill instructors in other branches of the military. They were tough but fair, and I don't know, but I would bet that their performance was excellent in making good sailors out of raw recruits during the Korean war. My company commander was soft spoken but firm, but the chief, who was the company commander of the adjoining company was loud and boisterous, and kept everyone, including himself in a turmoil. The Chief that saw me walking toward the head in my baggy underwear and a rebel cap, looked shocked, and he reacted accordingly,

"Halt!," he shouted.

I halted, just as I approached the swinging door leading into the head.

"Up against the wall, sailor," he said, still shouting.

"Yes Sir," I replied, as I moved against the wall and stood at attention, facing him.

"Just who in the hell are you suppose to be?" he asked.

"Nobody, Sir," I replied, really not knowing what else to say.

"Nobody?" he asked.

"No, Sir," I replied.

"Well, Mister nobody, I'm gonna ask you again, who are you?" he asked.

"Seaman Recruit Davis, Sir," I answered, loudly. Then, I quickly remembered to add, "Serial number 3190186, Sir."

The chief looked at me like he would like to bite my head off. Whatever the rules were that I had broken, or the laws I had violated, he acted like he was taking the infraction personally.

"What the hell you trying to do, son, start another war?" he asked.

"No, Sir," I answered.

"Well, that's what it looks like to me." he responded. Then he said, "Alright, at ease, sailor."

I immediately relaxed into an "at ease" posture. I was hoping at that point, he might laugh and tell me to destroy the cap and to get my behind back to my area and get dressed. That didn't happen. I was dreaming.

"You're in a lot of trouble, Sailor," he said. He then turned to the guy on guard duty and instructed him to, "Keep your eyes on this man. He's not to move from that spot. He's not to talk to anybody, and nobody is to talk to him. Do you understand those instructions?" he asked the guard.

"Yes, Sir," he answered excitedly, in a southern drawl worse than mine, as he pointed his rifle at me.

"Damn, I don't want you to shoot him. Just guard him while I go find out what the hell I'm suppose to do with him," the chief shouted at the guard, who was just a recruit like me. Actually, the gun wasn't loaded anyhow. It was an old, obsolete, 30 caliber Springfield, left over from World War II. The chief disappeared into the Regimental office.

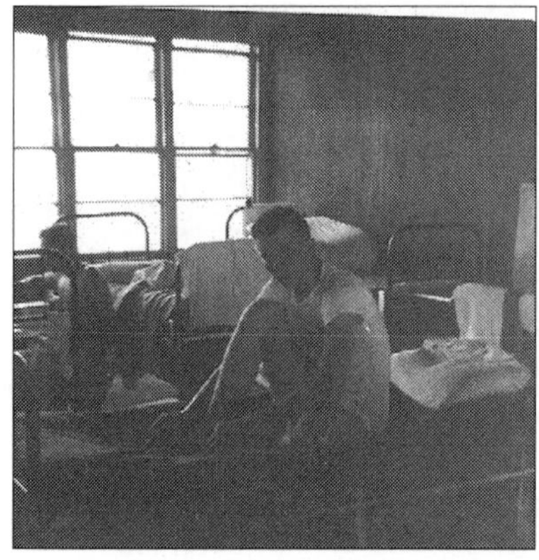
Charlie without his uniform

As soon as the chief closed the door to his office, several guys came flowing out of the head. They had been listening to what was going on but hadn't been able to see anything. They walked past me, quietly laughing to themselves, making smart remarks, like referring to Robert E. Lee's heritage, etc. A fellow recruit, Buddy Lepera, an Italian American guy, whom I had earlier befriended, stopped, saluted and made a remark that caused both of us to laugh.

"Hey!" "Hey!" shouted the guard. "Get the hell out of here, Lepera. You're going to get us all in trouble." he said, in a loud whisper.

Fifteen or twenty minutes went by, and the chief was still in the office. I didn't think too much about the two Shore Patrolmen when they entered the barracks, and knocked on the Chief's door, after taking a long, quizzical look at me. I must have looked somewhat comical, not just because of the rebel cap, but I had put on my brogans, without socks, because I didn't want to walk on the floor in my bare feet.

The Chief came out of the office and led the two Shore Patrolmen over to where I was standing, and said to them, "You are to escort this prisoner over to the Regimental Headquarters, and be quick about it." He then added, "The Officer of the Day is waiting." The chief turned to walk back to his office, but he paused, turned back around and looking at me, but obviously speaking to the Shore Patrolmen, he said, "And, he is to wear that cap." Then, looking directly at the two, he added, "You got that?"

"Aye, Aye, Sir," they responded, and stood at attention as the Chief returned to his office.

The word, "prisoner" got my attention, immediately. The two Shore Patrolmen appeared to be a bit reluctant as they made a couple short steps toward me. It was only then that I realized they were seamen recruits, just like me and that nervous redneck guard. It's true that I was known to be somewhat hardheaded, and it was a good possibility that I could be dense on occasions, and that, obviously, was one of those occasions. I thought, okay, it's just a cruel joke they've been playing on me, because these two guys aren't regular Shore Patrolmen, they're still in boot camp like all the rest of us. I was wondering why they picked me to be the goat. Obviously, I wasn't getting the picture.

I had trouble believing that wearing that cap could bring out the U.S. Navy's "gendarmes," and that I was actually under arrest. Well, whether or not I believed it really didn't matter, because it was true. The recruit Shore Patrolmen did what they were ordered to do, they proceeded to marched me across the "grinder," the drill field, on a cold, late afternoon in the snow to the Regimental Headquarters, but only after first, being stopped by another chief. We had marched only a short distance from the barracks, when a chief seemed to appear from nowhere, and stopped us. After a short explanation, he ordered them to return me to the barracks and for me to get back into uniform. A short time later, the march continued, with me in the uniform of the day, except for the hat. It was a long march, which caused a lot of Navy guys to stop and stare. The two fellow recruits, both Yankees, hammed it up, making me march six paces in front of them, and keeping their weapons pointed at my back. My comments to them during this "Prisoner's March" didn't make them want to do me any favors.

When we reached the Regimental Headquarters and entered the building, I was directed to a door down the hall. Not knowing what to expect, I opened the door, and all I saw was this guy's fist speeding toward my face. He was obviously waiting for me. I instinctively ducked, but he connected with the top of my head, knocking the hat off. The fist belonged to a short, stocky Lieutenant Commander, who was mad as hell. The room had chairs along the walls, occupied by a dozen or so chiefs, who observed everything the Officer of the Day said and did. His first words were, "We whipped youse asses once! Do you want us to do it again?"

The rest of what happened is a blur to me, but I do remember he chewed me out, unmercifully and I thought at the time that he was over-reacting and performing for the benefit of the chiefs. I recall some, but not all of them, laughing. I also recall him telling me that the procedure was a "Regimental Mast," a military judiciary procedure. I don't even remember returning to my barracks. The two Shore Patrolmen were gone, so I must have returned alone, out of uniform, because I didn't have a hat to wear.

I don't remember anything else about that incident, but about two weeks later, an officer came to our barracks, and I was summoned to the Chief's office. He instructed me to get dressed, in my dress blues, and report to the Regimental Headquarters immediately. When I arrived at the Headquarters. building, I was instructed to enter the same room where the Lieutenant. Commander. had taken a swing at me. I entered the room, expecting the Lieutenant Commander. to be huffing and puffing as before. Instead, I was shocked to see two Navy Captains, one whom I later learned was the Base Commander. The large room was lined with Navy chiefs. All the chairs were occupied. The Lieutenant Commander was there, but he looked a little subdued. It appeared that some type of formal procedure was in process. Frankly, I was scared. I assumed they were about to send me to the brig. All because of that damn cap Jack sent me.

All eyes were on me, as the Captain motioned me to come forward. I approached to a spot where I assumed he wanted me to be, and stood at attention.

"What is your name?" asked the Captain.

"Seaman recruit Davis, Sir," I replied.

"At ease," the Captain said to me, as he looked over toward the Lieutenant Commander, and then addressing me, he said, "The Commander has something to say to you."

The Lieutenant Commander. came forward and stood in front of me, looking like he was sweating bullets, or, as Jack would have said, "He looked like he had been dragged through a knot hole." As I can best recall, he said, "I had no right to strike you, and I had no right to take your personal property away from you. I was wrong, and I apologize."

Charlie in Washington D. C.

He then, ceremoniously handed me Jack's rebel cap, and once I had possession of it, he did a snappy about face, which placed him, at attention, face to face with the base commander. The Captain had some very important looking papers in his hands, and it appeared that he was about to read out loud to the Lieutenant Commander. Obviously, the Lieutenant

Commander. was having a Regimental or Captain's Mast of his own. I would liked to have remained there for awhile, just to watch the diminutive Lieutenant Commander sweat, but I was instructed to return to my barracks, which I did, with the rebel cap tucked under my peacoat, safely out of view.

I am grateful to the chief, or chiefs, who reported the incident to their superiors. I was later informed by letter from the Navy, that the incident and the Regimental Mast had been expunged from my record. The rebel cap was promptly mailed back to my brother, Jack. Perhaps it was some form of personal protest, but I continued to wear the baggy pair of "holy" drawers, even after being assigned to the U. S. Marine Corps. at Parris Island; that is, until I got tired of explaining the burn holes.

Charlie and some of his buddies from his military service days.

45

Schools

Those of us from East Pensacola Heights attended A. V. Clubbs Junior High School, which was located on 12th. Avenue. It was a good school, and the principal, Miss Lena Nobles, was obviously a good principal because she was a fixture there for many years. The teachers at "Clubbs" were all good teachers. The ones I remember well were, Mrs. Shell, Ms. Barrineau, Ms. Bayless, Ms. Lee, Ms.Greenhut, Ms. Parker, Ms. Wickersham, Ms. Pfeiffer, Mr. Priest and Mr. Responi. There are others I'll think of right after this book goes to print.

I'll always remember Mr. Eugene Responi, the Physical Education teacher. Everyone liked "Resi," as he was referred to by the students. As I've written elsewhere in this book, when he saw me, on my first day of school at "Clubbs," He said, "Oh, no, not another Davis kid!" Three brothers and one sister preceded me, so I was in trouble before I arrived. I don't remember who told me this story, but I believe it was "Resi," and it's about my brother Bill. Either "Resi" or one of the other teachers happened to see smoke coming out of one of the trees on the school grounds. It was my brother, Bill, perched on a limb, up in the top of the tree, smoking a cigarette. I didn't do anything that got me in trouble with the school, and I was relieved when the school didn't turn my two younger brothers away after I graduated.

L to R: Charlie Davis and Mary Ann Keller (Kickliter). Sarah Thomas and June Browder (Merritt) in the background

Clubbs Junior High School didn't have organized sports back in the forties, while I was there, but one group that many of us joined was the T.O.C. Club, which was an acronym for "Teens of Clubbs." It was a social group, and weekly meetings were held at Bayview Park, upstairs in the pavilion. It was a good group, and we had dances, games, horseplay, and some things we were not suppose to have. Each year there was a coronation for the King and Queen and their court for the year, followed by dancing. Overall it was a positive organization. Back at the school we had our usual functions in the auditorium, where talent was or was not often recognized. On the talent side was a duet formed by Frank Cagle and Bob Cary, and they were good. No, they were great! All I can say is that some unknown talent scout missed an opportunity. I think of those two guys every time I walk into the Marina Oyster Barn Restaurant where Frank is a permanent fixture behind the cash register.

Our class of 1951 was in the old PHS campus at the top of Palafox Hill, and Mr. McCord was the principal. PHS was "downtown," as it had been for years, just like Catholic High School and Washington High School were, and being downtown, there was little campus grounds, especially for PHS. As I recall, the school building and outside equipment accounted for most of the one square block. The center of commerce was still in downtown Pensacola, so after school let out, many students headed down Palafox hill toward "downtown" or to "Hoppy's," a favorite hangout for students, owned by the Hopkins family. Our

Boys, L to R: Bob Cary, Mickey Gilmore, Bob Kelley (King), Bill Kelley and Danny Gerow
Girls, L to R: JoAnn Owens, Shirley Smith, Diane Dashiell (Queen), Ann Martin and Madelyn Overstreet
Courtesy of Mary Ann Miller

favorite soda jerk was E.W. Hopkins. "Hoppy's" was located near the YMCA, which was another hangout for many of us.

I decided to transfer to Tate High School for a part of one school year, which I really enjoyed. Tate High School was a friendly place, and I made lifelong friends with many fellow students, plus I made good grades. However, it didn't take me long to realize that it was just too far to go, when PHS was so close to my home in East Pensacola Heights. It was one of those bad ideas that seemed good at the time. I don't regret it because of the friends I made. Mr. Lipscomb was the principal, and all the teachers I had at Tate were outstanding. After only a few months, I transferred back to PHS

Pensacola High School's football team was a powerhouse back in the forties and fifties, and there were many outstanding games at the old Legion Field ball park on West Gregory Street. Harold "Herky" Payne, Art Sabota and others made us proud at the old ball park, just as Larry Scott and company did later at the new PHS Stadium. PHS students always had a lot of good school spirit, plus we had excellent teachers, but I won't attempt to name them. During my years in high school and college the most popular hangout with our dates or as singles for most of us was the Scenic Terrace on Scenic Highway in East Pensacola Heights. It was the place to go to on the weekends. The year, 1951 was a time of concern for everyone in this country as the Korean War escalated, and it wasn't long before most of us from the Class of 1951 were in the military. Many of us returned for the fiftieth reunion in 2001, looking good, of course.

After two years at Florida State University, I transferred to Pensacola Junior College in 1955. I really enjoyed PJC, as it was a big change from what I was used to at FSU. My grades were very good, but not because the classes were any easier than at FSU. I almost felt like I was back in high school, because in 1955 PJC was located in the old Pensacola High School Building. I really enjoyed that year of college, but I was ready to return to FSU.

I returned to FSU and after satisfying the requirement for a degree in Zoology, except for a few hours of elected credits, I changed my major and dreams of going to Dental School and moved from the School of Science to the School of Business, graduating in 1959 with a degree in Real Estate and Insurance Marketing. I was ready to go to work because by that time I was married with two wonderful children.

Charlie in cap and gown

Fraternity brothers at a get together during the Sigma Alpha Epsilon Fraternity Weekend .
L to R: Tuffy Parson, and date, Raymond Weekley and date, Al "Nook" Davis and date, Joe Tarbuck and date, and Charlie Davis and date

Photos from Pensacola High School's 50th Reunion.
Above Left: Ted "Fuzzy" and Mary Peaden.
Above Right: Charlie and Sandra Davis

46

The Sinking of the Rampage

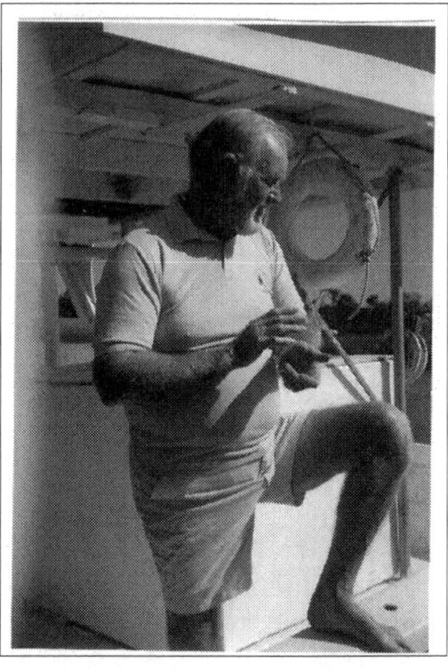
Capt. Bill Davis on the *Rampage*
Courtesy of Chris and Sharon Bridges

There were many interesting things about my brother, Bill, but the one that stood out the most by the people who knew him, was his love of boats, especially fishing boats. I don't ever remember him not having a boat, except during the years he was flying missions over Nazi Germany. Not long after he was discharged from the Army Air Corps, he took me along on a fishing trip on the Yellow River, just east of Milton, Florida, when I was about thirteen years old. We arrived at Miller's Bluff fish camp late in the evening and slept in the back of his bright, red pickup truck, after removing his outboard motor and fishing tackle. I

Capt Bill on board the *Rampage* at Sioux Bayou
Courtesy of Chris and Sharon Bridges

was a Boy Scout about that time, so I was used to sleeping outdoors, but not in the steel bed of a truck, with a small piece of canvas for a cover. I was too young to realize at that time that comfort and good weather conditions were not his requisites for a fishing trip. He could go to sleep anywhere, under most any conditions, and was subject to head out into the Gulf of Mexico, when most other skippers would remain in port due to unpredictable weather. Over the next fifty-seven years, from age twenty-three to age eighty, Bill owned and operated numerous small fishing boats suitable for river and bay fishing, two or three houseboats, a commercial barge and at least four commercial fishing boats. Owning and operating a boat of any size can be dangerous, and Bill almost lost his life while fishing alone in the Gulf of Mexico, through no fault of his own.

Several years after selling the *Flossie A* commercial fishing boat I write about in another section of this book, Bill had a strong desire to go snapper fishing, so he borrowed a commercial boat from his friend, Allen Williams, owner of Allen Williams Seafood Company. He had a volunteer crew of his five brothers, which included me, his eight year old son, Dickie, who loved to fish, and our dad, who had a bad habit of getting seasick. In fact, he once got seasick at the Saenger Theatre while watching "Mutiny on the Bounty." We were not the best of crews, but we were cheap. All of us loved to fish, and we had no illusions of making any money on the trip, but if we did we wouldn't be unhappy.

Allen Williams with Lina and Allen , Jr. at the Allen Williams Fish house
Courtesy of Mrs. Mary Williams

The boat he borrowed was not some high tech snapper boat with all the modern comforts; it was what the commercial fishing industry at the time called a Ching. I don't know the definition of a Ching, to differentiate it from other commercial fishing boats used along the Gulf Coast in the 1940's and 1950's. Frankly, I believe it would fit the description of a Chinese Junk, or at least the ones I've seen in movies and books. It could, in my opinion, be best described as "Junk."

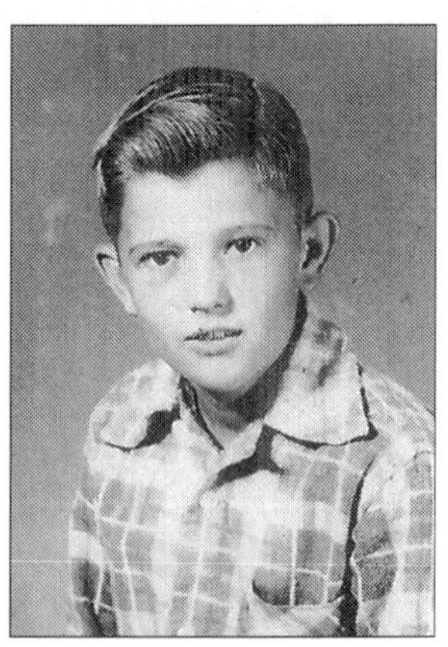

Dickie Davis
School picture , A. K. Suter

The Ching was the most uncomfortable boat I've ever been on, and we spent several days out in the Gulf of Mexico on this particular trip. It had a jib sail, which we didn't use, but it also had a center mast, which indicated that at some time in the life of this scow it was powered by sails. However, she had been refitted with a powerful diesel engine, which was naturally below deck with everything else, including the galley, the bunks and the fish holds, where the fish we planned to catch would be iced down for safe keeping. Everything below deck smelled like a mixture of dead fish and diesel oil, which, along with the constantly rolling of the boat, didn't help much with Dad's propensity for sea-sickness. Our last night out, we were struck by a bad windstorm, and had to anchor and ride it out. During the height of the storm the top portion of the mast suddenly broke off and made a frightful sound as it crashed to the deck. My dad, who was in the galley, had shouted something to one of us, and my youngest brother, Tom, who had been sleeping below in one of the bunks, thought dad had fallen overboard, and he almost panicked. We were all climbing around the debris in the dark checking on each other when we discovered that Bill was sound asleep and had not been disturbed by the storm, or the mast crashing to the deck. To paraphrase Walter Cronkite, "That's the way it was," and always was with our brother, Bill. He could "lie down beside the stilled waters," or the stormy waters, it didn't seem to matter to him. The storm broke, and by the time the sun rose our compass reading was "due north" to the Pensacola Pass. It was an "interesting" trip, to say the least, but this was not the end of Bill's love affair with fishing and fishing boats.

Tom Davis on the bow of one of Bill's boats
Courtesy of Fannie Davis

Bill was serious about catching fish when he was in search of red snapper, and he was good at finding fish once he and his crew arrived in the proximity of the fishing grounds. He usually had profitable trips, but he wasn't opposed to having fun, which was usually at someone else's expense. He was a practical joker, and on one occasion he almost went too far. Someone at the fish house had played a joke on him by placing a naked mannequin on board a boat he was operating for Allen Williams Seafood Co. shortly before he and his crew were to shove off for several days fishing in the Gulf of Mexico. Being the jokester that he was, he had one of the crewmen tie the mannequin to the top of the mast. To get through the pass and into the Gulf, they had to pass by the Pensacola Naval Air Station, where the Coast Guard Station was located. Before they reached the pass, having passed by the Naval base, a U.S. Coast Guard Cutter caught up with them, sirens screaming, and bull horns ordering them to stop. Some alert soul had notified the Coast Guard that "a woman had been hanged from the yard arm of a boat." Fortunately, the crew of the Coast Guard boat had a sense of humor, and began laughing once they realized the "woman hanging by the yard arm" was only a mannequin.

In the mid 1970's Bill purchased the Native Dancer, a fifty foot, former sports fishing boat with a wooden hull that had been converted to a commercial snapper boat. It was a good looking boat, safe, well equipped and comfortable. He enjoyed the Native Dancer, but he sold her upon retirement from the Escambia County Health Department as a Registered Sanitarian and head of the Solid Waste Department. Following retirement, he moved to Luvern, Alabama where he built a new home on several acres he had acquired. He obviously missed being on the Gulf coast, so he purchased a beautiful partial of waterfront property on Sioux Bayou in Gautier, Mississippi, and after building a home, he and his family moved to Gautier. It wasn't long before the call of the sea got the best of him again, and he began shopping for another commercial fishing boat to purchase.

Bill Davis at the wheel of the *Native Dancer*
Courtesy of Mrs. Fannie Davis

Bill bought the *Rampage* from her owner in Daytona Beach, Florida, and brought her home to Gautier, where she was moored at his own dock in his back yard on Sioux Bayou. The *Rampage* was a thirty-two foot "Downeastern" style lobster or crab boat, powered by a 671 Detroit Diesel engine. She was already equipped for hydraulic equipment use, so he removed the equipment for pulling up crab or lobster pots, and installed hydraulic fishing reels. Once he installed a large icebox, radar and other essential electronics, he was ready to go snapper fishing. We brothers joined him for several days' pleasure fishing aboard the *Rampage* around the Chandelier Islands. It was a memorable trip. His step-son, Chris Bridges, was a "regular" aboard the Rampage, and his other sons, Dickie, Billy, Ken or Rusty would often join him on his trips out into the gulf, but he didn't hesitate to go alone. Fishing was his passion, and he was good at it. It was during one of those long trips alone, when he was about seventy-five miles off the coast of Mississippi

Bill on board the Rampage
Courtesy of Chris ans Sharon Bridges

Chris Bridges
Courtesy of Chris and Sharon Bridges

Deb & Billy Davis

Karen & Ken Davis

Rusty Davis
Courtesy of Bob and Marilyn Davis

in the Gulf of Mexco, that he experienced what all boat captains fear most.

In the summer of 1989, Bill had been out in the Gulf on the *Rampage* for a few days, and was having a good trip. Around 7:00 a.m. he was enjoying his morning cup of coffee, having anchored overnight, and was contemplating the day ahead. He had noticed the shrimp boat in the distance, and was aware that it was heading in his direction, but he wasn't too concerned, since he figured the captain of the shrimp boat could see that he was anchored. Also, Bill was aware that the shrimp boat was not dragging for shrimp at the time, although the outriggers were down, so he knew the captain was free to maneuver the boat in any direction he wished. The shrimp boat continued on the same course at running speed, and was perilously close, when Bill suddenly realized that nobody was in the pilothouse of the shrimp boat. He immediately started the *Rampage's* engine in an attempt to escape an obvious collision, but it was too late. The outrigger struck the *Rampage* on the starboard side, pushing her sideways until the anchor rope tightened, causing her to roll over and sink, with Bill trapped inside. The *Rampage* was sinking fast as Bill struggled to free himself, and he finally did so at about fifty feet below the surface. He thought he was going to drown, but fortunately he was still a good swimmer at age sixty-six, and he made his way to the surface. What he saw as he surfaced almost paralyzed him with fear, for unfortunately, the shrimp boat was heading away from him on the same course and at the same speed prior to the collision. He saw the crew on the rear deck, separating shrimp from the by-catch, but they seemed oblivious to what had happened. He saw the shrimp boat's name, *Ella Lee*, emblazoned on the stern, as the distance between him and the shrimp boat rapidly increased. Bill must have experienced a feeling of helplessness and fear as he watched the *Ella Lee*, get further and further away. All he could do was focus on the *Ella Lee* as he held onto a large portion of the *Rampage's* wood canopy that was torn off by the Outrigger.

The Ella Lee

On board the *Ella Lee*, a major fire was extinguished earlier due to a faulty fuel line. Tim Adams, Captain of the *Ella Lee* had determined that the fire was so severe that the shrimp boat would have probably been totally destroyed if it were not for the steel construction. A short time before the collision, Captain Adams put the *Ella Lee* on auto pilot while he checked out the engine room, which he was in the process of doing at the time of the collision. Unknown to Bill, one of the crewmen saw him when he popped to the surfaced, along with much debris from the *Rampage*, and he immediately notified Captain Adams, who quickly turned the *Ella Lee* around and returned to the scene. Captain Adams said, "It scared the hell out of me when I saw only one person in the water. I was afraid I had wiped out a whole family." As he approached the location where Bill was hanging onto a large piece of the *Rampage*, he said, "There was so much stuff floating in the water, I could hardly see him." Not only did he return to where Bill was, but he jumped overboard to assist him. It was a dramatic moment for both of them.

Once Bill was aboard the Ella Lee, and the authorities and others notified, Captain Adams set a course for Mobile, Alabama, the home port of the *Ella Lee*. On the long trip to Mobile, Bill and Captain Adams made a discovery that surprised both of them.

At one point on the trip in to Mobile, Captain Adams said to Bill, "You know, I almost killed you back there, and I don't even know your name."

"My name's Bill Davis," he answered. "What's your name?"

"Tim Adams." He replied. Having learned that Bill was originally from Pensacola, Tim informed Bill that his dad was born and raised in Pensacola.

"What's your dad's name?" asked Bill.

"James Adams," Tim responded.

"Was your grandfather's name also James Adams?" asked Bill.

"Yeah, it was," he answered, somewhat surprised.

"Did your grandfather work for the railroad?" asked Bill.

"Yes he did, how'd you know that?" asked Tim

"Because we're cousins." answered Bill, as he laughed

Bill knew that James Adams, son of our first cousin, James Adams, lived in Elberta, Alabama, and he quickly made the connection. The revelation that the two of them were cousins must have been a real shock to both Bill and Tim. This really gives a new meaning to the saying, "I ran into my cousin…"

The Jimmy Adams family. L to R: Jerry, Susie (Adams Kichler), Jeff, Pam (Adams Moreno) and Tim. Left inset: Jimmy Adams. Right inset Stephen Adams, Tim's son.

Top: *The Open Sea,* Bon Secour, Alabama.

Right: Capt. Tim Adams, currently Owner/Operator of *The Open Sea,* formerly Captain of the *Ella Lee.*

Cousins visit in the pilot house of *The Open Sea,* July, 2009.
Jimmy Adams, (Tim's Father) , Tim Adams, Ben Davis, Charlie Davis and Bob Davis.

Cousins on the deck of *The Open Sea*
Tim Adams, Charlie Davis, Ben Davis, Jimmy Adams and Bob Davis

47

The Swamp House

Long before it was the Swamp House Marina & Landing, it was simply the "Swamp House," our family retreat on the Escambia River. It was the scene of many weekend parties and cookouts. My dad especially enjoyed using the "Swamp House" to entertain his employees from the Tax Collector's office. He loved that little cabin in the woods. On the weekends he could shed

The Swamp House, May, 1965
Courtesy of Fanny Davis

his "courthouse attire," put on his short britches or his bib overalls and relax, go fishing or just do nothing. The name, "Swamp House" was adopted permanently when Louise Barrow, Deputy Tax Collector, gave Dad a gift, which was a rustic wooden sign with the words, "Ben Davis' Swamp House," carved into the wood.

Dad acquired the property from relatives, Henry and Cleo Brown, in the early fifties. They owned and operated Brown's Fish Camp for many years, which was on the right, before crossing over the Highway 90 Bridge, as you travel toward Milton. (It is now Smith's Fish Camp") The Swamp House property is on the left before crossing over the bridge, and is situated on Old Highway 90, which now ends where the old, former wooden bridge began.

Both fish camps are located on Ferry Bayou which flows into the Escambia River a short distance down river from the bridge. In the years before the bridge, a ferry operated between Floridatown, across the bay in Santa Rosa County and Ferry Bayou, providing transportation between Escambia and Santa Rosa counties. The general area around Ferry Bayou back then was known as, "Delta," but for obvious reasons it eventually became known as "Ferry Pass."

Dad cooking on the grill at the Swamp House

In the sixties, my brother Ben acquired the property from our mother, and developed it into the "Swamp House Fish Camp." He dug a canal from Ferry Bayou up to the building, and constructed a large parking lot, boat slips and a boat ramp.

We can all remember "stupid things," we've done, and each time I think about the "Swamp House" I remember an episode that took place there years ago, which is high on my list of "stupid things." My friend, Billy Miller, and I decided to jump overboard at the landing to cool off after a hot day of fishing. It was so refreshing; we decided to swim up the bayou a few hundred yards. That night, I went "frogging" with my brother, Ben, in the same area and we saw thirteen alligators. Some of them were small, but others were large enough to have taken us home for supper.

Bill Miller
Courtesy of Ray Wheat

The current owner of the "Swamp House" is Gerald Mills, and he's developing it into a first class marina and boat landing. Dad's small cabin is now the "Swamp House" restaurant. There are many fishing tournaments that are held from the Swamp House, because the river and the bay is much cleaner than it was years ago, and consequently the fish are much more plentiful.

Progress and change is inevitable, but the memories remain. I remember the good times our family and friends had at the "Swamp House." I remember the parties and the cookouts. I remember the fishing trips, the hunting trips, the alligators and snakes, and the boat rides on Escambia River. I remember all the old stories, lies and tales that were told around the kitchen table, especially on the many weekend mornings when we brothers would visit with my dad, and often tell the same old stories we told the weeks before. Most of all, I remember how much my dad and mom enjoyed and loved that place.

Dad sitting on Bill's houseboat at the Swamp House

Dad and Uncle Bob fishing on the Escambia River
Note Dad "sculling" the boat.

48

Swimming the Bayou

I learned to swim when my brother, Bill, threw me and my cousin, Jack Brown, out of the boat while we were in the middle of Bayou Texar. His encouraging words were, "Swim or drown, boys." We swam. Swimming seemed to come naturally for most of us in the "Heights," probably because we spent so much time playing in the bayou. The guys and gals from East Hill, our "city friends," also spent a lot of time in the bayou, especially at Bayview Park, which they could get to by walking, riding their bikes, or skating. For most of us, the easiest way to get to Bayview Park was to swim across the bayou, so, we had to be good swimmers. There were many good swimmers from the "Heights," back when the water was clean and safe to swim in, but, in my opinion, two of the best were Mary Ann Keller and Joe Schiller.

Mary Ann Keller (Mrs. Ben Kickliter), apparently had no fear of the water, because at age ten or twelve, she was "swimming the bayou" from East Pensacola Heights to Bayview Park on a regular basis. Now, I'm not sure her parents knew about her "trips to town" early on, but I do

Mary Ann Keller Kickliter

know they had a lot of confidence in her, because when she was very young, she was allowed to take her younger siblings, Susan and Billy, swimming at Black's wharf. It was a common sight to see Mary Ann, with Susan and Billy in tow, walking down 10th. Street, (Now, Lee Street) heading for Black's wharf for their daily swim. She taught both of them to swim and dive, and all three were like frisky otters frolicking in the water.

Joe Schiller
Courtesy of Mrs. Janette Schiller

Joe Schiller was an all around good athlete, and he honed his swimming skills in the waters of Bayou Texar and Pensacola Bay. Joe and his cousin, Bert Delehanty, grew up together, and both were well respected for their accomplishments in athletics, but Joe excelled in long distance swimming. He was unmatched in swimming Pensacola Bay, and his family has the trophies to prove it. One trophy, in the hands of Joe's widow, Janette Schiller, reads as follows:

PENSACOLA BRIDGE TROPHY
1st Annual Three and One-Half Mile Swimming Race
Pensacola, Florida
First Place Joe Schiller
September 13, 1935

Joe Schiller
Courtesy of Mrs. Janette Schiller

To get to Bayview Park from East Pensacola Heights was about three miles on our bicycles, but as the crow flies, it's only about two thousand feet across from Hyer's Point. Back in the forties and fifties, we kids regularly swam across Bayou Texar

Virginia Gomez and Betty Harris boating in Bayou Texar with Bayview Park in the background
Courtesy of Virginia Gomez Newsom

to Bayview Park, where there were always more girls than we had at "Black's wharf", our favorite "swimming hole." The girls were not any prettier than the girls from the "Heights," but there were more of them. Maybe it wasn't the pretty girls, maybe we swam the bayou to prove we were men at ages twelve and fifteen; or because "it was there," or like the chicken, we needed to get to the other side. Whatever the reasons, we swam it, and if you wouldn't swim it, you were considered a "sissy," so "swimming to Bayview" was a guy's rite of passage into manhood.

On one occasion the law of averages almost caught up with me. I borrowed my brother, Bob's, swimming fins, and midway across the bayou, I developed cramps in both legs. My legs were useless, so I began "dog paddling." I was scared and in excruciating pain, and wasn't sure I would make it. Exhausted, I finally reached the swimming area, but my legs were hurting so bad that I knew I couldn't climb the ladders at the swim tower or the wharf, so I headed for the beach area.

Three guys I knew were on the top floor of the swim tower as I painfully paddled by, trying desperately to reach the beach area. They were "Crow" Crooke, Jimmy Hayes and Bob Kelley. I saw that they were watching me, and I assumed that they realized I was in trouble, and they were about to come to my rescue, but as I looked up all three were in the air, balled up into a "cannonball" position, shouting, "Bombs away." I forgot about the pain in my legs, I forgot about losing Bob's swim fins, because all I could think about was diving as deep as I could. I wasn't quick enough. All three scored a direct hit. If I had been a German U-Boat, they would have earned medals. What little air I had in my lungs was knocked out of me as they drove me to the bottom. Now, I really thought I was going to drown. I scooted along the bottom in the direction of the beach, and surfaced, gasping for air, among a group of kids and their parents. Somehow I made it to the beach. I don't remember now, but I hope I thanked God for my personal miracle of surviving the cramps and the "East Hill dive bombers"

After removing the swim fins, I rested and reflected on how close I came to being a statistic that beautiful summer day. Later, I walked, not swam, home to East Pensacola Heights. I did continue to swim the bayou, but never again alone or wearing swim fins.

Bob Kelley
Courtesy of Mary Ann Miller

James "Jimmy" and Hazel Hayes
Courtesy of Kristi Edgar

Richard "Crow" Crooke
Courtesy of Tommy Crooke

The Bayview Park diving tower
Courtesy of Jack Brown

49

Tom Davis and the SWAT Team

The A.C.L.U. is not one of my favorite organizations, but I agree with their opposition to "Operation TIPS"--the Terrorism Information and Prevention System -- one of the initiatives of the Bush administration's "war on terrorism." The government will initially recruit one million workers in ten cities, who will be trained to spy on their "neighbors," and report any unusual events and suspicious activities. Just think, millions of "peeping Toms," such as letter carriers, utility employees, repairmen, etc., some, whose imaginations will have been stroked to a level of fanaticism, will generate more false reports than the government's databases can process. In my opinion, this system will stomp all over the Fourth Amendment to the U.S. Constitution, which among other things has to do with protecting us against "unreasonable searches and seizures." Everyone will be suspect......not unlike the Nazi's Third Reich. A good example of the negative effects of an overactive imagination is an episode that happened to Tom Davis and his fishing partners on an early, foggy morning in 1989.

Tom Davis and his boat the *Tom Katt*
Courtesy of Tom and Sue Davis

In those early morning hours "an off-duty volunteer fireman," called the sheriff's department to report that, "Several men, armed with Uzi's, are loading drugs onto a boat docked at one of the waterfront homes." He did his duty, and waited!! He didn't have to wait very long. The Escambia County Sheriff's Department, upon receiving the report activated their SWAT team, a paramilitary squad, employed in many high risk and dangerous situations. They soon had the house and area surrounded, even though it was dark and foggy.

Tom Davis

Tom Davis was aboard his boat, the *Tom Katt,* a 38 foot sports fisher, moored at his dock on Escambia Bay. He developed Mackey Cove subdivision, had built his and several of the neighbor's waterfront homes, and was proud of the quiet privacy they all enjoyed. His crew and fishing partners were his son, Alex, and his good friend, Steve Flack, his nephew, Artie Shimek and his friend, and fellow attorney, Frank Sheppard. Entered in the Annual Billfish Tournament, they had loaded the fishing equipment, food and ice aboard earlier, but had to wait for the fog to lift to get under way. They were unaware that they were being watched.

The Crew
L to R: Alex Davis, Steve Flack, Artie Shimek, and Frank Sheppard
Courtesy of Tom and Sue Davis, Steve Flack and Alan Sheppard

Alex already had the "*Tom Katt's* two, powerful "cat," diesel engines humming, and they were ready to shove off, so Tom secured the house, and hurried toward the boat. He heard the unfamiliar voice, about the same time he saw the dark image of an individual next to one of his trees, and almost instantly, he saw that there were others behind him. Then, as if on command, the neighbor's yard seemed to come alive with armed troops. The heavily armed SWAT team was an awesome sight, and the element of surprise had its effect, but fortunately, Tom had the presence of mind not to raise his flashlight for fear of being shot. The leader of the SWAT team had probably already surmised that this was a "false alarm," which was confirmed minutes later. The SWAT team had raided innocent fishermen, loading ice, not drugs, who were carrying fishing rods, not Uzi's; thanks to someone else's overactive imagination.

With no apologies offered, the group's leader requested permission to search the boat, "since we're here," he said. Tom's reply was, "I'll have to check with my attorney first," and after pausing, said, "that's him over there," pointing toward Artie Shimek. Artie's affirmative, but unprintable reply was shared by the others, since an unnecessary search would make them even later getting under way.

Later that morning, the "Tom Katt" and her crew were trolling for blue marlin in the Gulf of Mexico. The day ended about as weird as it began. They hooked a large, blue marlin.....in the eye, and unfortunately that was all they caught....a huge eyeball!

Tom, wife Sue and grandson, Andrew
Courtesy of Tom and Sue Davis

Top: Alex Davis, wife Margaret, daughter, Christine and son, Alex, II. Courtesy of Tom and Sue Davis

Below: Tom Davis, Jr., his wife, Beth, daughter Laura and son, Andrew. Courtesy of Emma Jean Redding

Steve Flack and Family
Courtesy of Steve Flack

50

The Turtle Hunt From Hell

It was 1946, and at age thirteen, I went on my first, and my last sea turtle hunt. It was also the first time I had ever heard of, or had ever seen, a beach buggy, which, Ed, our neighbor in East Pensacola Heights had constructed from a Model A Ford roadster. The "great white hunters" I was privileged to accompany, in addition to Ed, were my older brother, Bill, and his friend, Bubba Johnson, who also lived in the "Heights." It was less than a year since both Bill and Bubba had returned from some pretty tough action in World War II. It was that time of the year when the female green turtles deposit their eggs on the Gulf of Mexico beaches of Northwest Florida. Our objective was to catch the female on the beach, either before or after she had buried her clutch of about one hundred eggs, and before she could return to the Gulf.

It was late afternoon when we left the Heights and crossed over the old Bayou Texar Bridge. Ed shifted down to second gear and gunned the engine as we climbed the steep Gadsden Street hill in front of the Mirador Apartments. I was excited, and thought of the books I had read by Martin and Osa Johnson, about their exploits in Africa. They traversed the remote areas of Africa in open Land Rovers, in search of wild game to photograph. We were in an open beach buggy, and in my mind, it was like we were on a safari to an area that was truly remote, and we were in search of wild game. I couldn't have been more excited if I had been riding with the Johnson's, Frank Buck and Stewart Granger. Only minutes later, we were crossing the narrow Pensacola Bay Bridge as the sun, a perfect circle of bright, orange was descending in the western skies somewhere behind downtown Pensacola. By the time we crossed over Santa Rosa Sound on the old wooden bridge to Pensacola Beach, the sun had totally disappeared. It would have been dark by then, if it had not been for the rising full moon, which appeared to be suspended just above the sand dunes.

Brother Bill in uniform visiting Rome, circa 1944
Courtesy of Bill and Shirley Fay Bryant

Charlie
A. K. Suter School
photo

Bubba Johnson
Courtesy of Thomas "Bubba" Johnson

The Casino and the adjoining fishing pier were the only structures on the western twenty plus miles of Santa Rosa Island, other than Fort Pickens at the west end, and the nearby "fish hatchery," which, today, houses the Environmental Protection Agency. If you wanted to travel east or west of the Casino, you had to walk because there were no roads in either direction. We stopped at the Casino parking area just long enough for Ed to tinker with the motor, and for the three of them to light up a cigarette. As we eased off the hard surface of the asphalt onto the beautiful sugar white sand, I believe we all held our breath. This was the maiden voyage for the beach buggy, which Ed had finished building only a few days before. To my relief, we continued moving forward as he maneuvered around a couple large sand dunes and down onto the beach. We each looked at each other and laughed, not that anything was funny, but it was our synchronized, approval of the performance of Ed's creation. It was almost dark, and Ed turned the lights on and pointed his miracle machine eastward, down the beach, and for the next couple hours we drove toward the full moon. We were there. We had arrived. We were on a safari after wild game, the elusive green turtle.

At age thirteen, conservation was not part of my vocabulary, nor was it a term I understood. It's safe to say that neither Bill nor Bubba, then, in their early twenties, had much concern for conservation of turtles. They were both avid outdoorsmen, and were in their teens when they volunteered to go away to war. As for Ed, he was an "old man," probably in his early thirties. He had moved to Pensacola about the same time Bill and Bubba entered the service. In retrospect, fifty-seven years ago, none of us were concerned about what effect we would have on the population of green turtles if we were successful that evening. As for me, I assumed God made turtles for men to capture and eat. It's like banana pudding at Barnhill's Restaurant: if God had not intended for me to eat a second helping, He wouldn't have put it there in the first place.

Santa Rosa Island stretches from Fort Pickens, at the mouth of Pensacola Bay, eastward to Destin, at the mouth of Choctawhatchee Bay, a distance of about forty miles as the crow flies or as the turtle swims. We did travel about five or six miles east of Pensacola Beach before Ed's marvelous machine broke down. This wasn't as bad as being up that well known creek without a paddle, but it was pretty close.

We were stranded in that one spot, of course, and my three partners were giving advice to each other on how to get the motor started and running again. Then, the battery became too weak to crank the motor, so Ed apparently decided that the best thing for him to do was to get totally drunk. It was known in the neighborhood that Ed had a wee bit of a drinking problem. Now, in reality, I don't really believe it was much of a problem for Ed, but it had become a real problem for us. He could afford to buy all the booze he wanted, as he was from a wealthy family up in north Alabama. They had encouraged him to move to Pensacola with his very pretty wife and son. He didn't work at a job; he just tinkered in his oversized garage with mechanical stuff, such as an old Indy style race car and the beach buggy. On that night, I never saw him take a drink, but he obviously had a bottle stashed in the beach buggy.

So, what started out to be an exciting night of turtle hunting, developed into "a real disappointing mess." The problem was a dead battery. The real problem was the approximately twenty miles back to East Pensacola Heights.

Of course, all of us could have simply walked the five or six miles back to Pensacola Beach, and then called for help. By that time, it would have been another business day, and we could have gotten some sleep and then decided what to do about getting the beach buggy back home. Unfortunately, the real, real problem was Ed. Not only was he unable to walk, he could barely talk, and dragging him all that distance back to the Casino, was not a good option. He had begun to sound like a refugee from the Tower of Babel. So, Bubba volunteered to walk back to the Casino, get a ride to Pensacola, pick up a battery, and somehow get it back to us. Then, we began our long wait. I didn't realize at the time what a burden this placed on brother Bill. He had to "baby-sit" a kid brother and a babbling drunk, and there was no food and no water, and the sun would be showing itself in a few hours. If a turtle had walked upon us at that point, I am certain we would have completely ignored her.

The full moon had worked its way over toward the west, and with the headlights turned off our eyes adjusted, and it appeared to be almost daylight. I watched Bubba for a long time as he walked back up the beach. The moon lit up the beach and the sand dunes, and it appeared as though it was about to become daylight, which was still several hours away. Bill suggested I get some sleep. I tried, but I was still so excited, that I was wide awake and sleep was impossible, especially with Ed's sporadic outbursts, as he jousted with his demons. Bill could sleep anywhere and soon he was sound asleep in the front seat of the beach buggy. An hour or so later, Ed finally stopped talking to his phantoms, and went to sleep on the ground, under the beach buggy, using his jacket as a pillow.

Still unable to sleep, I decided to walk along the beach, and became fascinated with the phosphorescence in the water. It was unbelievably quiet, and there was a gentle breeze. The only noise, other than the "singing" of a pesky mosquito, was the gentle lapping of the small waves as they rolled in and out, creating a light show with the natural glow of the phosphorescence. The small fish and crabs looked as though they were electrified as they moved about in the shallow water. I recall so vividly today how I felt that moonlit night so many years ago. I was disappointed, of course, that the hunt had turned into a disaster and sorry that Bubba had to walk the beach all the way back to the Casino. I was sure that Bill was disappointed for me, as he had brought me along to share in the excitement of the hunt. I was truly sorry that Ed was on another planet, and I wondered what he would be like a few hours later. I regretted our predicament, but I wasn't sorry we were there, or more specifically, I wasn't sorry I was there. I wanted to savor that time on that moonlit beach, when everyone and everything was asleep except me, God and those mosquitoes. It was like being stranded on some distant South Pacific island, all by myself, and for the first time I had learned to smell the roses. It was a memorable experience out of adversity, which I have relished recalling thousands of times over the past sixty-four years. It was one of those times when I unexpectedly felt close to God.

I did manage to get some sleep before daylight arrived, but it was almost impossible to drift off for more than a few minutes at a time, because the mosquitoes were terrible. Exhausted, I had curled up on the back end of the beach buggy, and finally went to sleep. The mosquitoes must have gone on break. I was later awakened when Bill began moving around in the front seat as he cursed the mosquitoes, scratching and swatting as he tried to get comfortable. I heard a "bump in the night" as Ed, still sleeping under the beach buggy, bumped his head on something pretty solid. Apparently the mosquitoes were working on him pretty bad, because he bumped his head a couple more times, each followed by some loud cursing, and fussing at somebody as though it was their fault. We were all scratching like a bunch of hunting dogs in a kennel. I dozed off again, and woke up to Ed's voice, as he searched for something in the back of the buggy. He was hunting for something to drink. I didn't know if he was after booze or water, but it really didn't matter, because he didn't have either one.

The wind had died down completely, the Gulf was calm, and the mosquitoes were having a ball. It was finally getting daylight, and Bill and I got out of the beach buggy and walked down toward the water, looking west for a possible sign that Bubba might be on his way back. There was no sight of him, so we decided to get in the water to avoid the mosquitoes. We simply floated in shallow areas with our noses protruding above the water just enough to allow us to breathe. I learned that if I totally relaxed, allowing only my heels to touch the bottom, that I would float, with only my face exposed to the mosquitoes. We stayed there for a long time, because it was a wonderful relief. To my surprise, I would doze off while in that relaxed position, but only for a few seconds each time. With my ears under the water, I discovered that while relaxed and calm, I could hear sounds emitted by the marine life. There were "grunts" and "clicks" and many other odd sounds. It sounded like the "grunts" were communicating with each other, but the "clicks" seemed to be clicking just for the heck of it. Also, we encountered another pest, which was irritating, but not nearly as bad as the mosquitoes. As we floated motionless in the shallow waters, dozens of little fish pulled at the hairs on our legs and arms, which was more irritating than painful. By the time we got out of the water, the sun had gone from a perfectly round, orange ball to an object too bright to look at.

Ed was gradually sobering up, but he was complaining of thirst, which prompted him to do a real stupid thing. We watched him as he crawled under the beach buggy, opened the little petcock at the bottom of the radiator, and proceeded to swallow the water as it drained directly into his mouth. As he should have expected, some of the liquid flowed into his nose, causing him to choke and cough like he was in real trouble. Then the pain he experienced must have been real bad, as the chemicals apparently got into his sinus cavities. We thought he was about to die, and I believe he thought so too. His face swelled up immediately, and he could hardly see. His face was as red as blood, and he was a real mess. I suspect he was more after the alcohol content in the radiator than the water, but either way, he got more than he bargained for.

We were well into the second day without water or food, but fortunately the mosquitoes had let up a little. The sun was unbelievably hot, and there were no clouds and little hope of rain. There were no trees in sight, and the only shade was under the beach buggy, and neither one of us even considered crawling under there with Ed. The hot sun can drive you crazy, and that's what I thought had happened to Bill on the afternoon of the second day. He had walked about two hundred feet toward the northern shore of the island. The body of water on that side of the island is Santa Rosa Sound, and there was a small, shallow slough that projected into the middle of the island, fanning out in several directions at high tide. Suddenly, Bill, clad only in a pair of U. S. Army drawers, began running around in the shallow water that had fanned out from the slough. He was whooping and hollering and kicking at the water. I was frightened, because I was sure the sun had cooked his brain, and I would end up with two derelicts on my hands. I ran towards him, and he continued to run in circles and kicking at the water; then, just as I got near him, he kicked a large mullet out of the water onto the sand. He could have been a great bare-footed soccer player. He immediately built a fire and cooked that most welcomed fish,

A Mullet

having impaled it on a stick. It was delicious. I have eaten a lot of fish in my life, cooked in many different ways, but I have never eaten fish that tasted as delicious as that mullet did. Bill is an avid fisherman, and in the ensuing years has owned several commercial fishing boats, and has caught tons of fish, but I am certain that is the only fish that he ever "kicked" out of the water.

After eating his share of the fish, Ed showed evidence of returning to the real world, although he still looked like a survivor from a bad train wreck. We watched as he jacked up the right rear wheel of the beach buggy until the wheel was clear of the sand. Then, without saying a word, he got up and turned the switch key "on," and shifted the gear to "high." Returning to the wheel, he strained as he turned it to the right, causing the engine to "turn over," and immediately Henry Ford's Model-A engine "cranked up," and the smoke and noise was wonderful. Five minutes later we were headed west toward the Casino. Why in the heck didn't Ed think of doing that earlier? His actions were just the opposite of the quote my mother often used, which was, "What soberness conceals, drunkenness reveals."

We were almost to the Casino, when we met up with Bubba, who looked like he had been "dragged through a knot-hole." He had just set out on foot to rescue us, carrying a heavy car battery and a bag of goodies, consisting of sandwiches, cookies, cokes, potted-meat and Vienna sausages. It was the best gourmet meal anyone could ask for. Unfortunately, Bubba didn't get to observe Bill's new fishing technique, and he didn't get to attend our one-fish cookout, plus, he missed all of Ed's unusual forms of entertainment. He experienced his own challenges, hitching rides and locating a battery. It's at a time like that that you find out who your real friends are...which is another story. Bubba attempted to rescue us by riding his motorcycle on the beach, causing great damage to it. He managed to return to the Casino parking lot, where he parked his motorcycle. He then began walking, his only option.

It was a memorable trip, but it was truly a turtle hunt from hell. Perhaps it was God's way of calling our attention to the importance of conservation. I took the warning seriously. I never again went on a turtle hunt. I now do all my turtle hunting on the Discovery Channel.

The Turtle Hunt From Hell
Illustration by Steve Blair,

51

U-Boats In The Gulf of Mexico and Disaster On the Mississippi River

Ben L. Davis Jr., and Sr. registering for the draft. Courtesy of The Pensacola News Journal

When the United States entered World War II, following Japan's attack on Pearl Harbor, my dad tried desperately to get back into uniform, but he had a few obstacles to overcome. He had served in France and Germany with the U. S. Army during World War I, and even though he was forty-two years old, he immediately registered for the draft. He and my oldest brother, Ben, Jr., were the first father and son in Escambia County to register together. An obstacle other than his age was the fact that he was an elected official, serving in his third term as the

Escambia County Supervisor of Elections. His biggest obstacle, however, was that he had lost part of his foot in an accident while working for the L & N Railroad prior to entering politics. He tried every way possible, but even with the help of U. S. Congressman, Lex Green, he was rejected, not because of his age, but because of his handicap. He was still determined to personally do his part, even though two of his sons were in uniform. He was especially proud to display the flag with two stars in our window. He decided to devote his vacation time to working aboard tugboats involved in the war effort, which were owned by his brother-in-law, Shirley Brown, of Brown Marine. As it turned out, he was probably exposed to more dangerous situations on board the tugboats than he would have been, if his request to serve had been granted by the U. S. Army.

Shirley Brown on the magazine cover, *Via Pensacola*
Courtesy of Bill and Shirley Fay Bryant

On one particular occasion in the summer of 1942, Dad volunteered to accompany Uncle Shirley to Tampa aboard the tugboat, “Venture” to tow a large, crippled ship, loaded with asphalt to Pensacola. The trip exposed them to the danger of German U-Boats in the Gulf of Mexico. When they first arrived in Tampa, they were notified by the U. S. Coast Guard that German U-Boats had been spotted in the Gulf of Mexico, so they were not allowed to depart Tampa Bay for the next two days. A short time earlier, in May of 1942, U-506 and U-507 were the first U-Boats to enter the Gulf of Mexico. The first sinking of an Allied ship in the Gulf was by U-507, on May 4, 1942. The U-Boat commander, Captain Harro Schacht, fired one torpedo into the 2,500 ton freighter, *Norlendo*. Reports were that the crew of the U-Boat provided the survivors with cigarettes, tobacco, crackers and drinking water before departing. Over the next eighteen months, U-Boats scored 56 sinkings and damaged 14 merchant ships in the Gulf. The last ship sunk by a U-Boat in the Gulf of Mexico was on December 4, 1943, off the southwestern coast of Florida. U-193 sank a brand new tanker, *Touchet*, which was carrying 140,000 barrels of oil.

When permission was finally given to the Venture by the Coast Guard, they were cautioned to stay within the "ten fathom curve," which is an area in the Gulf that was considered too shallow for U-Boats to operate in safely. To stay within that curve, required them to hug the coast of Florida all the way back to Pensacola, and not only would it increase the distance and take more time, but it would be more expensive. Shirley Brown's good business judgment, one of the reasons for his long record as a successful business man, was obviously evident back in the early forties. More expenses meant less profit, so he set the course as a straight line to the mouth of Pensacola Bay. This, of course, placed their tug and tow in the deeper waters of the Gulf and the possibility of being targeted by a German U-Boat. That possibility soon became a reality.

Several hours after leaving the mouth of Tampa Bay, with the large ship in tow, they were due west of Clearwater Beach, but still several hundred miles from the mouth of Pensacola Bay. The trip at that point had been uneventful, and they had observed nothing unusual, until, suddenly, six navy planes approached from the east, flying low. All six flew directly over the *Venture* and her tow, rocking their wings in some sort of acknowledgment, or warning, as they passed overhead. Each of the planes dropped depth charges several thousand feet in front of the tug. "It shook the hell out of us," said Uncle Shirley, when talking about the event in 2005, prior to his death. "Later," he said, "we read in the Pensacola News-Journal that a U-Boat had been sunk in the Gulf." I never heard my dad talk about that incident, but I was only nine or ten at the time, and I only learned of it recently.

About six months later, Dad was again serving as the engineer on the *Venture*. They had traveled to Baton Rouge from Pensacola, pushing three empty barges, and on the return trip back down the Missisippi

River, with the three barges fully loaded with oil, the captain failed to properly negotiate a bend in the river near New Orleans. Known to tugboat captains as the “Avondale Curve,” it is just one of the many difficult and dangerous curves and bends in the Mississippi River that experienced and licensed tugboat operators have to contend with all the way down to the Gulf of Mexico, or all the way up river to St. Louis, Missouri and above. It’s the same river and the same curves that Mark Twain had to negotiate while piloting riverboats out of Hannibal, Missouri, however, the famous story teller didn’t have to contend with bridges, and he wasn’t pushing several hundred feet of loaded barges ahead of him.

What made the “Avondale Curve” more difficult than most curves, was that the captain not only had to negotiate the bend in the river, but he had to line up the barges to pass thru the Huey P. Long bridge, just several hundred feet below the curve. If that wasn’t enough to keep him busy, he had additional hazards: it was night time, and they were going down river, which makes it much more difficult and dangerous to operate in the fast flowing water. He had his hands full, but his situation was no different from what other tugboat captains before him and the ones after him had to contend with. It was a dangerous situation, and required the experience and skill he was entrusted with, but something went wrong. Like airplane pilots, tugboat captains have to make split-second decisions that have far reaching effects on lives and property. Among other things, pilots must consider the wind currents, and tugboat captains must allow for the river currents.

I don’t know just what went wrong, if it was the captain’s error, or if it was unavoidable, but almost immediately, the barges swung around, striking the tug, nearly capsizing her. My dad was in the engine room, and shortly before the collision, the captain had called for full power. The huge diesel was screaming, and Dad knew something had gone awry. He was apparently on an elevated metal grid deck, common in tugboat engine rooms, which positioned him just above the huge diesel engine. The engine’s valve covers had been removed earlier to help cool the engine, exposing the many huge valves, rapidly moving up and down along the top of the engine. The impact of the collision knocked him onto the top of the engine, subjecting him to the constant jabs of the valves in motion. It was a miracle he was able to exit the engine room before the tug sank on the shallow banks of the river. He was bruised from top to bottom, especially the bottom. Those valves had really worked over his posterior. Several days later, he was showing his brother, Bob, his injuries, and Uncle Bob commented that his behind looked like the rear end of one of those female monkeys at the zoo. I wasn't present when he displayed his injured derriere, which in itself, must have been a sight to behold.

I don't know of any other scary trips or voyages Dad might have made to do his part for the war effort. It's possible that the incident with one of Adolph Hitler's U-Boat's, and bouncing around on top of the diesel engine while the tug was sinking in the Mighty Mississippi, might have been enough to scratch his itch for the rest of the war.

The U-Boat Incident in the Gulf of Mexico in 1942
Illustration by Steve Blair,

52

The Walker Family and Walker's Boat House

WILLIAM WILMER WALKER

Courtesy of Ted Brown, President, Brown Marine Service, and Pelican Roost Marina

Ever since I can remember, there has been two Walker's Boat Houses on Bayou Texar in East Pensacola Heights. Both were there in 1937, when our family moved to the Heights, and they each looked then like they had been there for many years. Actually, both are still there today, although the smaller boat house, built and owned by Mr. William Wilmer Walker, the patriarch of the Walker family of commercial fishermen, was transformed into the Marina Oyster Barn Restaurant.

Miss Lillian Harvey Gomez at seventeen . Walker's Boathouse in the background in the 1920s. Note also the trolley bridge. Courtesy Virginia Gomez Newsom

To most people, he was known as Mr. "Willie" Walker. It was his boathouse that people normally referred to when speaking of Walker's Boat House. The Walker family was prominent in the seafood industry throughout northwest Florida and south Alabama, and Walker's Boat House was a favorite among seafood lovers, fishermen, boaters and most of us kids who grew up in East Pensacola Heights. Mr. Willie Walker had four sons, Douglas, Wilmer, Maurice and Oliver, and three daughters, Ethel, Lois and Kathleen

The larger boathouse, which was a unique building, was built by Douglas Walker. The first floor was all boat stalls, each of which was rented to boat owners. The entire second floor was one big room, a boatwright shop for boat building and boat repairs. What was unique about his boathouse was it had an elevator which extended over one of the larger boat stalls, and could be lowered into the water, so a boat could not only be lifted out of the water, it could be lifted up to the second floor for repairs. Also, boats crafted in the shop, and ready to be launched, could be lowered into the water below. Doug kept his two commercial boats, the *Carolyn* and the

Walker's Boathouse in the mid 1940's
Courtesy Tom Brown, Jr.

Jo Ann, which he named after his two daughters, moored inside his boat house.

He was obviously a good businessman, as he also owned the Sea Breeze Cottages in Gulf Breeze for many years. In addition, he was in the shrimping business in a big way in South America, along with John Pace, one of the area's most successful and wealthiest entrepreneurs at the time. His son, Billy Walker, followed his dad into the fishing and seafood business. He operated two commercial party boats, the *Gulf Breeze* and the *Gulf Stream*, and later owned and operated a retail seafood business in Gulf Breeze, Florida.

Wilmer Walker, whom we kids called "Mr. Wilmer," was in the building trades, but he also operated a shrimp boat out of Walker's boat house. He supplied most of the shrimp that was sold at the boat house to consumers for the table and to fishermen for bait. The older kids, who were lucky, earned extra money by shrimping with him out in Pensacola bay. Bill Early, while still a teenager in school, operated Mr. Wilmer's shrimp boat for him while he was at work, and he became just as good, if

Walker's Boathouse 1962
Courtesy of the Marina Oyster Barn

A young Colonel Butch Redding on Fisher's dock. with Doug Walker's Boathouse in the background. (Coursen's Boathouse) in the late 1950s.

not better, than Mr. Wilmer at shrimping. He later owned his own shrimp boat, which he operated while managing his long, successful career with the Pensacola News Journal.

Maurice Walker was a commercial fisherman all his life, and at the time of his death, he and his wife owned and operated a fish house at the foot of "B" street, sandwiched in between Clyde Richburg's American Seafood Company and Allen Williams Seafood Company. In the early years, while we kids were hanging around the boat houses, Maurice owned and operated the "Patsy," a commercial boat, taking fishing parties out into the Gulf of Mexico. My brother, Bob, at age twelve, worked for him as the bait boy, deckhand, fish cleaner and anything else Maurice wanted him to do. It was a great experience for a kid, plus he made a little "spending money." The "Patsy" was also moored at one of the inside boat stalls at Doug's boat house.

In the mid 1950's Maurice was the Captain of one of the two party boats, the *Gulf Wind* and the *Gulf Breeze* that his nephew, Billy, operated from the docks at the foot of Palafox Street. While home between semesters, my fellow F.S.U. students and fraternity brothers, Joe Tarbuck, Bob Bell and I went deep sea fishing in the Gulf of Mexico with Maurice. In addition to the three of us, and a few other local citizens, the charter also included a senior class from somewhere up in Indiana. Those kids were eating everything they could get their hands on, including greasy hamburgers, and unfortunately half of them were seasick before we went through the pass into the Gulf. As the captain, Maurice was a bit unhappy with half the kids throwing up in his boat, and the other half tangling up the fishing lines of the serious fishermen. He was born with a cleft lip, a condition colloquially known as a "hair -lip." At one point I was trying to maneuver through several seasick teenagers, and Maurice seeing my predicament, shouted above the noise of the engine and the kids, in the vernacular of a person with a hair-lip, "Charlie, if they get in your way, get a stick and knock 'em overboard!" As I recall, Joe, Bob and I had an enjoyable fishing trip that day, but I don't remember us catching many fish. But, I do, remember that the kids from Indiana were glad to get back onto dry land.

Joe Tarbuck
Courtesy of Judge Joseph Tarbuck

Bob & Joy Bell
& Cindy

Mr. Willie Walker was very religious and he was always well armed with pamphlets and religious tracts. He was a hard working man, and I don't believe I ever saw him in an attire other than bib overalls, summer or winter. I know he went to church often, and I'm sure he wore something other than bib overalls to church. If any of us let a curse word slip out in his presence, we got a lecture and a pamphlet. It wasn't a hard, stern lecture, because he was a gentle man. Some of us accumulated quite a few pamphlets over the summer months.

Many of us kids worked for Mr. Walker, especially those of us who lived in the neighborhood, or nearby in the Heights. Our family home was only a block away. We would handle the rental of his boats and keep them bailed out, plus sell the shrimp and mullet he kept iced down in the boat house. Unlike today, many avid fishermen didn't own a boat and motor on a trailer, to be launched at some boat ramp when they wanted to go fishing. Instead, most owned only an outboard motor, which they kept in their truck or the trunk of their automobile, and when they went fishing, they rented a boat from places like Walker's Boathouse, but used their own outboard motor. The boats were also rented to people without an outboard motor, and they would row to where they wanted to fish, or some would simply spend the day relaxing on the bayou. The price per pound for mullet at the boathouse was ten cents, and fifteen cents per pound for shrimp. At the end of the day, we would turn the money in to Mr. or Mrs. Walker at their house, which was across the street from the boat house. I don't remember how he determined how much to pay us, but we never worried about being cheated. Not by that man.

Mr. Walker kept his mullet boat moored inside the boathouse, where there was a cutout slip for his boat. His boat was a large open skiff design, with moveable partitions to hold ice for icing down the fish, pieces of canvas for shelter from the weather, fuel for the gas engine, food, water and a coffee pot. The gill net was folded up on the stern deck, designed so the net would be pulled off as he made a large circle around the unsuspecting mullet. The boat, like many mullet boats at the time, had an inboard "Pop Pop" engine, which was probably a five or six horsepower Briggs & Stratton motor, situated in the center of the boat. It was commonly referred to as a "Pop Pop" engine, because owners usually installed a "straight" exhaust pipe which ran through the side of the boat. With no muffler, the noise was loud, and usually went pop,

pop, pop, pop, etc. The noise reverberated for miles on a quiet day or night. He would go out and fish all night sometimes, with either a gill net or a trammel net, usually along the shores of Pensacola and Escambia Bays. He normally went alone, but often he would take someone with him. My brother, Bob, always ready to make some pocket change, went with him several times. What I thought was interesting was, if the mullet were not running at the time, he would go to sleep on the beach and wait awhile. As I understand from Bob, Mr. Walker made a couple sleeping bags out of canvas, and when it was time to take a nap, they would just slip into the canvas bags, which were a little too thick for the mosquitoes to bite through, and go to sleep on the beach. As a young boy, Bill Early also fished with Mr. Walker, and he and Bob have great memories of their commercial fishing trips in the bays around Pensacola with a kind and gentle man.

53

The Wednesday Night Fish and Grits Club

In the mid fifties, the Mosquito and Rodent Control, a division of The Escambia County Health Department, built a small cabin and storage building on the Sound side of Santa Rosa Island near Big Sabine. As the seagull flies, that's about five miles east of Pensacola Beach. This was prior to construction of the road between Pensacola Beach and Navarre Beach, and the only normal way to get to that

Mosquito and Rodent Control cabin on Santa Rosa Sound

cabin was by boat or a four-wheel drive vehicle. The cabin served as a base of operation for employees as they battled the mosquito's breeding grounds on the island. It also served as a great place for the employees and their friends to gather, especially on Wednesday nights, to cook freshly caught mullet, hushpuppies and grits, and watch the fights on TV. What started out as a small group of employees and their friends eventually became a big crowd, with local politicians, professionals, plant managers and others in attendance. The group was proudly referred to as "The Wednesday Night Fish and Grits Club."

Getting to the cabin was half the fun, if you owned a beach-buggy, or hitched a ride with someone who did. Beach-buggies were a craze in the fifties and sixties. Many people built or bought one, and there was no law against driving on the beach back then. Otherwise, you had to have a truck with wide tires and low air pressure, but even then, somebody would manage to get stuck in the soft beach sand. It was just part of the trip. The not so normal way to get to the cabin, if you just had to get there, was to drive your car. That's right; you could actually drive your car right down the beach, on the Sound side, not the Gulf side. What was important was getting there! Of course, you had to first let about half the air out of each tire. Some made it, some didn't. We were all lured by good cooking and good times with a group of great guys on a pristine stretch of Santa Rosa Island, inhabited only at the time by wild animals and birds.

Bill's beach buggy. L to R: Billy, Bill, Rusty and ken.
Courtesy of Fanny Davis

The little cabin had all the necessary amenities, such as electricity, running water, a bathroom, a kitchen and a TV; plus sand, mosquitoes and a whole lot of smoke on Wednesday evenings. The first order of business was to catch the fish, and with guys throwing castnets into the Gulf, the Sound, the Sabine, the canals and sloughs, enough fish were always caught. Occasionally people would bring other things to cook, such as chicken, steaks, wieners, etc. We could always depend on a local veterinarian, to bring something interesting, like fresh "mountain oysters" for the guys to cook. As for me, I'll stick to bay oysters. There was always more than enough fish, etc. to eat, and those who wanted something other than water and coffee to drink, brought their own. You could get caught up to date on jokes, lies, who is doing what to whom, the local political climate; plus witness a few pranks before the serious business of getting your dollar in the pot if you wanted to bet on the fights.

After the fish, the fun, and the fights, then it was time to worry about making it back to the nearest paved road at Pensacola Beach. It doesn't seem possible, but those good times were over a half century ago, and many of the participants have gone on to "the great fish fry in the sky." In retrospect, those Wednesday nights were conducted in a respectable, sportsmanlike manner, and was just plain enjoyable fellowship and camaraderie. However, if we did some of the same things today, such as use county property, or drive up and down the beach in our vehicles, we would all probably end up in the "pokey."

54

"What did you do in the war, Grandma?"

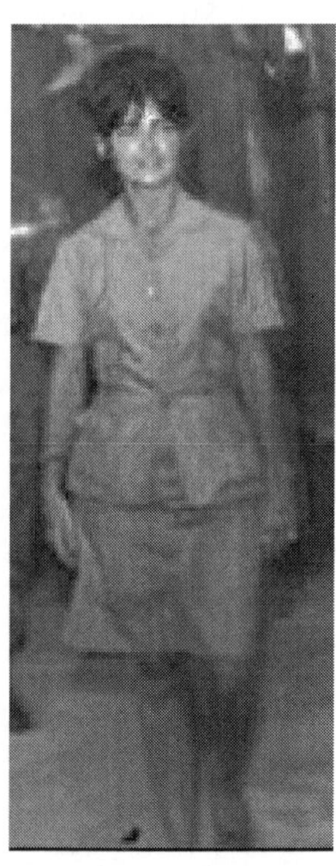

Sandra in the U. S. Army Special Services uniform

I'm not disappointed that my grandchildren haven't inquired about my military experience during the Korean War. If my memory serves me correctly, I didn't earn any medals or citations as a dental technician attached to the Marine Corps at Parris Island. However, if they should ask my wife, Sandra, "What did you do in the war, Grandma?" she would have some great stories to tell about her experiences in Vietnam.

I used to kid her by saying such stupid things like the army must have sent her to Vietnam to teach our soldiers to fight dirty. That wasn't true or funny. The truth is she wanted to go, because going off to war was a family tradition, as her father, LTC William J. Lockney, was a fighter

LTC Willam J. Lockney, USAF

pilot in World War II, Korea and Vietnam. She really didn't go to Vietnam to fight. She was a member of Army Special Services, and had already served a tour in Korea, and subsequently served in Vietnam from March, 1967 to April, 1968. There was a big difference, since the Korean War had ended several years before she got there, but the Vietnam War was in full bloom when she arrived. Her tour of duty just happened to be during the time of the Tet Offensive by the North Vietnamese and the Viet Cong.

Sandra at the firing range with an M-16 rifle at 65th Medical Group Headquarters, South Korea, 1965.

Right: Sandra engaging some of the field troops in conversation at Stateside Service Club, DiAn , South Vietnam, 1967.

As a civilian employee of the U. S. Army, Sandra along with other women of Special Services staffed craft shops, libraries and service clubs, and coordinated an array of entertainment programs. They also coordinated USO tours of celebrity entertainers, produced, and directed little theater productions. That was the kind of duty she was promised, but as a bonus she endured rocket attacks, mortar barrages and

Sandra's "hootch" in DiAn, South Vietnam, 1967.

Sandra watching a Christmas parade with the troops at the Free World Service Club, Tay Ninh, South Vietnam, December, 1967.

commando raids mounted against her base camps. She had her "hootch" to live in, but often had to spend nights in rat infested bunkers. She traveled throughout South Vietnam by jeep and helicopters, and lived in such places as Tay Ninh, Cu Chi, Di-An and Long Binh. It wasn't the lifestyle that you would imagine of a "Marian The Librarian" type, but Sandra endured because, as she says "I'm from good ole tough, West Virginia mountain stock." Today, the former U.S. Army Special Services employee is Dr. Sandra Lockney-Davis, a retired District Department Head from Pensacola Junior College.

Over 265,000 military and civilian women volunteered to serve in Vietnam, risking their lives to serve their country in whatever capacity they were needed. Most of them were in their early twenties. More than fifty civilian women died in Vietnam. On November 11, 1993 Sandra was invited to attend the dedication of the Vietnam Women's Memorial at the site of the Vietnam Veteran's Memorial in Washington, D. C. At the dedication ceremony, Admiral William Crowe, former Chairman, Joint Chiefs of Staff, made the following remarks:

> "The moving piece we dedicate today stands not only as a reminder of a painful era, but more importantly, as a tribute to an exceptional group of American women who answered their country's call at an extraordinary time in our history and did so at great personal sacrifice.

It is, or course, with a great deal of pride that I show friends and family her pictures in the publication, *Vietnam Women's Memorial: A Commemorative,* and the personal Certificate of Appreciation signed by the U. S. Secretary of Defense, Les Aspin.

The presence of women in harms way existed in all of our wars. Vietnam was a new kind of war for our country, and once again, our leaders are adjusting to another "new kind of war" in Iraq and Afghanistan. Many of our young men and women are once again in harms way. Let us pray that our country, along with our Allies, will find a way to end the threat of terrorist attacks without a prolonged war. If not, there will be another group of young ladies, just like "Grandma Sandra," who will be ready, willing and able to serve their country.

Above:

Sandra gives a tour of the Free World Service Club in Tay Ninh , RVN to General Creighton Abrams, Commanding General , with General V. Tobias, Commanding General 1st PHILCAGV circa 1968

Left:

Sandra gives a tour of the Free World Service Club to another visitor with General Tobias, and one of Sandra's colleagues, Marilyn Ramge.

Julie
Ashley
David
Kelsea
Grandma Sandra
Lorelei
Hayden
Hunter
Davis
Sam

55

The Whitwell House

It was late April, 2009, and my wife, Sandra, and I had just enjoyed our favorite lunch: a delicious breakfast menu at Jerry's Drive In, a popular "wait in line" spot in East Pensacola Heights. While waiting at the traffic light at Cervantes Street and Perry Avenue, we noticed the little, nondescript "Estate Sale" sign nailed to the bottom of the telephone pole. The address on Desoto Street was just a couple blocks away. The light changed, and instead of turning left, as originally planned, and driving the ten miles to our home across the bay in Gulf Breeze, we proceeded straight ahead in the direction of Desoto Street.

When we arrived at the address, I wasn't too surprised to discover that the estate sale was at the house known to many of us as the "Whitwell House," a beautiful two-story colonial, situated on the corner of Perry Avenue and Desoto Street. Many years before, my parents knew the Whitwell family, and our family home was only three blocks away on Bayou Boulevard. My brothers and I walked past the well manicured yard each day on our way to and from Annie K. Suter School.

Situated in a community of smaller homes, the Whitwell house was one of only a few large, prominent homes in the area affectionately known as the "Heights" by the residents.

As a young child, I remember being in the big white house. It seemed so big. I recall that I watched in amazement as Mr. Whitwell, a friendly, small framed, white haired, elderly gentleman, decorated a large Christmas tree. It was the largest Christmas tree I had ever seen, and it reached all the way to the high ceiling of the living room. Real logs were burning in the fireplace, Christmas carols were being played from a Victrola, and the many different colored lights and decorations dazzled my young mind. It was like a modern day Christmas special on prime time television. Mr. Whitwell was a gracious and gentle host and seemed to be amused at my childish wonderment of the whole scene. Over the past seventy-plus years, I've recalled numerous times the memory of that wonderful experience with Mr. Whitwell. Even though that was the only time I was ever in their home, as far as I can remember, it left a lasting impression on my mind that there was a lot of happiness in that home, and that the joy of Christmas must have been very important to the family.

We were anxious to enter the house, so Sandra and I got in line with others who seemed as interested as we were to find out what items were for sale. The fact that I had been in the home over seven decades earlier didn't seem to impress anyone. Once inside, I tried to reconcile my memory of that visit years ago with what I was observing on this second visit. The living room didn't look much like what I remembered it looking like, and it didn't seem to be as large, although it is in fact a large room. We soon realized that the entire house was well stocked with antique furniture, art work, porcelain dishes and vases, etc., mostly of Asian origin. We had been looking for a small desk or table that would be suitable for use in our office at home, so we rambled throughout both floors. The antique appraiser responsible for the sale, informed us that, "Everything must go!" We found a couple interesting desks, but the prices quoted were out of line for what we were looking for, although we knew that once those items were cleaned up and sold at auction or from a showroom floor, they would sell for much more than what we were quoted.

The one thing that surprised us the most was that even though the appraiser said, "everything must go," we didn't realize he really meant,

"Everything." People were pillaging through drawers, closets, picture albums, and boxes of personal letters and many miscellaneous items of a personal nature. Photos and snapshots of individuals and group shots, which once must have been prized and coveted possessions, were scattered throughout every room in the house. It seemed sad to me that items, especially personal items, that were collected and saved over many years, and considered valuable and irreplaceable, would suddenly have very little value, due to deaths, separations, old age and many other reasons. I overheard several people make similar comments about how "sad" it is, especially when they observed the many snapshots of family members, and boxes and boxes of personal letters saved over the years and now scattered about on beds and tables for strangers to read and pick through.

I believe we learned a couple important lessons from going to the sale, although our primary purpose for going was to find a small desk or table, and to satisfy our curiosity. We didn't find a suitable table or desk, but we did satisfy our curiosity, plus we purchased an interesting, but simple little tea cart. The lessons we learned were perhaps, a bit more complicated. For example, I'm a pack-rat. I save everything! Occasionally, Sandra will shame me into getting rid of "stuff," and I will go through boxes in the attic, my closet, my desk drawers, notebooks and the tool shed, and will throw things away; but by the time I go to bed, I will have retrieved half the "stuff." As we went through the Whitwell house, I thought of how it might look someday if my house was being trampled through by hundreds of people, strangers and friends, going through all my junk, much of which had already been thrown away several times before. I now have renewed, good intentions of getting rid of "stored stuff" that I don't need now or probably won't need in the future, and I will seek membership in "Pack-Rats Anonymous."

Another lesson has to do with family photos and snapshots, and the many letters and cards stored away somewhere and not being enjoyed by anyone. One of the major frustrations I've had to contend with while preparing this publication had to do with obtaining photos to go with the stories. Most families have photos, but they can't find them. Modern personal computers make it possible to store your own pictures and important papers and letters on discs, and then you can make inexpensive copies for family and friends. I didn't notice if the people who were going through the many letters and boxes of pictures purchased any of them. Perhaps there is a demand from collectors for such items that I'm not aware of.

It was interesting to walk throughout this beautiful old home that housed several generations of the same family, most of whom have died or live elsewhere, but left evidence of their presence in the many different items for sale. Most members of the Whitwell generations have moved on, but the house remains intact, stately as ever, on the market, and ready for a new generation of owners and caregivers.

The Whitwill House,

56

"Yellow Perils" Over Pensacola

The Yellow Peril
Courtesy of the artist, Capt. Bob Rasmussen, USN, Ret.

For those of us who lived in Pensacola in the late thirties and early forties, it was a common sight to see numerous U.S. Navy, bi-wing, open cockpit trainers in the skies over Northwest Florida, and South Alabama. The trainer was designated the N2S by the U. S. Navy, and the PT-13 by the Army Air Corps, but generally was known around the world as the "Stearman." Because of it's traditional bright yellow paint scheme and it's somewhat tricky ground handling characteristics, it was nicknamed the "Yellow Peril." It was the only American aircraft that was completely standardized for both Navy and Army use. The sturdy bi-plane served in primary training schools throughout World War II. It was much loved by those who flew and trained in it, and by thousands of us kids, who, if we were lucky, got the pilots to wave at us as they flew by, low and noisy.

Ellis Davis sitting astride an N2S at Bell Flying Service, 1950s
Courtesy of Ellis Davis

One of those kids was Ellis Davis. He grew up on Palafox Highway, less than a mile from "Stump Field," the present site of "Car City," and one of the local grass fields the Navy used to train their pilots. Ellis said, "I woke up every morning, and went to bed every night to the sound of those planes landing and taking off at Stump Field." He said he was in "Hog Heaven" just being near those planes and their pilots. He reminisced about those days recently, telling me how he used to pack a lunch of sandwiches and chocolate milk, and spend the day at "Stump Field." He was bitten by the "flying bug," and never completely recovered. What really must have sealed his fate as a future pilot, was when he was twelve years old a navy "Check Pilot" broke all the rules and took Ellis up for a ride in one of the "Yellow Perils." It changed his life. At a very young age, he became a licensed pilot, and later an instructor. In 1970, at age forty-one, he purchased a 1940 "Yellow Peril," which he kept in mint condition and flew it around the

Ellis Davis
Courtesy of Earle Bowden

Ellis and his N2S
Courtesy of Tom Helms

country, often accompanied by his wife, Barbara. There's no way to know, of course, but the "Yellow Peril" he owned for over thirty years could possibly be the one he rode in at age twelve.

In the late thirties, about the time Ellis Davis was washing down his peanut butter and jelly sandwiches with chocolate milk, Glenn Lambert, was watching a couple Navy bi-planes from Pensacola land in a field near the old "Lambert Plantation" up around Uriah and Frisco City, Alabama. Glenn was bitten by that same "flying bug," and instead of becoming a farmer, he became a Midshipman at the United States Naval Academy, Class of 1944. He was briefly exposed to a "Yellow Peril," on pontoons, at the Academy. Upon early graduation in 1943, he married, Fran, his childhood sweetheart, and immediately the Navy shipped him off to war on board the U.S.S. Biloxi.

Capt. Glenn Lambert, USN
Courtesy of Fran Lambert

Glenn finally got his orders to report to flight school at NAS, Ottumwa, Iowa where he had a "hands on" experience with the

"Yellow Peril," and his dream of becoming a Naval Aviator became a reality. Glenn recalled that the weather was always a problem in Ottumwa and the student pilots had to wait for good weather in order to fly. On one occasion, the weather appeared safe, and he was flying solo. Unfortunately, the weather quickly changed and Glenn was lost in the clouds, and couldn't see to land at the base. He remembered that a train track ran by the base. Flying just above the rooftops, he found the track, and following it, he located the base, just barely clearing the gate. Glenn completed his training in spite of bad weather, got his wings, and later flew just about everything the Navy had. Along the way he was an Aide to three different Admirals, serving in both World War II and the Vietnam War. After thirty years of active duty, he retired in 1973, as Captain, Glenn E. Lambert. Like many Navy pilots, he had fond memories of the "Yellow Peril." He and Fran lived many happy years in their wonderful, waterfront home on Bayou Texar, and later moved into Azalea Trace.

When I was about ten or twelve, a couple of my cousins and I were picking blueberries in a field in the Ferry Pass area, back behind my grandmother's house. I was fascinated with all the yellow airplanes overhead. They were not very high up, and we managed to get some of them to wave at us. We heard the sound of a collision overhead, and suddenly one of the planes landed in the same field we were in. All the bushes were about four or five feet high. The little "Yellow Peril" plowed through them and came to a stop about a hundred yards from us. The pilot was coated with oil, but otherwise appeared to be unhurt. He asked if we would take him to a telephone, so we escorted him to my aunt's house, which was nearby. Several of his fellow pilots circled overhead. He didn't appear to be excited or upset. Navy personnel showed up right away. The next day they had the wings off and the whole thing loaded onto a truck, and it was hauled away.

Whenever I see a bi-wing airplane, I think of the U.S. Navy. Others, not familiar with Naval Air Training will probably think of "Barn Storming" or the heroic adventures of Eddie Rickenbacker. Either way, it's flying by the seat of your pants in an open cockpit, which is dangerous, but it must be exhilarating to those who love to fly. Glenn related an incident where the navy instructor looped the airplane, and the student pilot, who had neglected to fasten his safety belt, fell out of the cockpit. Fortunately, he was wearing a parachute and his life was spared.

Ellis recalled a similar but amusing incident when he took his friend, Frank Conti, up for a ride in his "Yellow Peril." At an altitude of several thousand feet, he flew the plane through a loop, which according to one seasoned pilot, was "like being invited to a suicide that you didn't want to attend." At the point where the airplane was upside down, Frank's seat gave a little, causing him to think he was falling out, "scaring the hell out of him," said Ellis, as he laughed when telling me about the incident a few years ago. Ellis further explained that, "Frank had a death grip on the steering cables on both sides of the fuselage and wasn't about to let go, which made it a little difficult for me to control the plane." The story always gets a lot of laughs, but it was no laughing matter to Frank at the time.

Frank Conti
Courtesy of Frank and Mary Alice Conti

Over ten thousand "Stearmans" were built during the late thirties and early forties, and over two thousand are still flying today. The Museum of Naval Aviation at N.A.S., Pensacola has two of them on display. Sold by the thousands after World War II, the "Stearman" has had a long and full career as a trainer, crop duster and air show performer.

Those who earned their wings by first training in the N2S belong to an elite group of Naval aviators. They learned the basics of military flying in tough little airplanes made from steel tubing and wood framing, covered over with fabric. From the "Yellow Perils" they graduated to fighters, dive bombers, torpedo planes and whatever else the Navy had for them to fly. They fought the battles, and helped win the wars. Some never made it home to their loved ones, some returned to civilian lives forever changed from the experiences, and some continued to "Fly Navy," later retiring as captains and admirals. They all began as young graduates from colleges all over the country, or graduates of the Naval Academy, or young officers from duty stations. Most of them, at some point in their career, flew into Pensacola, and some of them were the pilots we kids waved to so many years ago, as they flew their "Yellow

Perils" over Pensacola. To know only a smattering of naval aviation history makes one swell with pride, and to appreciate the full meaning of those words over a pair of doors at the Officer's Club at N.A.S., Pensacola, Florida , which are, "Through These Portals Walk The World's Greatest Aviators."

Right:
Capt. Glenn Lambert, USN, Ret. and a Yellow Peril at the Pensacola Naval Aviation Museum
Courtesy of Fran Lambert

Below:
Ellis Davis with cousins Ken and Brian Davis
Courtesy of Rose Marie Davis Kaiser

57

You Can Go Home Again

In deference to Thomas Wolfe, you *can* go home again. Today, my home is in Gulf Breeze, but for almost thirty years, East Pensacola Heights was home for me, my parents and my five brothers and one sister. We often hear that "home is where the heart is," and I know that is true, but part of my heart is still in the "Heights."

Three years ago, my wife, Sandra, and I were invited back to East Pensacola Heights for a picnic. The invitation, signed by Jean Wallace, was on a small post-a-note attached to a great little newsletter

East
Pensacola
Heights
Association 1998-2009

Spring 2009

Mission of the East Pensacola Heights Association:

To enhance, protect, preserve and promote the unique quality of life in East Pensacola Heights and to foster an inclusive and ever-deepening sense of community.

Help Wanted

Meet Your Neighbor

Dancing Through Heights History with Fran Bryson

By Dolly Berthelot

Fran Bryson

East Pensacola Heights Association Newsletter

published by the East Pensacola Heights Association. The message was, "Come to our picnic and see some of your old neighbors."

The newsletter contained a notice about the picnic, showing the address to be 720 Bayou Boulevard. Our old address was 700 Bayou Boulevard. This area was part of my paper route, which seems like fifty years ago...what the heck; it was more than fifty years ago. Obviously I couldn't remember which house was number 720, so I wondered if it was the old Broome family home next door, or the old Zur Lenden house down the hill on the bayou, or the Black family home at the curve, from whom "Black's Wharf," our old "Swimming Hole" got it's name. It was neither. It was the home on Hyer's Point, now owned by Edwin and Jean Wallace, which is probably the most beautiful piece of real estate in Northwest Florida.

Hyer's Point was our usual jumping off point when we swam across the bayou to Bayview Park. Recently, I mentioned this to Edwin Wallace, Mrs. Hyer's grandson, and he responded with this unintentional funny comment: "Yeah, I know, we used to swim over to Bayview Park for swimming lessons." We could always count on catching a lot of crabs between Hyer's Point and Zur Lenden's dock. But, what I really

The Hyers House on Hyers Point. Courtesy of Ed and Jean Wallace

remember most about Hyer's Point was Mrs. Hyer herself. Mrs. J. Whiting Hyer, that is. She was a very nice lady, of course, and the first thing you would notice about her, other than a nice, friendly smile, was that she often wore men's pants. She probably wouldn't look unusual today in a pair of men's khaki pants, because women now wear

The Hyer Family
L to R Back Row: John Hyer, Jr., J. Whiting Hyer, J. L. Hall (Mike) nd Edwin Wallace, Sr. Middle Row: Mrs. J. W. (Em) Hyer, Margaret Hyer Hall, Em Tucker Wallace. Front Row: Frances Hall Summit and Edwin Wallace.
Courtesy of Ed & Jean Wallace

just about anything, but this was long before the Bermuda shorts craze hit this country. Some women did wear slacks back then, styled to fit the female body, but Mrs. Hyer seemed to be content with a pair of Mr. Hyer's pants, and a large belt to hold them up.

Mrs. Hyer in typical attire
Courtesy of Ed and Jean Wallace

Another interesting thing about Mrs. Hyer is that she obviously loved animals, because she had a lot of them, especially the flying kind. She had the usual number of ducks and chickens, but what interested us kids most was her large flock of white geese, and an equally large, if not larger, flock of guinea fowl. If you can imagine the noise a flock of about two dozen geese can make, you should hear the noise from a large flock of guinea fowls. It was always interesting to hear the noise coming through the woods from Hyer's Point when the geese and guinea fowl were trying to outdo each other. They flew all over the neighborhood, and occasionally Mrs. Hyer would round them up and herd them home like sheep.

When I was about eight or nine years old, the geese were in our yard and Mrs. Hyer, with stick in hand, was trying to shoo them back across Bayou Boulevard into their large wooded property. I volunteered to help her catch a recalcitrant old gander which just refused to go home with the others. I was the official "chicken-neck-ringer" at our house, so with my experience, I figured it wouldn't be much difference in catching geese and catching chickens. I was unaware that a gander, especially an old, large one has a bony or calcified knot about the size of a golf ball on each wing, plus unlike chickens, a goose can bite the heck out of you. It took that old gander about ten seconds to bloody my nose and scratch me all over. Mrs. Hyer was very concerned and sympathetic, but I bet she had a good laugh when she got home.

By the way, the picnic was great, but I knew only three of the people there, and only one of them lived in the Heights when I did. We've returned each year for the Association's annual picnic, and although we don't usually know all the people there, their friendliness and their relationship with each other was just like it was years ago when we had Easter egg hunts at Suter School, political rallies, fish fry's and many other events at the Community House. It's obvious that the friendly ways of the people in East Pensacola Heights never change, even though the residents come and go.

Right: Ed and Jean Wallace with daughter Nancy Wallace Robichaub,

Courtesy of Ed and Jean Wallace

NAMES INDEX

Made in the USA
Middletown, DE
11 December 2019

80505402R10219